DATE DUE			
No 16 1991			
APR 18 1995			
OCT 7 1998			
FEB - 7 2000			

Sagas of
Old Western
Travel and
Transport

Sagas of Old Western Travel and Transport

BY H. WILBUR HOFFMAN

SAN DIEGO · Howell-North Books · CALIFORNIA

First Edition
Manufactured in the United States of America

For information write to:
    Howell North Publishers, Inc.
    11175 Flintkote Avenue,
    San Diego, CA 92121

Library of Congress Cataloging in Publication Data

Hoffman, H   Wilbur.
    Sagas of old western travel and transport.

    Bibliography: p.
    Includes index.
    1.   Transportation — The West — History.
2.   The
West — Description and travel.   I.   Title.
HE210.H63   380.5'0978   80-14407

ISBN 0-8310-0002-3

1 2 3 4 5 6 7 8 9   84 83 82 81 80

Contents

DEDICATION

*I dedicate this book
to my wonderful wife Ruth
whose help,
suggestions, and encouragement
were indispensable.*

Introduction

Hewn in stone over the portico of a state building in Sacramento, California, are these words: "Bring me men to match my mountains." The West has mountain ranges that reach for the skies, mountains of solid stone and granite so tough and durable they defy subjection to the elements and the incursions of man. Though these words allude to California's mountains, and men who figuratively matched them, this metaphor could be extended to include all of the Old West; that part of America stretching from the 100th meridian westward to the Pacific Ocean and north and south from the Canadian border to the Mexican border. This vast land not only contained numerous mountain ranges, but also endless prairies, shimmering deserts, bleak wastelands, and, in the mid-nineteenth century, Indians, some of whom were hostile to the white man. Here also were millions of acres of rich farm and grazing land, boundless timber, uncounted tons of precious metals, and other natural resources, all untouched. These assets were the prize that men sought.

Thousands from the already crowded Eastern United States, including immigrants from across the Atlantic, swarmed westward during the mid-nineteenth century to this land of promise, to, hopefully, a better life. Not since the migrations across Europe after the fall of the Roman Empire has a migration been so vast as the flow of emigrants to the Old West. (In America, those pioneers who migrated to the West were known as emigrants.) Perhaps never have as many converged on such an unsettled, remote place in so short a time.

The Old West enabled the United States to absorb hosts of oppressed and impoverished immigrants from Europe as well as thousands of Americans from the East Coast. Few immigrants came directly from Europe to the West. Most settled first in Eastern America, then migrated westward by wagon, steamship, sailing vessel or, after 1869, by railroad.

The Old West was the land of opportunity, but it exacted a high price for its riches. Sparsely inhabited in the 1840's, the region was almost as remote as another planet. It took months to reach the Far West overland by ox-drawn wagon, three to six months by windjammer over 17,000 miles of often raging seas. Primitive ocean steamers brought passengers from the East Coast to Panama, where they proceeded overland across malaria-infested jungles to reboard a San Francisco-bound steamer. Upon arrival at their destination, immigrants found their situations uncertain. The few Spanish Indian missions, American Indian missions, and fur-trading posts lay widely scattered. Disease, especially cholera, stalked the wagon

9

trains and early settlements. Several estimates have been made of the number of graves along the Oregon Trail; one estimate states an average of one grave every eighty feet. Many families were separated never to meet again. Work was hard, long and frequently unremitting. Building the Old West was neither for the weak, nor for the timid.

As with any successful nation or region, transportation was the key. Transport facilities in the early West were as primitive as those at the dawn of history—pack animals, animal-drawn carts and wagons, and wind-driven ships. True, America had railroads and river steamers by the 1840's, but only in the East. These were introduced later into the West only after Herculean effort, as were the thousand miles of stagecoach routes and the Pony Express.

Never before had Americans coped with such long distances in so bleak and inhospitable a land. Stagecoach and wagon-freight lines stretching fifteen hundred to three thousand miles were built and stocked. Several groups of Mormons pushed handcarts westward fifteen hundred miles. Rivers of marginal navigability were sailed with comparatively primitive steamboats; or equally crude steamships or windjammers sailed treacherous seas to the Far West. A Pony Express 1,988 miles long was organized to expedite communication between east and west before telegraph wires stretched between these points. And finally, the Pacific railroad was laid between Omaha and Sacramento over wild prairies, deserts, and towering mountain ranges that were the highest and most inaccessible ever conquered by railroad builders.

The men who built these transport systems had available engineering techniques far less advanced than those of today. Then too, most heavy freight had to be shipped from the East Coast to the West Coast seventeen thousand miles around Cape Horn. Complicating the problem of logistics was the sudden migration of about 100,000 emigrants to California during the gold rush in 1849.

Much of the Old West prior to 1846 was not even American territory. Until that year Great Britain and the United States jointly administered the area north of the California Border to 54°49′ latitude and east to the Continental Divide. The Southwest and California had been Spanish and, after 1821, Mexican territory.

Organizing, constructing and operating these Old Western transport systems required men with stamina, vision, courage, perseverance, skill, and a willingness to risk their capital and energy against great odds. The stakes were high, but the odds were great. Some organizers, builders and operators of transport systems became wealthy; others lost fortunes. Almost all participants, whether stage drivers or relay-station operators, muleskinners, steamer or windjammer crewmen, railroad men, Pony Express riders, or entrepreneurs, were unusual men who helped build the Old West into a great empire. They were men who matched her mountains.

The story of travel and transport in the Old West is replete with sagas of hardship, sacrifice, peril, heroism, triumph, adventure, romance and typical wry Western humor.

Acknowledgments

Special acknowledgment is due the following:

To my friend Dr. John Wilhelm, Professor of English, California State University, Sacramento, for suggesting I write the book.

To Dr. Edwin H. Carpenter, Chief Western Historian, Huntington Library, San Marino, California, for his excellent suggestions.

To Mrs. Waddell Smith of the Pony Express History and Art Gallery, San Rafael, California, for permission to reprint several lines from her late husband's book *The Story of the Pony Express.*

To Mrs. Alice Soderberg, Former Director of riculum, Sutter County Schools, Yuba City, California, for her encouragement.

To the librarians and attendants of the following libraries and institutions for their splendid cooperation: Packard Library, Marysville, California; Sutter County Library, Yuba City, California; Bancroft Library, University of California, Berkeley; California State Library, Sacramento; Wells Fargo Bank History Room, San Francisco, California; Pony Express History and Art Gallery, San Rafael, California. Especially helpful were the first two mentioned libraries in obtaining books and photocopies of periodical articles through the interloan library service.

To the several museums and historical societies as a source of many pictures, sketches, and maps. Due credit is given on each picture, map, and sketch as they appear in the book.

And last, but of prime importance, to the reader. A book is not really complete unless it is read. So to the reader, pleasant reading!

Wilbur Hoffman
Yuba City, California

Sagas of Old Western Travel and Transport

1

Pack Trains

The first white men to journey overland to the Old West were members of the Lewis and Clark Expedition. In 1804-06, under the leadership of Captain Meriwether Lewis and Captain William Clark, this party of Americans journeyed by perogues and canoes on the Missouri River from St. Louis to its headquarters in the far reaches of the Rocky Mountains. Then traveling with horses, the party then crossed the Rocky Mountains and floated down the Clearwater, the Snake and the Columbia rivers to the Pacific Ocean. After wintering there, they returned to St. Louis via the same route in 1806. On their heels followed the fur trappers — better known as mountain men and sometimes frontiersmen. They followed various trails across the Great American Desert to the mountains of the West. (The Great American Desert is considered to be the area of the high plains that stretch westward from approximately 100 degrees longitude to the Rocky Mountains, a region that was considered uninhabitable.) The main quarry of these frontiersmen was beaver, which thrived abundantly along Western streams. Trappers pushed further westward as beaver streams became trapped out. These pioneer men of the West soon learned the trails and the ways of the Indian. They blazed the overland path for traders, miners and settlers. The earliest mountain men carried supplies on the backs of pack animals — mules and horses. Only after the main trails had been explored by these hardy men, did the wagon trains roll westward to the Pacific.

Beasts of burden continued to move the freight in the Old West wherever wagons or boats were unable to navigate. During the 1850's, most Western towns were beyond the reach of wagon roads or river transport and thus were dependent solely on pack animals for supplies. Even by 1848 the West was but a wilderness and sparsely inhabited by Indians and a few whites; a year later thousands of men swarmed into the foothills of the Sierra Nevada in search of gold. Steamers carried supplies from San Francisco up river to California ports like Sacramento, Stockton, and Marysville. From these communities thousands of pack animals dispatched freight to the gold diggings.

The pack animal overwhelmingly preferred in the West was the mule, although horses and burros were widely used. Mules possessed several superior qualities that made them ideal pack animals. Sired by a jackass and born of a mare, mules seem to have inherited the most desirable characteristics of each. Mules are, however, unable to reproduce. It has been said that they have no pride of ancestry, nor hope of posterity.

The popular conception of a mule is that he is stupid. True, a mule's stolid countenance, expressionless eyes, long ears that impassively wig and wag, and manner of braying do convey an appearance of gross deficiency of intellect. Notwithstanding, mules are surprisingly intelligent.

Though not an eager pupil, a mule can learn all necessary tasks from a patient trainer. Once learned, a mule will remember and perform duties well without further guidance. Mules require less forage than horses and do not overeat or over drink, an attribute not inherited from the gluttonous equine side of their family.

Smaller than horses, the mule, nevertheless, is sturdy and will perform a more complete day's work than a horse. He will plod along at a steady, less fatiguing pace that will enable him to carry more weight for a longer period of time. When ladened with a full pack (200 to 250 pounds), the trained pack mule will fall into his ambling gait. The mule quickly learns this gait will not rock his load, enabling him to travel five or six miles an hour without undue fatigue. And unlike horses, mules work better in hot weather.

Mules are not without faults. No animal is more ornery or stubborn than "them 'ere mules." They can be cantankerous and unpredictable. On the trail they may suddenly stop for reasons known only to the mule; then it takes a skillful muleteer, utilizing the most glowing profanity, to get the obdurate beast under way once again.

A mule is shy and sudden movement around his hindquarters will produce a kicking tantrum dangerous to anyone in close proximity. For this reason mules were often blindfolded while being loaded and while on the trail, should the pack require adjusting. Frightened mules will tend to bunch up especially while crossing streams.

An effective way to control and calm a mule is with the bell mare. A strange affinity exists between a mule and a mare. The reason might be that a mare is a mule's mother — he associates the bell tied around the bell mare's neck with his own beloved mare and will follow her anyplace. At night the bell mare is often tethered amongst the mules and her closeness, assured by the occasional tinkling of the bell, comforts pack mules and quiets their fears.

Spaniards and Mexicans packed with mules along the trails of Old Mexico long before this beast of burden was introduced into America. In 1823 Stephen Cooper, returning to Franklin, Missouri, herded four hundred mules, jennies, and Spanish jacks purchased during a Santa Fe trading expedition. These jacks sired the first Missouri mules. From this modest beginning ultimately sprang a great herd of thousands of mules that became renowned, desired, exploited, loved, and hated according to circumstance. Although mules are unable to reproduce, their rapid expansion is quite remarkable. In fact, the Missouri mule, as ornery as he is, qualifies as an American institution.

Warily avoiding its hindquarters, muleteers adjust a blindfolded pack mule's load.

During the California gold rush of 1849, the mule was of great economic importance to pack trains operating out of Marysville, California, bound for remote gold diggings in the Sierra Nevada. Marysville soon became an important shipping center to the gold country. On easterly trails out of this settlement in the early 1850's, mile-long columns of dust drifted from the hooves of a thousand mules plodding toward the distant Sierra Nevada. "All along the Yuba Road at any hour of the day droves of pack mules can be seen on their way to the hills," reported the *Marysville Herald* on March 29, 1851.

Following the discovery of gold in the northern Sierra Nevada in 1848, thousands of gold-hungry emigrants swarmed into the area. By 1852 the population of the Marysville region had swollen to nearly forty thousand. These pioneers were not only hungry for gold; they were eager for supplies. Provisions for the gold miners were funneled through Marysville via a long, treacherous, expensive route. Beginning on the East Coast, freight was loaded aboard sailing vessels for the three-months trip around the Horn to San Francisco. It was reloaded onto whale boats, skiffs, small schooners and steamers that plied the Sacramento River to Sacramento, then transshipped via smaller vessels up the Feather River to Marysville. At this point modern transportation ended and primitive began. Because of insufficient roads, it was 1853 before wagon-hauled supplies rolled out of Marysville.

Mule train taking on water in the Sierra Nevada.

Thousands of mules were needed to transport the thirty-five thousand yearly tons of supplies from the Marysville dock to the gold fields. Soon Marysville acquired the distinction of being the pack-mule capital of California. So many mules were stabled around the town (over four thousand) that the mule population often exceeded the human inhabitants. The cacophonic braying of that many mules must have created a din worthy of the town's unique distinction.

The Marysville animals had been imported from Mexico and were also owned and driven by Mexicans. The average Mexican understood the beast and knew his unpredictable moves. Not long after, many local residents and merchants purchased their own mules, learned how to handle them and organized their own packing companies. One Edward McIllhany, perhaps the best-known and most enterprising, began with a string of thirty mules purchased from a Mexican for five thousand dollars.

Since freight packing was lucrative and in demand, the business of mule trading soon developed in Marysville. The Lower Plaza region and even street corners echoed to the cry of mule auctioneers. Prices varied from $100 to $150 per head.

The number of mules in single pack trains increased rapidly. During 1850 some Marysville merchants were sending one hundred pack mules at a time to the mines, while other traders sent as many as five trains of ten to thirty mules each. By the end of the year, at the height of the freight season, as many as one thousand mules made the run from the Marysville Plaza to the mines with each mule carrying 200 to 250 pounds. Two hundred pounds of freight and fifty pounds of forage, such as barley, was a normal load. (General Crook, of Indian-War fame, demonstrated that by lavishing love upon the humble mule and providing him with a special harness, the animal could be persuaded to carry 320 pounds. So great was Crook's admiration for this animal that he charged into battle astride one.) A train of one thousand mules could pack between 150 to 200 tons at a time. Since steamers at this time unloaded over two hundred tons daily at the Plaza, the animals were hard pressed to keep the freight moving. As Shakespeare wrote about the lowly ass, they had to "groan and sweat under the business. . . ."

Mule freight rates varied greatly, ranging from one dollar per pound during the early 1850's to four or five cents by 1856, when rates had stabilized. The winter season, of course, brought the highest tariff. McIllhany charged seventy-five cents a pound for hauling freight to Onion Valley in November 1850. Just one year later he charged one dollar per pound for a load he took to Downieville. Rates such as these brought wealth to early mule packers.

Though mule packing was profitable, it was also perilous. Danger lurked on trails to such remote mountain areas as La Porte, Port Wine, and Spanish Diggings. Road agents, covetous of the expensive cargo and mules, often lurked along the trail. Renegade Indians were especially fond of mule meat. So serious was this threat that packers at times fought pitched battles with the Indians. Some muleteers even preyed on their own kind. The trails became more treacherous deeper within the mountain country. Normally sure-footed mules at times slipped from narrow trails to fall hundreds of feet. So hardy were these animals that frequently such falls failed to injure them.

The most hazardous time in the Sierra was winter. Packers tried to avoid winter travel, but high packing rates and near starvation in the mountain country attracted the more venturesome. Miners in their lust for gold failed to realize the severity of winter in the Sierra Nevada and were often unprepared. Then there were times when steamers and pack trains were unable to move sufficient supplies to mines during regular freighting season in order to provide winter stockpiles. Severe privation, hardship, and near starvation became a specter during winter.

In November 1850, Edward McIllhany and his Mexican muleteers with a train of three hundred mules were moving badly needed provisions (and Christmas supplies) to Onion Valley high in the Sierra Nevada. One morning two feet of snow covered the trail and a blizzard cut visibility to about seventy-five feet. The lead bell mare was unable to follow the trail, so McIllhany, who knew the trail well, mounted a large mule and broke trail. In the howling blizzard, a Mexican muleteer and seven mules disappeared. On McIllhany's return trip to Marysville, he fed his mules on one-dollar-per-pound barley. He managed to get his mules to Marysville, and later the Mexican returned, but the seven missing mules had frozen to death. More unfortunate, during the same winter, was another pack train on the trail to La Porte. Before reaching their destination, eighteen men and sixty mules had frozen to death.

The most disastrous winter for pack teams was that of the 1852-53 season. An extreme shortage of provisions in the mountains and high freight rates lured many packers to the trail. The ventures, however, proved costly. For example, forty-two mules perished in snowdrifts between Little Grass Valley and Onion Valley. Another train had to be abandoned above Foster's Bar. By the following summer, the bleached bones of many unfortunate mules were strewn along the mountain trails.

After 1855 wagon roads had been built from Marysville to foothill points. As roads were extended, mule trains leaving Marysville gradually diminished until Downieville, La Porte, and Oroville became the main mule-packing centers. Mules were used for many years from wagon road termini into the far reaches of the Sierra Nevada.

Pack mules ascending the summit of the Sierra Nevada in 1861. California State Library, Sacramento.

Mules packed newly mined gold from the diggings to stagecoach stations. They also packed gold eastward across the Isthmus of Panama, gold which had been shipped to Panama City from San Francisco. On their return westward over the Isthmus, these same mules carted supplies to Panama City for reshipment to San Francisco. One momentous treasure-packing convoy over the Isthmus involved nearly one thousand mules laden with $2,600,000 in gold. Five hundred armed guards and homeward-returning miners accompanied the pack mule train that strung over a mile through the twisting jungle trail. Suddenly screaming bandidos emerged from the jungle, pistols blazing. Prospectors and guards opened fire. The easily excitable mules reared and kicked. Some broke from the line and bolted into the jungle. Four bandits were killed and the others driven off, but not before they had stolen over $100,000 in gold from the animals that had bolted.

The U.S. Army used pack mules to good advantage during campaigns against the Indians. On forced marches the beasts were able to keep up with the troops, whereas slower-moving freight wagons could not. Mules also packed supplies over terrain impassable to wagons. On night marches the mule's highly developed sense of smell kept him on the trail.

When pack mules accompanied the cavalry, they were at a disadvantage at the beginning of a march. In the morning the spirited cavalry mounts eagerly pranced along the trail, outpacing the slow-plodding mules. But after thirty miles of march, the mules kept pace with the horses. In a march of seventy-five to one hundred miles, the mules retained their original plodding pace, leaving the tiring horses far to the rear.

General Custer praised his mules: "don't ever flatter yourself . . . that a mule hasn't sense. He's got more wisdom than half the horses in the line." During the initial phases of the ill-fated battle of the Little Big Horn, Custer's last dispatch to Benteen was an urgent request to bring up the pack train quickly.

For many years these lowly beasts of burden plodded their way over the desert and mountain country of the American West packing vitally needed supplies. They helped tame the West and create a great empire.

Twenty-mule borax team plodding through Death Valley.

2

Traversing the Trails by Wagon

Whips snapped sharply and teamsters shouted urgently at 4, 6, 8 and even 20-mule or -oxen teams as they strained to pull heavily laden freight wagons westward along the endless trails of the high plains, across vast deserts and over towering mountain ranges. In caravans from two to over a hundred wagons the teams relentlessly carted supplies and people to faraway Western military posts and the distant frontier of the enchanted West, where settlers dreamed of finding a better life.

Two main trail systems stretched westward to the far ends of the continent over which these wagon trains rolled. Neither trail was a single road, each having short cuts and various branches. They were the Overland Trail and the Santa Fe Trail. Though the former trail did carry freight, it was primarily an emigrant road, while the Santa Fe Trail was primarily a commercial highway.

The great Overland Trail included the Oregon Trail, the Mormon Trail, the California Trail, the Bozeman Trail, and several other branches and short cuts. About two thousand miles long, it has been described as a rope frayed at each end. The eastern ends terminated at such Missouri River towns as St. Joseph, Independence, Kansas City, Atchison, and Leavenworth. Only at a point near Kearney, Nebraska, running westward to Julesburg, Colorado, did the trail unite as a single trunk road. During the 1860's, branches from this trail sprouted northward from Fort Laramie and Fort Hall to service the gold rush towns of Virginia City, Nevada and Helena, Montana. The branch northward from Fort Laramie was known as the Bozeman Trail and ran through Sioux Indian hunting grounds. The U.S. Army constructed a series of forts along this trail, but because of determined, bloody and incessant wars waged by the Sioux for

Principal wagon freight routes.

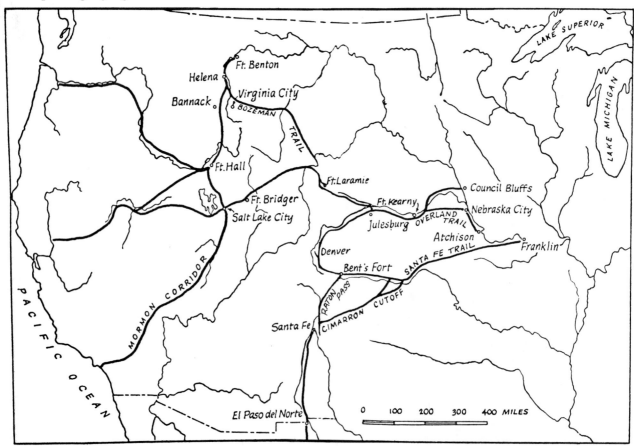

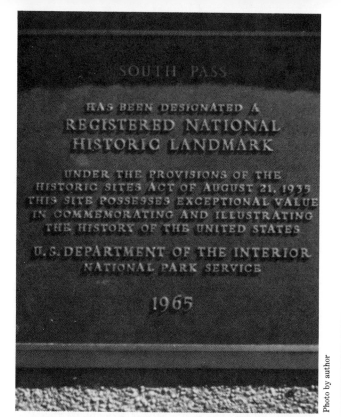

Original ruts mark the Oregon Trail's Lander Cutoff in Wyoming.

TOP: *A commemorative marker at the summit of South Pass in present-day Wyoming.* BOTTOM: *Commemorative marker indicating the Lander Cutoff, a trail (improved in 1859) crossing the Continental Divide north of the regular trail at South Pass. As the wording states, ". . . to avoid dry wastes of the road to the south and provide more water, wood, and forage. . . . Thirteen thousand people . . . passed this way in 1859 and for thirty years thereafter was used as heavily. Setting the destiny of an empire, these wagon tracks and lonely graves for miles beyond, a great landmark of history."*

intrusion of their hunting grounds, the Bozeman Trail proved to be the bloodiest of the western trails and was abandoned in 1868 after only two years of operation. The branch northward from Fort Hall ran to Virginia City and Helena and Fort Benton, Montana. Other western fringes of the Overland Trail wound on to Oregon and California, fringes that included several cutoffs and short cuts.

The central portion of the Overland Trail followed the North Platte River for about 140 miles and then followed the Sweetwater until the trail gradually sloped upward to South Pass on the Continental Divide in what is now the state of Wyoming. south Pass is on a sage-covered plain about twenty miles wide at an elevation of over seven thousand feet. Here was the gateway to the Far West beyond which various trail branches led on to either Oregon or California.

OPPOSITE TOP: A series of wagon tracks on the Oregon Trail ground out during the mid-nineteenth century, wend their way westward and upward on the eastern slopes of South Pass in present-day Wyoming. OPPOSITE CENTER: Original ruts along the Oregon Trail in Wyoming. Cattle and sheep ranchers occasionally use the road today. OPPOSITE BOTTOM: One of several California or Oregon cutoffs on the Oregon Trail in Wyoming.

The first white men over this trail were trappers in the 1820's. They operated singly or in companies; the Pacific Fur Company and the American Fur Company were the most prominent. Fur trappers first traversed the trail with pack horses or mules, but by 1832 Captain Bonneville had taken a wagon train through South Pass and across the Green River to the mouth of Horse Creek. That same year Nathaniel Wyeth led a pack train to the mouth of the Walla Walla River on the Columbia. Thus was traveled, by wagon or pack train, the original Oregon Trail from Independence, Missouri, to the mouth of the Walla Walla, where the Hudson's Bay Company had built a fort in 1818.

On the heels of fur traders and mountain men came missionaries sent to the Oregon country by various Presbyterian, Congregational, and Methodist mission associations. The objective, to convert the "heathen" Indian to Christianity. The most notable missionaries were Dr. Marcus Whitman and his wife Narcissa Prentiss Whitman. In the fall of 1836 they established a mission named Waiilatpu, twenty miles from the mouth of the Walla Walla River in the valley of the Columbia now known as the Walla Walla Valley. The modern city of Walla Walla lies about six miles eastward from Whitman's former mission.

History has seldom produced a more sincere, selfless, religious man or woman than Dr. and Mrs. Marcus Whitman; they willingly and completely dedicated their lives to a divine mission of converting a barbarous people to Christianity and teaching these heathen a more meaningful way of life. Narcissa was a gracious, vivacious lady with sparkling eyes and a ready, heartwarming smile. Though humble, almost self-effacing, Mrs. Whitman was

Very old marker along the Oregon Trail near South Pass in present-day Wyoming.

Original wagon tracks worn in the 1840's on the Oregon Trail can be seen alongside the Whitman Mission near Walla Walla, Washington.

possessed of an inner strength that enabled her to overcome severe hardships and privations. Her religious faith sustained her, as a passage from a letter to her mother illustrates:

> *. . . I should have fainted under it. Then the promise appeared in full view 'as thy day is so shall they strength be' and my soul rejoyced [sic] in God and testifys [sic] to the truth of another evidently manifest 'Lo, I am with you alway.'*

Narcissa Prentiss Whitman was as much at home in an elegant drawing room of an Eastern city as she was in a crude hut in hostile frontier thousands of miles from civilization. She not only was Dr. Whitman's wife but also was qualified by education as an assistant missionary.

Dr. Whitman was equally devoted and dedicated. In order to qualify as a missionary, he attended medical school and received a degree. Thus he could serve the physical and spiritual needs of the natives. Both he and Narcissa gave of themselves, asking nothing in return except the opportunity to help their fellow man. Both possessed moral and physical courage, remaining faithful to their calling rather than exploiting the economic opportunities that their environment offered.

Whitman, soft-spoken and humble, nevertheless possessed qualities of leadership he used when necessary. In spite of dire warnings about extreme hardships too difficult for women to endure, Dr. Whitman and his fellow missionary, Henry Spaulding, brought their wives, the first

29

white women over the Oregon Trail, to Fort Walla Walla in the summer of 1836. Accompanied by a farmer and a carpenter, they attached themselves to a fur trade supply caravan of seventy rough and tough frontiersmen led by Tom Fitzpatrick. Also accompanying the caravan was a party of genteel English sportsmen bound on a buffalo hunt looking for a "rousing bit of sport." Perhaps no more contrasting group ever passed over the Oregon Trail. At first, the uncouth frontiersmen shouted ribald remarks about the two women within earshot of the ladies. These remarks outwardly shocked Mrs. Spaulding but not Narcissa Whitman. She had heard such language in her judge father's courtroom and so overlooked it. In fact, Mrs. Whitman became a favorite of these frontiersmen; they soon respected her and cleaned up their language when in her presence. They treated her like the lady she was. She forgave their rough manners and knew that behind their tough façades were human beings.

At Fort Hall, a Hudson's Bay Company outpost, Whitman was forced to abandon the last of two wagons he originally had insisted on taking to Walla Walla. They—Whitman, Spaulding, their wives and the farmer and carpenter—arrived in good shape at Fort Walla Walla in September 1836. The area was so distant and isolated from home that Mrs. Whitman wrote her sister in New York that they must "calculate three years' time" to hear

from one another. What mail arrived came by occasional sailing vessels that stopped in the Northwest.

In her diary Mrs. Whitman vividly recorded the view as the party descended the Blue Mountains:

While upon this elevation, we had a view of the valley of the Columbia river. It was beautiful. Just as we gained the highest elevation and began to descend, the sun was dipping his disk behind the western horizon. Beyond the valley we could see two distant Mountains, Mount Hood and Mount St. Helens. These lofty peaks were of a conical form and separate from each other by a considerable distance. Behind the former the Sun was hiding part of his rays which gave us a more distinct view of this gigantic cone. The beauty of this extensive valley contrasted well with the rolling mountains behind us and at this hour of twilight was enchanting and quite diverted my mind from the fatigue under which I was labouring.

Never again from this vantage point would she gaze upon the valley where her mission was to be erected, nor upon her home in the East, because tragedy struck suddenly in November 1847. The Cayuse Indians, whom the Whitmans had been ministering to, murdered Mrs. Whitman, her husband, and all men connected with the mission. The remaining women were taken prisoner and the mission buildings burned. It is ironic that these missionaries, who neither asked for nor took anything from the Indians, but tried to Christianize them, educate them and teach them how to farm, should have been so treacherously dealt with by the Cayuse. Smallpox had killed many Cayuse, and some historians believe the epidemic was blamed

NARCISSA
PRENTISS
WHITMAN.
ELIZA.HART
SPALDING.
FIRST WHITE
WOMEN TO
CROSS THIS
PASS
JULY 4.1836

Very old marker along the Oregon Trail's South Pass in present-day Wyoming.

on the good doctor and his wife. The Indians, according to tribal custom, executed their witch doctor if he could not control an epidemic. Possibly the Indians equated Dr. Whitman with a witch doctor. This may be true, but the exact answer for the massacre is forever lost in history.

In the winter of 1842, Dr. Whitman had made a journey on horseback to Boston to discuss mission business with his board, but he also went to Washington, D.C. to talk to government officials. This trip undoubtedly had a profound influence on the political future of the Oregon Country which from 1818 had, by agreement, been jointly administered by the United States and Great Britain. Oregon Country included Washington, Oregon, Idaho, those parts of Montana and Wyoming west of the Continental Divide, and the Canadian province of British Columbia. In 1840 about one hundred Americans living in the Willamette Valley began agitating that the United States be the sole administrator of the Oregon Country.

In February 1843, Whitman proposed to the Secretary of War that the government establish military posts along the trail. Some historians feel

*Monument dedicated to those massacred by
Cayuse Indians at the Whitman Mission in 1847.*

Whitman also urged the United States to assume sole jurisdiction over the Oregon country at least as far north as the forty-ninth parallel instead of granting Great Britain sole jurisdiction north of the Columbia River, a rumored proposal.

While on his trip East, Dr. Whitman encouraged the formation of a wagon train to leave Independence, Missouri, for the Whitman mission on the Walla Walla in the spring of 1843. This caravan, subsequently known as "The Great Emigration," was guided by Whitman west of Fort Hall, a point on the trail west of which wagons had never rolled. The English factor of this Hudson's Bay Company fort tried to discourage movement of wagons to the west by warning that the wilderness passage of wagons was impossible. Some believe the factor wished to prevent Americans settling in the Oregon country, settlement that would weaken Britain's claim to the area. Whitman, however, was adamant in his conviction that wagons could indeed proceed westward. Preceding the train in his wagon, he guided the caravan through rugged wilderness to the Whitman mission, arriving there on October 10, 1843. The wagons then proceeded to Fort Walla Walla, then down the Columbia to The Dalles, and finally by boats to the mouth of the Willamette.

This train was large for its time. Whitman wrote to Secretary of War Porter that it contained "no less than two hundred families consisting of 1000 persons of both sexes ... 694 oxen and 773 loose cattle." The caravan contained 120 wagons. More important, it had proven that wagons could roll westward from Fort Hall to the Pacific. This Great Emigration, the two larger ones that followed, and various newspapers that agitated for a settlement finally convinced Great Britain to relinquish any claim to the Oregon Country south of the forty-ninth parallel. But as historian W. J. Ghent has said, Oregon was taken at Fort Hall." Whitman's

Scotts Bluff, a landmark in Nebraska used by many thousands of emigrants on the Oregon Trail.

vision, courage, and perseverance demonstrated the historical axiom that, "The flag follows the settlers."

Traffic westward along the Overland Trail then increased yearly until the discovery of gold in California in 1848, at which time emigration swelled to a torrent and the California Trail cutoffs bore much more traffic than did those to Oregon. Discovery of gold in Montana in the early 1860's also shunted heavy traffic into that area.

The California gold rush expanded the Oregon Trail into a multilaned thoroughfare. Innumerable columns rolling in parallel formation stretched for miles along the trail, their canvas tops fluttering, weaving, and bobbing like the waves of a gigantic sea. Wheels ground dust to the depth of six inches, dust that welled upward casting a dense pall over the area. By mid-May 1849, nearly forty-five hundred wagons had passed by Julesburg. The *St. Joseph Gazette* reported that on June 22, 1849, 10,500 wagons had passed Fort Laramie, and thousands more were yet to follow. It is said that a single traveler could have ridden a thousand miles along the trail and been certain of food and lodging. Bancroft estimated that more than forty thou-

sand persons arrived in California by land that year, with most of them traveling by way of South Pass. By 1852 over one hundred thousand people had reached California via the Oregon Trail.

Many thousands crossed the Oregon Trail in safety and in good health, but for thousands of others, illness, privation, suffering, and death stalked the trains. Cholera struck with devastating fury in 1849. Restricted to the plains portion of the route, the disease created panic and gloom. Many emigrants returned eastward to escape the malady. It felled weak and strong alike. Families were decimated, leaving widows, widowers, or orphans to continue the journey alone. Death or recovery was usually determined within a day. Estimates are that five thousand unmarked graves are strewn along the trail, victims of cholera during that year alone.

The *St. Joseph Gazette* offered some practical advice for California-bound emigrants in May 1852. They were advised not to overload their teams at the start of the journey because the trails were still

Original ruts mark a section of the Oregon Trail in Wyoming. The road is still used occasionally by cattle and sheep ranchers.

Parade ground at Fort Laramie, Wyoming. A key United States Army fort, the post was also an important supply depot for emigrants and freighters going westward on the Oregon Trail.

soft and miry in the spring, and streams high. And secondly, not to push their teams too fast at first when the oxen had neither learned to work as a team, nor adjusted from a diet that included grain to one that was exclusively grass. The article mentioned that it was unnecessary to load heavily at the start of the journey because supplies could be purchased at Forts Kearney, Laramie, Bridger, and at Salt Lake City. At Forts Laramie and Kearney, stocks of government supplies were sold to emigrants at cost. On the other hand, many wagon masters required that each wagon carry three months' provisions. So "You pays your money and you takes your pick."

Other problems faced by wagoners included howling wind, battering hail and electrical storms, lack of sufficient grass for the oxen, and wagon breakdowns. The forty waterless miles across the hot, shimmering desert between the Humboldt Sink and the Truckee River in Nevada exacted its toll of thirst on men and oxen. Rugged mountains of Idaho, Oregon, and Washington debilitated men and animals. On the California branch loomed the Sierra Nevada, a formidable barrier of sheer granite. So high and perpendicular towered these granite walls, that wagons had to be dismantled and hoisted by rope, piece by piece, over precipices seven thousand feet above sea level. On some wagon trains, supplies ran low or became exhausted. Aid from California saved hundreds of destitute and emaciated pioneers. The story of the ill-fated Donner party that lost half its roster to starvation, freezing cold, and deep snows just east of Donner Pass in the Sierra Nevada is well-known. The great westward adventure was not for the

35

weak, the timid, the infirm. One emigrant graphically recorded a small incident along the trail:

On the stormy, rainy nights in the vast open prairies without shelter or cover, the deep rolling or loud crashing thunder, the vivid and almost continuous flashes of lightning, and howling winds, the pelting rain, and the barking of coyotes, all combined to produce a feeling of loneliness and littleness impossible to describe.

Hostile Indians, of course, were always a hazard, but this danger was not as severe on the Oregon Trail as on the Santa Fe Trail, the second major westward trail. Defense tactics against Indians were similar on both trails, tactics that will be described later in this chapter.

The Santa Fe Trail was primarily a commercial and supply road. Few settlers used it; during the California gold rush, only about eight thousand Argonauts followed it because of the extreme danger of Indian attack. Prior to 1821, any non-Spaniard caught on the trail was imprisoned as a spy by the Spanish, who had political jurisdiction over the territory through which much of the route passed. In 1821 Mexico won its independence against Spanish rule and welcomed traders south of the Arkansas River (at that time the Mexican border), and encouraged them to sell their wares in Santa Fe. At the same time, Mexico allowed American trappers in the southern Rockies, the Sangre de Cristo.

The eastern termini of the Santa Fe Trail slowly moved westward from Franklin, Missouri, to Independence, to Westport, and to Kansas City.

Its western terminus was romantic, exotic Santa Fe, New Mexico, a drowsy city of about thirty thousand Mexicans, located approximately 870 miles from Franklin. Much of this distance lay through trackless deserts baked under a torrid sun to temperatures up to 120°F and dominated by fierce Cheyenne, Comanche, Kiowa, and Arapaho Indians. Thousands upon thousands of buffalo roamed much of the area, animals that were almost the sole source of food for these Indians. The original trail blazed by trappers followed the Kansas River in central Kansas, branched southward to the bend of the Arkansas River, followed this river to present day La Junta, Colorado, skirted the eastern foothills of the Sangre de Cristo Mountains, passed over Raton Pass, and then bore southeastward to Santa Fe.

As early as 1815 a few American merchants carried on a lucrative trade with Indians of the area, particularly the friendly Osage tribe, trading trinkets and other articles for buffalo robes and horses and mules (stolen from the Spaniards). After 1821 trappers and hunters caught beaver and buffalo in New Mexico, using Taos, an ancient Spanish trading post on the trail west of the Sangre de Cristo Mountains, as a supply and trading center. Several famous trappers (also known as frontiersmen or mountain men) not only pioneered

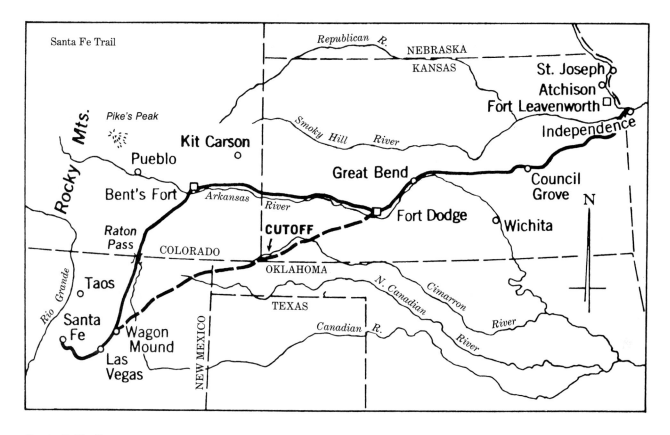

Santa Fe Trail

the Santa Fe Trail, but also other western routes. Among these staunch, independent and capable men who loved the lure of the wild, lonely, sparsely settled early West were Kit Carson, Tom Fitzpatrick (who led Marcus Whitman over the Oregon Trail), David Jackson, and William Sublett.

The first known trader on the Santa Fe Trail, sometimes referred to as the father of the Santa Fe Trail, was William Becknell of Franklin, Missouri. An expert frontiersman, he had traded with Indians prior to 1821. Loaded with goods Indians liked, he left Franklin with several other traders in September 1821 and followed the Arkansas River to La Junta, Colorado, but he learned that the Indians had already disposed of the furs, horses and mules they used for trading. Discouraged, Becknell turned south over Raton Pass and there encountered a troop of Mexican soldiers who welcomed him to Santa Fe, informing him that Mexico

was now independent and that the Spanish governor was gone. Becknell and his party then led their pack mules into Santa Fe and sold their merchandise at fantastically high prices. Even so, these prices were a bargain for Santa Fe residents previously charged much more for similar merchandise by Spanish merchants who had been shipping goods northward from Chihuahua, 540 miles south in old Mexico over the old Spanish Trail, since the early 1600's.

Most of the men in Becknell's party spent their Spanish silver dollars frolicking with the enchanting, sparkling-eyed Santa Fe señoritas. The colorful *baile* with its strumming guitars, lively accordion airs, and laughing señoritas was enhanced by the enchantment of soft light and dark shadows cast by a full moon on the hills of the Sangre de Cristo. But for Becknell the lure of profits overcame the lure of the fiesta. Becknell

37

Mid-nineteenth century wagon ruts on the Santa
Fe Trail near Fort Union in present-day
New Mexico.

packed his saddlebags with Spanish silver dollars and hurried away from such gaiety for home to organize another trading expedition to Santa Fe. Such will power was perhaps also needed to build the West.

An example of these bonanza profits is that of Fanny Marshall, who loaned her brother $60 toward the amount needed to buy his pack horse and trade goods; her share of the profits was $900. In the early days of trading, $30,000 invested in merchandise could turn a profit of $150,000.

News of these profits spread fast and the following May, Becknell and twenty other traders left for Santa Fe. While the others used pack animals, Becknell hauled his goods in two wagons, the first over the Santa Fe Trail. He knew that negotiating Raton Pass with a wagon was almost impossible, but he had heard that a river called the Cimarron ran almost parallel to the Arkansas River sixty miles south of it. If he could veer southward to the Cimarron, he could then follow it westward to the Canadian River and thence into Santa Fe. This

route would bypass Raton Pass and also would be about one hundred miles shorter. But this cutoff presented a very dangerous problem. Between the Arkansas and the Cimarron lay sixty miles of torrid, trackless, waterless desert. Anyone losing his way here would be almost certain to die of thirst, and sixty miles was more than twice the distance draft animals normally pulled in hot weather without water. In the face of this hazard, Becknell forded the Arkansas River about five miles west of present-day Dodge City and headed southwest with only a pocket compass as his guide. The only water his party carried was in their canteens. At first it was a gradual uphill six-mile climb in miring sand shimmering with torrid heat. By evening the canteens were empty. All night the caravan creaked along. Animals weakened and dropped along the trail. Several men had also slumped to the burning sands. By noon the following day their plight was desperate. Those still afoot staggered forward racked by thirst and weakened by heat. Suddenly one of the stronger men walking ahead spotted a

Josiah Gregg's COMMERCE OF THE PRAIRIES *depicting the arrival of a caravan at Santa Fe in 1844.*

From Arthur Amos Gray's MEN WHO BUILT THE WEST, *a publication of the Caxton Printers, Ltd., Caldwell, Idaho.*

buffalo with damp mud clinging to its legs. Realizing the animal's belly was gorged with water, he shot the buffalo, drained the water from its stomach into canteens and carried this normally obnoxious drink to his friends. Thus refreshed, they reached the Cimarron and ultimately Santa Fe, where they sold their merchandise at the usual huge profit. The new route Becknell blazed became known as the Cimarron Cutoff and was used almost exclusively by traders until 1834 when the Bent brothers built Bent's Fort as a trading post on the Arkansas River near La Junta and widened the trail through Raton Pass to accommodate wagons. The Raton Pass route was safer from Indian attacks than the Cimarron Cutoff and so, after 1834, only large, well-organized outfits used the Cimarron Cutoff.

During the spring and summer of 1846, as a result of the Mexican War, the Santa Fe Trail became a military road to the West. Colonel Stephen Watts Kearny's "Army of the West" passed over the trail en route to California and paused in Santa Fe, proclaiming New Mexico as territory of the United States. The United States Army established several forts along the trail and garrisoned thirty-five hundred troops in Santa Fe. These troops, along with the Mexican population who were now American citizens, had to be supplied by the United States. As a result, caravans on the trail increased and transport companies grew larger. Many traders began shipping their merchandise by professional caravan operators instead of in their own wagons. The United States Army also relied on private transport operators. A few of these outfits grew into gigantic transport companies. The largest were the Diamond R and those of Russell, Majors and Waddell.

They pulled freight, not only across the Santa Fe Trail, but also over the Oregon Trail into Montana and to Salt Lake City. Some wagon freight crossed the Sierra Nevada into California, but most freight to the West Coast arrived aboard sailing ships until the completion of the Pacific railroad in 1869. A few traders also followed the old Spanish Trail south of Santa Fe serving settlements in Texas and old Mexico.

In 1859 Horace Greeley, the famous New York newspaper editor, rode west on the Central Overland Mail stagecoach and stopped at Leavenworth, Kansas, headquarters for the now combined huge wagon transport company of Russell, Majors and Waddell. So impressed with this operation was Greeley that he recorded the following remarks in his journal:

> *Russell, Majors & Waddell's transportation establishment, between the fort and the city, is the great feature of Leavenworth. Such acres of Wagons! such pyramids of extra axletrees! such herds of oxen! such regiments of drivers and other employees! No one who does not see can realize how vast a business this is, nor how immense are its outlays as well as its income. I presume this great firm has at this hour two millions of dollars invested in stock, mainly oxen, mules and wagons. (They last year employed six thousand teamsters and worked forty-five thousand oxen.)*

A teamster camp at Santa Fe in present-day New Mexico.

As wagon caravans creaked westward over the Santa Fe Trail, the iron horse puffed not far behind. By 1872 rails had been laid to the point where Becknell had crossed the Arkansas River to mark the Cimarron Cutoff, near Dodge City, Kansas. Slowly, but relentlessly, the rails crept westward by way of Raton Pass until on February 9, 1880, the first train clattered into Santa Fe, and thus the wagon caravans of the Santa Fe Trail rolled into history.

One of the most widely used vehicles for hauling freight and emigrants was the popular Conestoga wagon, named after the town of its birthplace, Conestoga, Pennsylvania. This famed freight carrier was sturdily built of Yankee oak and ash. It had a certain grace and charm. Sagging in the middle, it rose majestically fore and aft like a ship. Ends flared outward at a rakish angle. A high, rounded canvas top followed this rakish contour.

The wheels were heavy and wide-rimmed for mud and sand. Front wheels measured four feet in diameter and rear wheels, six. Capacity was about four tons. Americans built other commendable freight wagons, the Chattanooga, the Carson, and the Studebaker, but all were fashioned after the Conestoga.

After teaming had developed in the Far West, teamsters there decided that Eastern-built wagons were inadequate for far-western transport, and soon California manufacturers were building wagons that met local freighting conditions. The beds of most California-built wagons measured sixteen to twenty feet long and forty to forty-eight inches in beam. The sides, painted red or blue, rose at a ninety-five degree angle four to eight feet above the bed. Side gates opened for loading and unloading. End boards slanted outward at forty-five degrees. Rear wheels spanned a diameter of seven feet, which put the wagon floor three and one-half feet off the ground. Front wheels were three to four feet in diameter. Since side boards often rose seven or eight feet, full height of this mammoth

A bull freight train in Nebraska City.

freighter towered eleven or twelve feet. These vehicles weighed from twenty-two hundred to thirty-eight hundred pounds empty, six to ten tons loaded.

Braking these fully loaded behemoths proved difficult. On the leading edge of the rear wheels, wooden brake shoes six inches wide and twenty to twenty-four inches long were installed. The shoes were connected to a vertical pole fastened at the rear of the wagon in such a manner that a teamster pulling on a rope fastened to the top of the pole could engage the brake shoes. Chock blocks, hung over the trailing edge of the rear wheels, could be dropped to brace a packed wagon against rolling backwards.

Freight wagons often pulled trailers during heavy freighting seasons. Attached to the team-drawn vehicle by a tongue, they were referred to as backactions. Trailers usually were 25 feet long, 5 feet wide, and 8 feet high and were equipped with the same type braking system as wagons. Outfits pulled by six- to eight-mule teams often measured

over 120 feet from the lead team to the trailer's rear board.

Such rigs packed large loads. Most six- and eight-mule teams hauled five tons of freight to the summit of the Sierra Nevada, including one-half ton of barley or oats as feed for the teams. Some outfits, however, stowed up to seven tons. Heaviest merchandise was packed in the bottom and light goods on top. If a trailer was used, heavy freight was loaded on the wagon with light goods in the "backaction," making the proportion of weight stowed by wagon and trailer at five to three.

After the introduction of trailers, many freight wagons were designed with a verticle instead of slanted front and rear. This design required shorter hitches, enabling wagon and trailer to ride closer together. The sides of this wagon were also upright. In order to stow the same payload, the beds of these wagons were wider. All freight wagons came equipped with canvas tops to protect freight from the weather.

To be a good teamster required great skill.

42

Freight trains leaving Nebraska City for Denver in the early 1860's.

Handling teams of six to twelve oxen or mules drawing a towering twenty-foot wagon and a twenty-five-foot trailer, with load and vehicles weighing up to seven tons, across endless prairies or over narrow, sharply curving mountain roads was no mean task. For this reason Western society of the day ranked teamsters just below steamer captains and stagecoach drivers in esteem.

Mules or horses were hitched in a manner that facilitated negotiating curves. Protruding forward from the front wheels was a tongue to which was harnessed the strongest team. Called the wheelers, this team directly steered the wagon and helped brake when going on the downgrade. Directly ahead of the wheelers was a team called the pointers. Positioned ahead of the tongue, this team pulled on the tongue with the wheelers.

Attached under the front axle was a chain (known as the swing chain) that extended under the tongue to the lead spans; a span being the pair of animals that worked as a team. Each span in front of the pointers pulled on the swing chain by traces attached from their collars to doubletrees fastened crosswise to the chain. Teams between the pointers and leaders were known as swing teams. On curves the inside animal of a pointer team stepped over the swing chain and pulled straight ahead on the tongue while the leaders and other swing spans pulled on the swing chain diagonally to the wagon. These forward spans moved along the outer edge of the road. They pulled diagonally because they were rounding a curve that the pointers and wheelers were just coming into. This was the only way to prevent the wagon from scraping a bank or dropping over a cliff or, in town, from running across a sidewalk.

The driver either rode the left wheeler or walked along the left side of the wagon. He controlled the teams with a single line. Known as a jerk line, it passed along the left side of each span through a ring on their collars to the lead team.

The line then ran from the bit of the left lead animal along a narrow wooden rod to the bit of its partner. This line was also fastened to the bits of the pointer team since they had to pull with the wheelers on curves. A steady pull on the line meant left turn and a series of jerks meant right turn. Many teamsters in later years used double reins to each team and controlled from a seat perched high on the wagon.

Most California teams consisted of mules, although horses and some oxen also pulled freight wagons. Mules, surprisingly intelligent, were particularly adapted to wagon freighting. In general they required less care than horses, were steadier workers, and healthier, ate less, and were less excitable or affected by hot weather. When properly trained and handled by a good teamster, mules proved excellent draft animals.

In addition to the jerk line, drivers controlled their teams by voice and bullwhip. Mules learned to recognize their driver's voice and the moods it reflected. If the teamster's voice expressed laxity, so did his mules; an urgent tone generally caused them to strain against their collars. If sterner efforts were needed, the teamster smartly cracked his long bullwhip over any recalcitrant mule, but seldom did a good teamster indiscriminately beat his animals. There were exceptions, but most expert teamsters agreed that the better teams were treated, the better they worked.

OPPOSITE TOP: Bull trains and headquarters of John Becker, wagon freighter, at Belen (in present-day New Mexico), 1877. OPPOSITE BOTTOM: Bull teams at rest in White Oaks in present-day New Mexico.

A jerk-line freight team hauling freight in the Sierra Nevada.

Muleskinners and bullwhackers resorted to violent and eloquent outbursts of profanity. According to tradition, these outbursts caused a mule to dig in his hooves, to dip his back until his belly scraped the ground, and to strain to the utmost at the traces. Or in the case of the stolid ox, to heave against his yoke and slowly and ponderously pull the heavy wagon on its lumbering way.

Teamsters worked hard at developing profanity into an eloquent means of communication. Loud and long flowed a unique profusion of words, some new and some old, words that would shock or be unknown to more genteel souls, but that were readily understood and even appreciated by the lowly mule or ox. Good teamsters prided themselves on their individualistic style of verbal pollution and on their ability to vary their profane vocabulary and delivery as the occasion demanded. This unique and colorful but profane communication from man to mule or ox surpassed by far

Ten-team outfit.

current blasphemous invectives. With the passing of the teamster there is now no need for it.

Though references to such prolific blasphemy are undoubtedly exaggerated, its use was quite general. Some drivers were known never to curse except when they drove mules. An expert mule-skinner was deemed capable of making a sluggish mule twenty feet away jump against his collar by calling his name and strongly adding a few invectives concerning the mule's dubious ancestry.

Clarence King in his book, *Mountaining in the Sierra Nevada*, vividly recounts his witnessing a teamster waxing eloquent at a stalled team.

He [the teamster] began in rather excited manner to swear, pouring it out louder and more profane, till he utterly eclipsed the most horrid blasphemies I have ever heard, piling them up thicker and more fiendish till it seemed as if the very earth must open and engulf him.

I noticed one mule after another give a little squat, bring their breasts hard against the collar . . . till only one old mule . . . held back. . . . The teamster walked up and yelled one gigantic oath; her ears sprang forward, she squatted in terror. . . . He then stepped back and took the reins, every trembling mule looking out of the corner of its eye. . . .

. . . He said in everyday tones, 'Come up there, mules.' One quick strain, a slight rumble and the wagon rolled on. . . .

A notable exception to such profanity were orders given drivers for Russell, Majors and Waddell, whose freight-wagon trains lumbered westward over the Oregon and Santa Fe Trails in the 1850's. Driving sixteen-mule teams, pulling five thousand pounds of freight, these teamsters were forbidden by their employers to use profanity. In fact, they were forbidden many vices and pleasures taken for granted by most teamsters in the Old

West. These instructions attempted (probably in vain) to elevate teaming to a dignified and gentlemanly profession, a mode of conduct somewhat unique in the Old West.

Following is the "Instructions to Freighters" issued to each freight train manager:

a. We outfit and ration a trip for eighty days (expect that will be sufficient time).

b. We do not ride on Sunday.

c. You must deposit rations for return train at Ft. Laramie and Ft. Lauderdale.

d. We are not at war with the Indians.

e. Take good care of your trains — keep things in order, oiled, etc.

f. You are not allowed to destroy fence poles and crops (Manager held responsible and any losses reported charged to him).

g. You will not allow your men to mistreat an Indian or anyone else. It is wrong and will recoil upon us in some way.

h. No Indian stock is to be molested. If emigrant stock is found and you are able to take it forward, do so, and report at Salt Lake to Mr. James Rupe.

As a general thing there is not importance enough attached to your position. We trust you with more in value than is generally conveyed to a first class clerk in an extensive store. Your responsibility is treble that of clerks. You must for our interest and your own credit watch closely all points.

By care and good management you can save us thousands. While on the contrary, a trifling neglect may lose us thousands.

You and your men understand our regulations: No profanity, gaming, dissipation or other immorality must be allowed. No abuse of cattle tolerated. No traveling on Sunday unless in search of water or grass or the health of your camp requires it. There is a Bible for every mess which is to be read, especially on Sunday. The Managers are to read it as an example.

You are to send a man ahead as a lookout as grass is getting thin for grazing.

(Signed: *Russell & Waddell*
Leavenworth City, K.T. 1857)

Orders such as these look commanding on paper but on the trail, hundreds of lonely miles from headquarters, such orders were an exercise in futility. Few bullwhackers or muleskinners persuaded reluctant teams to stir without resorting to an occasional blast of blasphemy. The following incident illustrates the need of such a blast. A bullwhacker was vainly pleading politely with a team of unenthusiastic oxen to pull a wagon from a mudhole. Waddell happened to be there. In desperation the bullwhacker pleaded:

Boss, the trouble with them oxens is they don't understand the kind of language we're talkin' to 'em. Plain 'Gee' and 'Haw' ain't enough under the present circumstances. Now, if you could just find it convenient to go off on that thar hill, somewhere, so's you couldn't hear what was goin' on, I'd undertake to get them oxens out.

Waddell retreated from audible range. Blasphemy rent the air, oxen strained at their yokes, and wagon wheels squished from the mud.

Oxen in considerable numbers pulled freight, especially on the high prairies. This draft animal had some advantages over the mule, and bullwhackers and muleskinners often engaged in contentious arguments over the relative merits of their respective wagon pullers. An ox cost about half as much as a mule and the wooden oxen yoke cost considerably less than leather mule harnesses. The cloven hooves of the bovines gave better traction in mud or sand than the smaller hooves of the mules. And though mules and horses foraged on natural grasses, they required additional grain

*Eight-ox bull team pulling wagon and
backaction.*

feeds to keep in good condition; whereas oxen did not, they thrived and gained weight on natural forage. Additionally, Indians were not as eager to steal oxen as they were horses or mules.

On the other hand, oxen's hooves became footsore more readily. Oxen were more subject to diseases; infectious diseases could decimate a herd in a short time. Like mules, oxen could pull prodigious loads, but could not compete with mules in hot weather. In spite of their apparent stolidness, oxen "spooked" easily and stampeded violently. They were known to run a mile over rough rocks pulling a heavily laden wagon that ended up broken into pieces with its cargo strewn over a wide area. Another disadvantage of oxen was their short working life (average ten to twelve years). Mules averaged a working life of eighteen years. On the trail ox teams averaged only twelve to fifteen miles a day compared to fifteen to twenty-five miles for mule teams.

Freighters on the High Plains learned, from bitter experience on the trail, to organize their trains in a quasi-military fashion. Twenty-five wagons forming a single caravan proved to be the optimum number for defense and maneuverability. In charge of the caravan was a wagon master or captain, and under him an assistant or lieutenant. The wagon master was in command; his word was law. Freight operators of less than twenty-five wagons attached their trains to other small outfits to form caravans commanded by a wagon master and his assistant. Outfits with more than twenty-five wagons on the trail generally divided themselves into twenty-five-wagon caravans. They spaced their caravans about a day's journey apart to avoid excessive crowding of animals around water holes and grazing grounds at night. Alexander Majors' caravans had an extra wagon that hauled supplies and food for the outfit, a mobile headquarters.

49

The wagon master determined when the caravan would roll, where it would stop, and when the men would eat and rest. He would scout ahead of the caravan or ride up and down the line observing the progress of each wagon, assisting a teamster with a recalcitrant team. His assistant generally rode to the rear of the train giving help to any stragglers or making certain that the drovers were herding the spare animals.

A caravan of twenty-five wagons was manned with about thirty-one to thirty-five men. Included were the wagon master, his assistant, twenty-five muleskinners or bullwhackers, a night herder, two day herders, and several extra hands as replacements for casualties or deserters. Some caravans carried a cook for the whole crew. Some member of the crew usually was a blacksmith and repairman, a vital occupation for a caravan rolling through wilderness territory with hundreds of miles between forts or settlements. Sometimes the owner of the freight or his clerk rode in the train with an "office wagon."

If the caravan carried no cook, the crew divided into messes of eight to twelve men. One was elected cook and relieved of all other duties except handling his team. Basic rations consisted of bacon, flour, coffee and sugar. The flour was made into flapjacks, biscuits, or bread. Some outfits served beans and dried apples once a week. When a caravan rolled through country with game, especially buffalo, hunters were sent out to supply the crew with much-welcomed fresh meat.

Caravans carried a variety of supplies. Extra wagon parts such as spokes, rims, bolts, links, chains, and hubs were essential, as were spare harnesses, yokes, and animal shoes. Tools were always carried and usually a small forge was included. Some outfits stowed a medicine chest stocked with calomel, laudanum (for dysentery), and Epsom salts. Sundry items included water barrels, wagon grease, candles, rope, soap, pepper, salt, matches, nails and of course, muskets, rifles, and sidearms. Early trains, using muzzleloaders, had on board powder, lead, and bullet molds; later trains, ammunition for breech-loading weapons.

Most wagon trains followed a similar daily routine, although it could vary according to the whim of the wagon master or weather conditions. All trains formed a corral at night for protection against Indian attacks. To form a corral, wagons circled to form an oblong enclosure with the wagons angled next to each other and the front wheel of one wagon opposite the rear wheel of the wagon beside it. These wheels were then chained together, and openings at each end of the corral were closed by chains. A well-trained crew could corral in five minutes.

Mule team loaded with boilers and machinery weighing 54,000 pounds en route from Elko to White Plains in 1869.

In hostile Indian country, wagons were corraled with tongues facing inward where crews could harness or yoke animals in greater safety. If an Indian attack was imminent, animals were herded into and kept in the corral for protection. Since ten to twelve draft animals pulled each wagon, 250 to 300 mules or oxen plus thirty-odd spare draft animals crowded the corral. During hitching-up time, confusion was great. The shouting and cursing of teamsters, the braying or bawling of animals, the stomping of hooves and clinking of chains blended into a cacophony that reverberated far across the prairie. But after some time on the trail many draft animals learned to move quietly to their proper places and wait to be hitched.

Most outfits had eaten breakfast, hitched up, and were ready to roll at daylight. About ten in the morning, the caravans usually halted for about four hours. This pause was common when the outfit passed through hot country. Teams were then unhitched and allowed to graze so that the animals would rest all night instead of foraging. This practice also avoided disturbing the crew and herders and lessened the risk of animals wandering off in the dark.

During this midday halt, the men received their main meal, but very little rest. There was always work to be done such as greasing wheel hubs, repairing harnesses or yokes, and shoeing or nursing animals. Some outfits were fortunate to have a full-time carpenter to keep wagons in repair; if not, teamsters were required to perform this task. Teamsters might also be required to take their turns at herding if the caravan was short of herders.

The afternoon run began at about two o'clock and usually ended at six, the length of the run determined by the distance between water holes and grazing grounds. After the train corralled and the evening meal was eaten, the crew relaxed. The men smoked, played cards, or swapped tall tales around campfires. Someone always stood guard and a night herder watched over the animals.

A good wagon master attempted to travel as far as possible and yet spare his draft animals and men undue fatigue. Usually teams and men rested one day a week. Alexander Majors' orders were that his outfits rest on Sunday, unless the welfare of the caravan demanded that it run on Sunday. Overall distance covered in the shortest possible time depended on the condition of the animals; overworked teams could slow the caravan, cause needless delays, or ruin an expensive animal.

Day after day the heavy wagons lumbered onward, wheel rims ground in dust or sand, and the caravan squeaked and creaked as it jolted over the trail. Dust welled upward from each wagon mixing with the sweat of men and beasts. Bullwhips cracked over reluctant oxen; bullwhackers shouted, "Hi-up thar you sons 'o the devil! Hi-up!" It was hot, dreary, wearisome toil on desolate trails that wound hundreds of miles from civilized outposts.

Not only was freighting hard work, but also

perilous—perils that included windstorms, hail, flash floods, and hostile Indians. At times howling winds drove blinding dust or sand across the prairies that could rip asunder canvas tops and halt caravans for days. Cloudbursts converted dried stream beds into raging torrents within an hour. A train moving into the path of such a stream often suffered heavy damage to cargo, and wagons and animals were drowned or scattered. Hailstones as large as baseballs would suddenly plummet on a hapless train, shredding canvas and injuring or stampeding the animals. Often in such a storm, frightened teams ran off with wagons until the vehicle broke up or overturned, scattering freight about the prairie.

The greatest hazard facing a freight-wagon train was hostile Indians. Indian hatred of the white man flared along the Santa Fe Trail more than on the Overland Trail, especially after the Mexican War because of the behavior of some of Colonel Kearny's troops, which included the dregs of the West and of the East. Many of these soldiers felt the only good Indian was a dead one and so created many "good" Indians as they moved along the Trail. Many soldiers indiscriminately shot buffalo, the Indians' basic food. Part of the Army aroused the ire of the men of New Mexico because many soldiers violated the chastity of their women. To avenge these outrages, New Mexicans whipped the Indians' latent hatred of the white man to the burning point. After 1848, hardly a caravan that rolled across the Santa Fe Trail escaped Indian attack.

Indians usually attacked wagon trains for two reasons: if they felt the train was encroaching on their hunting grounds, or for plunder, more often the latter. They always wanted horses and mules and often drove these animals off, leaving a train stranded. Food and freight goods also interested the savages. Sometimes they demanded and received goods and food under threat of attack. This ploy worked on small caravans or those inexperienced in defending themselves. A well-organized and disciplined outfit, of at least fifty men under good leadership and willing to put up a fight, usually held its own against plundering Indians.

Even though he was an excellent fighter, the Plains Indian, with few exceptions, had no desire for a prolonged, stand-up fight. He attacked only when he possessed overwhelming numbers and broke off the fight when he faced a determined foe. His favorite tactic was the ambush, followed by a short decisive fight, after which he swiftly galloped out of sight, driving off the caravan's animals. He loved pillaging, but was not disposed to lose his life for loot.

Caravans usually rolled in single file, but when they approached hostile Indian country they formed a double file and ran close up, making it easier to corral. A good wagon master sent men ahead to scout for Indians. If a war party was reported, the train immediately corralled. Animals were herded into the corral and the openings chained. If they had sufficient time, the men then dug rifle pits; otherwise, all hands were stationed behind the wagons, loaded guns at the ready.

Almost from the beginning of trade on the Santa Fe Trail, traders suffered from attacks by warlike Indians. Not every fracas on the trail can be recorded here, but a few examples are given to illustrate the hazard. In August 1828, some fifty or sixty traders, their dozen wagons loaded with fur packs and Mexican silver, were returning home from Santa Fe. Following the wagons, drovers herded a thousand mules and horses in stifling heat and thick billowing clouds of dust created by four thousand hooves shuffling along the desert. Two scouts, riding far ahead seeking water, were ambushed and shot near a nameless creek by unknown Indians. Coming upon the scene, the traders found one scout dead; the other died before the caravan reached the Cimarron. At this point they spotted a small group of Indians riding toward them. These Indians were perhaps not those who killed the scouts, but the angry and fearful traders opened fire on them, killing all but one, who escaped to inform his fellow tribesmen—Comanches—of the engagement.

Soon shrieking, howling Comanches galloped toward the wagon train from all directions. Riding out of range of the white men's rifles, the Indians stampeded and drove off the entire herd of one thousand horses and mules—draft animals purchased in Santa Fe for about $15, but worth over $100 in Missouri.

Other trading caravans met similar fates. Among surviving traders were men of influence in Missouri who induced Senator Benton to ask for Federal troops to escort wagon trains on the trail. Finally in 1829, President Andrew Jackson dispatched four companies of infantry for escort duty on the Santa Fe Trail. But effectiveness of these troops was hampered by two problems: one, the soldiers could not cross the Arkansas River since that would be an invasion of Mexican territory; and two, the troops were foot soldiers. Foot soldiers are very ineffective in battle against Indians riding fleet ponies. At that time, the United States Army had no cavalry.

In the spring of 1829, traders assembled thirty-eight wagons at Independence and prepared for the long, dangerous trek to Santa Fe. They were to be escorted to the Arkansas by two hundred troops under the command of Major Riley. Unfortunately the troops included riffraff of the plains and the Major was inexperienced in Indian fighting. Actually there was little trouble as the train creaked and rumbled through Indian country to the Arkansas River except that one night unknown Indians crept up to the troop encampment and made off with the few horses that the officers used for mounts. The Major sent his men far and wide in search of the horses, but in vain. Since the area south of the Arkansas at that time was Mexican territory, the soldiers could proceed no further. Pleading by the apprehensive traders failed to prompt the Major to move his troops across the river. Instead he prepared a fortified encampment and awaited the return of the caravan. The Major did, however, loan the traders a small cannon to bolster their courage.

In the wagon train were the Bent brothers, Charles and William, two young fur trappers and mountain men turned traders. They were resourceful, persevering, courageous, and intelligent—natural leaders. And they were wise to the ways of the Indians. William possessed an uncanny knack of quickly learning the languages of various tribes and of gaining their respect and confidence. The Bents now assumed command of the train. With the caravan were several other experienced frontiersmen.

After fording the Arkansas and filling every barrel, keg, and canteen with water, the wagons ground southwest over the desert toward the Cimarron. William Bent, riding a mule, scouted ahead to the west of the wagons when suddenly his mule turned his head toward some nearby rolling sand hills and snorted. William knew that meant Indians. Immediately young Bent fired his rifle, shouted a warning, and spurred his mule. Within a moment scores of shrieking Comanches poured from a gully less than a hundred yards away and charged the wagon train. William and two other mountain men, firing, reloading and firing again, countercharged the howling savages, who, abashed by this audacious tactic, momentarily swerved from the caravan. Then from another gully swooped other Comanches. To meet this new onslaught, Charles and William Bent and eight other frontiersmen, yelling the mountain men's battle cry, charged on foot this second group of Indians, simultaneously firing their rifles. This remarkable display of courage blunted the Indian attack and gave Charles Bent time to order his teamsters to corral their wagons, dig rifle pits, and throw up crude breastworks. Fortunately the draft mules and other livestock were safely driven into the tight corral. The Indians now slowed their ponies to an untiring lope and circled the caravan beyond rifle range, taunting the white men and waving the scalp of an outrider who was unable to make it back to the wagon train. The problem ultimately facing the besieged wagon train on this barren desert was water, and the Indians knew this.

Charles Bent now decided to roll out the cannon, a weapon the Indians feared worse than an evil spirit. The piece was loaded with grapeshot. Bent called for two volunteers and gave them the fastest mounts. At dusk the cannon was pointed at the encircling Indians. With a roar, a flash, and billowing smoke, the cannon spewed shot into a wide segment of Indians and their ponies, both of whom were ripped and mutilated by the grape-sized pellets; other braves bolted for the hills to escape the terrible demon. The mounted volunteers now galloped through the broken Indian circle and into the enveloping darkness. When the Indians had regained their composure and resumed their encircling lope, the volunteers were well on their way to the encamped troops.

The next morning the troops arrived and the Indians rode off. The caravan moved on, but the braves returned and continued their harassment from a greater distance. On the second day, water in the kegs and barrels ran low; troops staggered over the hot sands; animals became thirst-crazed. The Major now decided that he would have to return to the Arkansas or lose his troops to thirst.

Day after day the thirst-crazed caravan plodded through the sand, still under harassment by Comanches who rode beyond rifle range. Finally, a group of Mexican hunters out of ammunition stumbled onto the wagon train. Knowing where there was water, they led the caravan to it while a few of their party rode to Taos for help. In response, forty mountain men, including nineteen-year-old Kit Carson, rode over the Sangre de Cristo Mountains and across the desert to relieve the beleaguered train. But by now more Comanches had joined the original horde and this combined Indian force proved too large. After a bitter fight, the forty mountain men were forced to retreat. Kit Carson volunteered to ride to Taos for reinforcements and he returned with fifty-five frontiersmen. Now numbering ninety-five, the men charged several hundred Indians and routed them. The train proceeded safely to Santa Fe. On its return trip it was again set upon by several hundred Indians, this time Arapahos, but thirty mountain men, who had joined the caravan to return with their furs, easily repulsed them. These skirmishes convinced the Bent brothers that frontiersmen were the best guards a caravan could have until the Army could provide well-trained cavalry. Many frontiersmen were subsequently hired as teamsters or themselves became traders.

An eight-mule jerk-line team pulling a wagon and backaction.

The United States Army now withdrew infantry from the Santa Fe Trail until mounted troops were available. Later such troops, called Dragoons, assumed escort duty on a limited scale and still later, the United States Cavalry occupied forts in the area. But there never were enough such troops.

Even when Dragoons escorted wagon trains, many caravans did not go through unharmed. One portion of the Santa Fe Trail wound through a bleak stretch of six hundred miles in which no forts or depots were located, a dangerous area for attack, especially from the fierce Comanches. One engagement involved a company of First Dragoons and a caravan attacked near Coon Creek in June 1847. Comanches had attacked a wagon train and run off or killed all the oxen. The commander of the Dragoons patrolling the area sent twenty-five men to aid the immobilized caravan. Upon reaching the scene, they dismounted but were suddenly surrounded by blanket-waving Indians who then ran off the Dragoon's horses. Teamsters and Dragoons repelled the attack, but the military lost five men killed and six wounded; four teamsters were killed.

Since military garrisons were at times under-strength, the escorting of caravans was spasmodic. Trains had to learn to protect themselves. Skirmishes between freighters and Indians continued for many years on the Santa Fe Trail. During one bad year, 47 American traders were killed, 330 wagons were looted and burned and more than 6,500 mules and other livestock were killed or stolen. But in spite of these attacks, the freight rolled westward in sufficient quantities to supply Western outposts, thanks mainly to the courage,

perseverance, organization and discipline of those manning the caravans. Outfits on other trails westward, such as the Oregon Trail, also experienced Indian attacks but not as continuously, with the exception of the Bozeman Trail closed after two years of bloody Indian attacks.

The sagas of western freighting would not be complete without mention of the colorful twenty-mule borax teams that made scheduled runs in the 1880's between Furnace Creek in Death Valley, California, and the railroad at Mojave, California — a trip of 164 miles. The trail ran from the hellish heat and wasteland of below-sea-level Death Valley, over towering mountains, and across the Mojave Desert to the railroad — sandy, rocky, barren desert all the way. Men and mules sweltered in temperatures that soared over 130°F in the shade, but there was no shade on the Death Valley trail.

To haul tons of borax over such a torturous route required special wagons, men and mules. Like a symbol of the Old West, the wagons were massive. These behemoths weighed 7,800 pounds empty and stowed 22,500 pounds of cargo. They

were 4 feet wide, 6 feet deep, and 14 feet long. Front wheels were 5 feet in diameter, rear ones, 7; the huge hubs were 22 inches long and 19 inches in diameter. The oaken spokes were 5-1/2 inches in diameter and tapered to 4 inches at the felloe that was 8 inches wide. Wrapped around the felloe was an iron rim 8 inches wide and 1 inch thick.

An outfit consisted of two wagons and a thousand-gallon iron water tank mounted on a standard undercarriage. Mules were large, especially trained California mules. The entire caravan: twenty-mule teams, two freight wagons, and the water wagon, strung out over 150 feet.

Two men handled the outfit, the muleskinner who was boss and a swamper. The skinner had to be an excellent teamster to handle twenty mules organized into ten spans. Each mule knew its place in the line and exactly what it had to do. The same teamster always worked with the same team. On some sharp mountain curves, half the team was out of sight of the skinner. In such a situation the lead spans were pulling in one direction while the wagons were rolling in another. When the swing chain formed an arc around the curve, the inside

mule of each span nearer the tongue successively jumped over the chain as the span pulled to the outside. Upon straightening out, each inside mule jumped back over the chain in reverse order. The muleskinner guided the team by a jerk line while he rode the saddled near wheeler and he also worked the brake line of the lead wagon. The swamper's duties included working the brake line on the trailing wagon; cooking; harnessing, feeding and watering the team; and handling, along with the skinner, any emergency such as repairing harnesses and broken wagon parts, and shoeing mules. In addition, the crew needed special psychological qualities to endure driving twenty mules over landscape akin to the moon and in heat akin to hell.

The teams made the round-trip run from Furnace Creek to Mojave Village in twenty days — 164 miles each way. No natural forage for the mules grew along the trail and very few water holes existed. There were several dry stretches of twenty miles and one of almost sixty miles. To quench thirst of men and mules between water holes, water was stored in a thousand-gallon tank on the

57

rear wagon and in water barrels fastened on the side of each wagon. Hay and grain were stored at unmanned stations spaced at an average of sixteen miles (a day's run) along the trail. Springs and water holes were improved. On the return trip to Furnace Creek, hay and grain for the teams were loaded on the wagons and cached at the way stations.

Pay was $120 per month for the skinner and $80 for the swamper. It was good money for the times with very little opportunity to spend it. On the trail, crewmen furnished their own bedding and food, that consisted of bacon, beans, Dutchmen bread, canned goods and coffee. These items were inexpensive and to prevent such valuable, hard-to-find men from indulging in a prolonged binge, they were given only an afternoon off at each end of the run. The next morning it was hitching up and then, with a shout of, "Come up thar you sons of Satan!" plus a few colorful words of blasphemy to encourage the mules and make them feel wanted, the heavy wagons rumbled down the lonely desert trail stirring up a wake of grimy, billowing dust.

What was it like to drive a wagon team hauling five tons in a wagon and trailer? Up to now you have been told about it; now you will experience it. You are about to hitch a ride on a five-day journey from a Sacramento Valley shipping center into the Sierra Nevada gold diggings of the 1850's. The teamster you will meet is preparing to leave Marysville for La Porte, a mining settlement seventy miles away in the Sierra Nevada. The same kind of trip could be duplicated from either Sacramento or Stockton.

Shortly after dawn, you cross the Lower Plaza to meet your teamster. The mournful wail of a steamer whistle sweeps across the Plaza. You gaze toward the Yuba River to see the *Governor Dana* drift from the levee and turn downstream. In a few moments she will reach the mouth of the Yuba and swing into the Feather River on her run to Sacramento. As smoke from her stack drifts away, you muse that Marysville bridges the gap between the relatively modern invention, the steamer, and an invention so old its origin is lost in the mist of antiquity, the animal-drawn wagon.

The teamster is checking his fully loaded trailer and wagon, which towers eleven feet off the ground, at a Marysville commission house. He greets you with a friendly smile and seems pleased to have company on the long trip to La Porte far up the Sierra Nevada.

After carefully inspecting the traces, double trees, and swing chain and at the same time talking to his mules, the teamster mounts the left wheeler and indicates for you to mount the right wheeler. This places you and the driver on the team immediately ahead of the front wheels. Should you tire of riding, you may walk, or perhaps find some room on the backaction (the trailer).

The teamster takes the jerk line and both brake lines (one from the wagon and one from the backaction), cracks his bullwhip, and shouts, "Come up there, mules!" Eight mules lurch against their collars; traces snap taut; wagon and backaction jerk forward and rumble along the dusty street.

Your attention is immediately focused upon six jingling bells resounding in the clear spring air. These dangle from a long metal arch secured to the manes of the lead team. Later you will learn that these bells alert drivers of other teams that may be approaching on narrow, winding mountain roads.

Your 120-foot caravan turns onto B Street. Reacting to a steady pull on the jerk line, the lead span turns left and swings wide around the outside of the curve. The next span (the swing team) follows suit. The next team (the pointers), however, pull forward on the tongue at a diagonal to the lead team. As the lead span rounds the curve, the left pointer steps over the swing chain that is now at a diagonal to the tongue since this chain stretches from the axle to the lead and swing spans. When the pointers come into the curve, they round the corner followed by the wheelers. The wagon and trailer then negotiate the curve until the whole caravan is again straight and heading north on "B" Street.

Early risers, especially boys, wave in admiration at the adeptness with which your driver rounded the corner. None of the wheels brushed the curbs.

At Sixth Street a stop is made at a feed barn to stow half a ton of oats as forage for the team. This now brings the total cargo to five tons. Barley rather than oats was sometimes carried; price determined which it would be. The cost, however, is now considerably less than the dollar per pound charged a few years earlier.

Three wagons are ready to leave ahead of you, and as yours is loaded, another comes up. "We'll wait till them three wagons is well ahead of us. No use eatin' their dust. Besides, we got lots of time," explains your driver.

When the wagon ahead is 150 yards down "B" Street, your outfit lumbers onto "B" Street. At Twelfth Street the driver yanks the jerk lines several times and the eight mules begin the complicated right turn toward the distant Sierra Nevada shimmering in the bright sunlight of a late spring day. You look back and notice the billowing dust of a trailing team and wagon.

Dusty and weary, you arrive about six o'clock at a roadhouse located near Stanfield Hill sixteen miles from Marysville. Immediately the teamster unharnesses his mules and feeds them hay. Then after shaking dust from your clothes, you soak the dust off your face and hands in cold water at a common wash basin and comb your hair with a comb hanging by the mirror over the basin.

Most teamsters gather around the bar for a dust-cutter or two before dinner. Here teamsters' normally loud voices rise in volume as they exchange tales about unusual teaming experiences, or boast about the tonnage their mules could pull. Depending upon the strength of the dust-cutters and the number consumed, experiences become most unusual and heavy loads grow to prodigious sizes.

After listening to this jovial banter, you and your driver with ravenous appetites enter the dining room. An excellent dinner of soup, salad, meat, potatoes, pie or pudding, and tea, coffee or milk is set before you. (All this for fifty cents.) One large table seats the guests and dinner is served family style. Serving dishes, heaped high with portions, are passed and teamsters seriously and quickly begin devouring huge portions from plates piled high with food.

Niceties of etiquette are unknown here; if a diner wants another helping, which is often, he does not ask (he knows better), he reaches for the dish. Many times a hand or arm flashes by your face or a fork, on its way to spear a piece of bread or meat, nearly jabs your arm.

With dinner over, your teamster cares for his mules. They have cooled down by now and can be watered. He brushes off the sweat and curries them. They are then fed barley or oats, tied to the wagon and bedded down for the night.

With this chore completed, you and the driver return to the roadhouse for a few moments of relaxation. He explains how atrocious and expensive meals and conditions of roadhouses were just a few years previous when the gold rush was young. With more roadhouses came competition and thus better conditions.

Sleep begins to hang heavily on your brow and that of your companion. For fifty cents each, you and the driver could bunk in the roadhouse, but if the weather is pleasant, your teamster prefers to sleep near his team. Tonight is balmy and clear, so you and he make beds of hay by the wagon. You lie looking at the emerging stars. As they grow brighter, your eyes grow dimmer until you are engulfed in deep slumber.

With dawn you awaken refreshed to resume your trip. After a hearty breakfast of hot cakes, bacon and eggs, and coffee, you are ready to start. An eight-mile grade rises ahead. The destination for today is a roadhouse sixteen miles away.

As each mule strains at the traces to keep the wagon and backaction (trailer) lumbering up the hill, the driver urgently calls and encourages the team, calling each mule by name, to keep them pulling together. His voice is firm and commanding. He explains that if he appeared indifferent in voice or action, his mules would sense it and become lax. Without the teamster, the team would bog down and finally give up.

The arduous toil of pulling upgrade finally tires the mules. Before they manifest undue fatigue, the teamster drops the chock blocks, located at the trailing edge of the rear wheels of wagon and trailer, and halts the team. A particularly steep hill rises ahead for several hundred yards, so wagon and trailer will be pulled separately.

Unhitching the trailer and making certain that no animal is panting or showing fatigue, the driver then shouts an order and cracks his whip. Since this portion of the grade is steep, the team is driven only about forty to sixty feet when the chock blocks are again dropped to allow the team to rest. Only when all mules are rested is the order given to start.

Each mule makes certain it has good footholds before starting. Then every animal squats down until the hair of its belly almost scrapes the ground and with a mighty effort strains at the traces until the wagon slowly rolls forward. Here is a good team driven by an excellent teamster. Every fifty feet the team is rested until the steepest part of the grade is ascended. Then it is unhitched and the backaction pulled up in the same manner.

eling down the Sierra Nevada in 1865.

About six p.m. you arrive tired and hungry at a roadhouse at the foot of Willow Glen Grade. Here the second night is spent under similar circumstances and atmosphere as the previous one.

Leaving shortly after dawn, the team begins the steep pull up three-mile Willow Glen Grade. Using the same procedure of the previous day of pulling and resting, the team consumes three hours reaching the summit. Here toll must be paid at the first Knox toll station.

Near the summit of Willow Glen Grade and during a rest period, the distant jingling of bells rings across the clear mountain air. Your driver determines that another team has just begun to descend the grade about half a mile up the road. Since roads are too narrow to allow teams to pass, and this type of freight wagon cannot back up, one team will have to stand at a turnout, a wide space along the road. Toll-road owners by this time had constructed several turnouts per mile. Some roads, however, had few turnouts.

Loaded teams, especially those pulling upgrade, had the right of way, but loaded or not, teams nearest turnouts had to pull onto them. As your team is only two hundred feet from a turnout, it pulls toward the widened portion. Here again skill is required to maneuver the eight-mule team, wagon and trailer to the end of the turnout which is just long enough to accommodate the caravan. This turnout is on the outside and over its narrow shoulder a cliff drops several hundred feet.

The distant jingling becomes louder until clouds of dust well up around the next bend and a team plods into sight. The rig is similar to yours. As it draws alongside, it stops and teamsters jovially greet each other. They exchange tales of passing difficulties encountered in earlier days. The stranger recounts a time when his and another's teams met on a road between turnouts. Neither team could back up nor could they pass. Finally the ladened wagon was unloaded. Then one wagon was set as close to the edge as possible while the other was pulled around it with only inches to spare.

Your companion tells of an incident calling for even more drastic measures. His team had met a light outfit on a road which was too narrow for passing even if the wagon were unloaded. To remedy this situation, the team of the light wagon was unhitched, heavy ropes were attached to the wagon and wound around tree trunks. The wagon then was lowered over the side of the road while the other passed by.

Teams and teamsters now are ready to resume their journeys. After hearty farewells, your teamster guides his team onto the road. Before reaching La Porte, several such passings would be negotiated.

On the morning of the fourth day, you ascend a heavy grade to Woodleaf where the second Knox Road toll is paid. A late spring rain then showers down, settling the dust but increasing the hazard of mud.

A few miles farther, at a low spot on the road, wheels begin sinking into mud, slowing progress until team and wagon are hopelessly mired. The driver shouts and cracks his whip and hurls a few blasphemous innuendoes, but to no avail. He realizes that his mules cannot pull through this quagmire; further use of the whip would be unduly abusive.

Lifting his cap and scratching his head, the teamster remarks, "There just ain't nothing to do now but wait till another team comes along. Runnin' a rig such as this takes patience. Not all teamsters has got patience, though. Some gets mighty riled up at times like this. One time a driver got stuck in mud and couldn't get his mules to go. He finally got so mad he took out his pistol and shot each of his mules and then blew his own brains out."

Shortly, bells westward herald another caravan. The new arrival halts behind your rig, and both teamsters confer.

They unhitch all spans except the wheelers from the newly arrived wagon and hitch them to your wagon. With a mighty effort fourteen mules struggle for footing and strain against their collars. Teamsters shout and whips snap. Slowly wheels begin to churn through mud until firmer roadbed is reached. The combined teams are now hitched to the trailer and it is pulled to drier ground.

The sky begins clearing and soon a warm sun brightens the evergreen forest. Roads are much drier and the sun soon evaporates moisture on those portions of the road that lie flat.

After a rather steep climb, the team rests at the brow of a knoll overlooking a deep, wooded valley. The road ahead steeply descends toward a sharp curve beyond which drops a deep chasm.

"I ain't goin' to trust the brakes to hold the wagon back on this hill," muses your companion as he unhitches the lead team. You watch curiously as he pulls an ax and saw from the wagon. With these tools and the lead team in tow, he proceeds to the back of the trailer and up a slope to a grove of firs. Stopping at a tree about twelve inches in diameter, he begins chopping. Suddenly several staccato cracks spit from the lower trunk and the tree smashes to the ground with a resounding crash. The lead team draws it to the rear of the rig where the butt of the trunk is tied to it. You now realize this immense tree is to act as a drag to brake the wagon down the steep grade.

While you and the teamster rest, he tells you the downgrade with its curve reminds him of an unfortunate team that pulled a wagon down a similar grade:

Two ten-mule-team freight outfits attempting to pass each other in the Sierra Nevada. Mud and the injured mule in the passing turnoff add to the teamsters' difficulties. CIRCA 1870.

"When the mules just about got around the bend, the brake shoes broke. The wagon shot down the road to the curve and rolled over the cliff. Them 'ere poor mules was tryin' to get a foot-hold to keep from bein' pulled over with the wagon. After scrapin' and stompin' for a few seconds, the weight of the wagon and load pulled them over the cliff. Only one mule wasn't killed."

Having rehitched the lead span, the driver takes the jerk line, calls his mules, pulls the brake line taut, and eases the caravan down the hill. He guides the team cautiously around the curve. So heavy a drag is the tree, however, that the team actually pulls somewhat going downgrade.

Later you reach another toll station where your driver pays his third and last toll on the Knox Road. That night is spent at North Star House. On the fifth day, after climbing North Star Hill, you pass Buckeye House and American House. The road is now a gentle grade into La Porte where you arrive at midafternoon.

Reluctantly you shake hands with your interesting and informative companion of five days and bid him farewell. With a smile and wave of his hand, he fades into history; you now become aware that time had merely been turned back over a hundred years in your imagination. However, you also realize that the teamster, mule team, wagon, and trip were not your imagination, but realistically symbolized the vital role they played in the development of the West. Without the freighters with their courage, determination, and disciplined organization operating under primitive conditions in dangerous, hostile country over trails thousands of miles long, it is doubtful whether the far-flung settlements in the Old West could have survived.

Knophus' statue of a family with handcart.

3

Westward by Handcart

Wearily pulling and pushing two-wheeled handcarts, nearly three thousand men, women and children trudged from eastern Iowa to Salt Lake City, deep into the pioneer West. Most were newly arrived immigrants from England and Europe. Recent converts to the Church of Jesus Christ of Latter-day Saints (popularly called Mormons), they traveled from their homeland by steamship, then by railroad to Iowa City, Iowa. Here modern transportation ended. Thirteen hundred trackless miles of treacherous desert, prairie, rugged mountains and hostile Indians lay between these Mormons and Salt Lake City, Church headquarters.

From 1856 to 1860 ten handcart brigades passed over this perilous wilderness. All ten endured severe hardships; two resulted in tragedy.

Prior to 1856, Salt Lake City-bound Saints (as Mormons referred to themselves) traveled by wagon trains, but this mode of transport was more costly than many could afford. During that year hundreds of indigent Mormon converts streamed into Iowa City, where the Church maintained an outfitting depot. They were welcomed and sorely needed by the fledgling Mormon community in Utah. To get them there economically, Brigham Young, President of the Church, proposed that handcarts replace teams and wagons.

Handcarts had some advantages over teams and wagons. They were faster and less cumbersome. Oxen were slow and required much precious time unyoking, rounding up, and hitching. They demanded considerable forage and water and to meet these needs wagon trains frequently wound many miles off their course. Then too, speedier handcart travel reduced sickness on the trail, according to Church officials who believed such illness resulted from too much time spent in one place.

Acting upon this suggestion, Mormon emigrants began constructing handcarts at Iowa City in the spring of 1856. Though their size and shape varied somewhat, handcarts presented a general uniformity of pattern. Resembling the two-wheeled carts of present-day railroad porters, their beds consisted of a small box three or four feet square and eight inches high. Two parallel wooden shafts, crosspieced at the end, extended forward. Little or no iron was used. Axles were hickory; hubs, elm; and beds, white ash. Wheels were tired with hickory, although some were hooped with iron. Canvas canopies similar to those on covered wagons protected some handcarts from the elements. Five persons (generally families) were assigned to a handcart. Two pulled while one pushed and helpers on each side twisted the spokes to keep wheels moving in sand, mud or up hills. On board only seventeen pounds of utensils, bedding and clothing per person was stowed, along with any who might be sick. Each brigade included several ox-drawn wagons that transported food, tents, and miscellaneous supplies.

During the spring of 1856, two companies built handcarts and outfitted themselves at Iowa City for the trek westward. On June 9 and 11 respectively, these companies consisting mainly of English converts left Iowa City. Edmund Ellsworth, age thirty-seven, led the first brigade; Daniel McArthur, age thirty-six, led the second. Both men were American missionaries who had served in England and Europe.

Reenactment of the Archer family leaving Iowa with a handcart company.

A total of 494 emigrants were assigned to one hundred handcarts. Nine wagons stowed twenty-five tents and sufficient food to last to Florence (now Omaha), Nebraska. Since handcart baggage was limited, many chests, dishes, and personals had to be left behind. On the journey these two companies associated closely and arrived at Salt Lake City the same day.

Eager and lighthearted, the emigrants pulled their carts across the dust-coated plains of Iowa. They logged only four miles the first day, but as they toughened to the trail they covered up to thirty miles a day.

Even though these two brigades and a third that followed on June 28, 1856, were considered successful, fatigue, hardship, hunger, sickness and death stalked them. At times food rations had to be lowered. Daily rations were reduced from one pint of flour per person to one-half pint, rice to two ounces. Weekly rations cut bacon to one-half pound and sugar to three ounces per person.

A few excerpts from the journal of Archer Walters, an Englishman and member of the first brigade, vividly illuminate how many fared. Being a carpenter, it became his lot to repair handcarts and build coffins.

June 11th, 1856. Journeyed 7 miles. Very dusty. All tired and smothered with dust and camped in the dust. . . .

June 15th. Got up about 4 o'clock to make a coffin for my brother John Lee's son. . . .
. . . and at the same time had to make a coffin for Sister Prator's child. Was tired with repairing handcarts the last week.

June 16th. Harriet [his wife] very ill. Traveled 19 miles.

June 17th. Traveled 17 miles. Made coffin for Br. Job Welling's son. . . .

21st. Bower died about 6 o'clock.

26th. Traveled about 1 mile. Very faint from

Courtesy Church Archives, The Church of Jesus Christ of Latter Day Saints, Salt Lake City, Utah

lack of food. . . . Made a child's coffin . . . for Emma Sheen aged 2-1/2 years.

July 7th. Thousands of buffalo. Traveled twenty-five miles. Camped late at night. Had to dig for water and it was very thick. Our hungry appetites satisfied by the buffalo meat. Got up soon to repair handcarts.

July 25th. Saw many Indians. Camped about 19 miles from Fort Laramie. Handcart axle tree broke on the road. Plenty of wood. Quite a treat after burning buffalo chips.

Aug. 31. Very poorly, faint and hungry. Traveled to Deer Creek, 22 miles. Brother Stoddard . . . died in the wagon on the road.

Relentless dust ground away the carts' wooden axles. Fortunately, a tinsmith had a box of block tin and by working morning, noon and night during stops he wrapped every axle.

Weary but happy the first company trod into Florence on July 20; the second followed four days later. They spent two weeks recuperating and repairing equipment, as nearly one thousand miles of wilderness lay ahead—exotic land inhabited only by unpredictable Indians and a few scattered U.S. Army forts.

As the emigrants trudged across Nebraska, new obstacles arose. Firewood became scarce, but was replaced by buffalo chips. Perhaps the most difficult problem was frequent fording of streams and the Platte River—as many as twenty crossings in a day. Carts had to be pushed and pulled across muddy or rocky river bottoms, through water at times several feet deep. Another impediment was deep sand that clutched at the wheels.

Pushing westward, they passed near present-day Scottsbluff, Nebraska; then into Wyoming, where they crossed the Continental Divide at South Pass. From here the trail veered southwest toward Fort Bridger, Wyoming, near the Utah border. This is approximately the route of the Oregon Trail where it branched southward at Fort Bridger. Most Mormon migrations, however, stayed off this famous westbound-emigrant trail (but within distant sight of it) because they wished to avoid the "Gentiles," as non-Mormons are called.

In sagebrush-blanketed Wyoming, Indians appeared more frequently. They presented a mental hazard, even though most proved friendly and sometimes helpful. On one occasion the brigade teetered near disaster when they encountered a war party of Indians. The company had stopped at the Platte River when Indians, decorated with war paint and appearing very hostile, approached the emigrants and demanded food. Captain Ellsworth asked the brethren to pray while he talked to the Indians. During their conversation, Ellsworth offered beads and the Indians departed in peace.

During the first week of September, at Deer Creek, about 150 miles northeastward of Fort Bridger, the two companies observed billowing clouds of dust to the southwest. Soon a five-wagon train hailed them. Sent from Salt Lake City as a relief train, each wagon was ladened with one thousand pounds of flour. Nourished in body and heartened in spirit, they joyfully hurried on. Within two weeks they were camped at Fort Bridger only 113 miles from their destination. Five days later the weary but exuberant emigrants, pulling their carts and praising God, triumphantly entered Salt Lake City. On hand to give them a rousing reception were Brigham Young, church dignitaries, brass bands and the city's inhabitants.

A third handcart company left Iowa City, June 8, 1856, and arrived at Salt Lake City, October 2. This party was led by another American missionary, Edward Bunker, and was composed of Welshmen for the most part. This company of 329 emigrants, 64 handcarts and 5 wagons, while suffering similar hardships as the first two, made what was considered a successful journey.

Inspired by the example of the first three companies and burning with religious zeal to reach their city of Zion, a fourth and fifth company left Iowa City, July 15 and 28, 1856. Both brigades were much larger than their predecessors. Company four numbered 500 emigrants, 120 carts, 6 wagons, 24 oxen, and 45 head of cattle and milk cows; company five consisted of 576 persons, 146 carts, 7 wagons, 30 oxen, and 50 head of cattle and cows. But freezing cold, blizzards, starvation and death were also to accompany them on their trek.

Four weeks after they left Iowa City, the emigrants arrived in Florence with no greater difficulties than had befallen their predecessors. However, the lateness of the season and the bleak one thousand miles ahead caused foreboding among some elders who favored establishing winter quarters at once. Others felt that the mission to push westward was divinely right. Most emigrants, ignorant of the country and its severe winters, were eager to proceed. Ignoring ominous warnings, company four, led by forty-one-year-old American missionary James Willie; and company five, led by thirty-seven-year-old missionary Edward Martin, left Florence August 15 and 28 respectively and proceeded to their rendezvous with tragedy. For a few days laughter and song permeated each campsite.

Before long trouble arose. Heavily laden handcarts began breaking down. Each cart had been loaded with an additional ninety-eight pounds of flour, since the wagons could not stow enough to last to their destination. Wooden parts broke and dust ground wooden axles in spite of their being bound with leather or tin. Since no proper lubricants were available, many Saints greased axles with lard and bacon to their later regret. Precious time was lost on repairs.

Food shortages now plagued them. Company four learned that expected provisions from Salt Lake City had failed to arrive at Fort Laramie, Wyoming. Flour rations were reduced from one pound to three quarters of a pound per day, since at the former rate of consumption supplies would be depleted three to four hundred miles short of their destination. Later the daily ration was again reduced when it was determined that food would not last to South Pass on the Continental Divide where supplies from Salt Lake supposedly awaited. Hunger and weakness were further aggravated when a buffalo herd stampeded and drove off many cattle and milk cows.

As company four struggled toward South Pass, the continuous rise in elevation and the passing of summer brought even colder days and nights. Clothing and bedding, sufficient for summer, were insufficient against the penetrating cold. Each day the snow level on distant mountains crept lower and lower toward the struggling Saints. Finally the enveloping mantle overtook them. Weakened by hunger and numbed by cold, they frantically tugged and pushed to keep wheels churning through snow and mud. To add to their burden, more and more sick were forced to ride the carts. Death now took an ever-increasing toll. Some emigrants died by their carts during the day; others passed away during the night. Many a father pulled a cart with his little children on it one day and died the next. Each morning burial parties were formed. Death not only brought sorrow; it depleted the needed manpower to pull carts, erect tents and perform other duties.

Exuberance of early weeks gave way to sorrow and wretchedness. No one could be certain that a relief train was en route or, if one were, that it could find them in this snow-blanketed wilderness. Spirits sank; some became mentally deranged. Deep religious faith sustained many and daily prayers for deliverance were offered.

One particularly torturous day, with a howling blizzard banking deep snowdrifts, company four was forced to a crunching halt at noon. Despair settled over the group until someone peering westward noticed shadowy forms moving eastward in the swirling whiteness. The forms slowly came closer. At last they were recognized as a light wagon bearing two young men. The men, Joseph A. Young (son of Brigham Young) and Stephen Taylor, had been sent eastward by a relief train to find the companies and inform them that help was coming. This news must have seemed like answered prayers.

Hopes now soared at the unexpected arrival of these two young men. Utilizing superhuman strength, the company rolled their carts westward in search of the relief train. Young and Taylor hurried eastward to find Martin's company that was several weeks behind number four and beset with even greater difficulties.

The relief expedition had been quickly dispatched from Salt Lake City after Brigham Young had been informed, by returning missionaries on October 4, that the two handcart companies were still on the trail. Surprised church officials called for immediate formation of a relief train. Response was spontaneous and even the poor donated unstintingly. Women darned socks and shawls; they gave underwear, blankets, clothing and utensils. Men loaned wagons and mules; blacksmiths shoed mules and repaired wagons. Young men volunteered to drive the wagons. From none too plentiful larders, flour, bacon, beans, corn, sugar and rice were cheerfully given.

In two days sixteen wagons drawn by four-mule teams were speeding eastward on their errand of mercy. Daily more wagon trains were organized until by the end of October an armada of two hundred and fifty teams was headed toward the stricken emigrants.

As company four resumed its journey in search of the relief wagons, its plight became increasingly desperate. Sparse forage dispersed cattle and milk cows; remaining cattle weakened and died. Finally another blizzard and deepening snow forced the brigade to halt. Food now was depleted except for two barrels of hard bread and a few scrawny cattle. Dysentery in epidemic proportions took its grim toll. The promised relief train had not materialized and hope of its arrival or of its finding the emigrants ebbed.

Willie, the company's captain, finally scouted westward in a desperate effort to locate the relief caravan bogged down by the same storm. Several days later on October 21, Willie stumbled onto the stalled wagons and explained to elders W. H. Kimball and G. D. Grant, leaders of the train, the emigrants' severe predicament. Kimball and Grant immediately moved eastward against howling winds and driving snow that stung like needles. Three days later Willie led them into his company's camp. Shouts of joy and hymns of praise greeted them. Strong men wept; others knelt and prayed in gratitude. Kimball remained with Willie's company with half the relief train and Grant moved eastward with ten wagons to find company five. Arrival of the relief wagons undoubtedly saved Willie's brigade from total destruction. Their ordeal, however, was far from over. Hundreds of miles of windswept, snow-covered prairies and icy mountains stretched before them.

In the meantime Martin's company was experiencing extreme hardships. Until it had left Fort Laramie (several weeks later than company four), this company had fared well. As with company four, troubles commenced westward from Fort Laramie. Here dwindling food supplies forced Captain Martin to lower rations repeatedly until each person was allotted less than one-half pound of flour per day. Scant forage weakened oxen and cattle.

Earlier, in order to increase their speed, members of company five had lightened their loads by abandoning clothing and bedding, thus reducing baggage to ten pounds per adult and five pounds per child. In two days they realized their tragic error. Weather turned colder at the last crossing of the North Platte River near the present-day city of Casper, Wyoming.

Josiah Rogerson of the company recorded the crossing in his journal:

The crossing of the North Platte was fraught with more fatalities than any other incident of the entire journey. . . . Blocks of mushy snow and ice had to be dodged. . . .

A Mrs. Elizabeth Jackson wrote about the crossing:

Some of the men carried some of the women on their backs or in their arms, but others of the women waded through. . . . My husband (Aaron Jackson) attempted to ford the stream. He had only gone a short distance . . . when he sank down through weakness and exhaustion. . . . A man on horseback conveyed him to the other side. My sister then helped me pull my cart with my three children and other matters on it.

Twelve miles beyond the crossing, a shrieking blizzard blasted the exhausted travelers. Winter now began in earnest. The determined emigrants staggered another twelve miles until exhaustion and deep snow forced them to halt.

Frayed clothing and shoes offered little protection against the biting cold. Snow measured nearly eighteen inches. No comforting word of a relief train had been heard; it now seemed doubtful that one could or would arrive. Daily prayers for deliverance were offered.

Deaths occurred at an alarming rate. During the nine days following the final crossing of the North Platte, fifty-six emigrants died. Mrs. Aaron Jackson, whose husband's passing resulted from his ordeal in crossing the icy North Platte, graphically describes his interment:

. . . oh, such a burial and funeral service. They did not remove his clothing —he had but little. They wrapped him in a blanket and placed him in a pile with thirteen others who had died, and then covered him with snow. The ground was frozen so hard they could not dig a grave. He was left there to sleep in peace. . . .

Joseph Young and two other men found the stalled brigade and announced that ten relief wagons captained by George D. Grant were at Devil's Gate, Wyoming. Electrified by this wonderful news, the emigrants mustered superhuman strength and pushed through eighteen inches of snow toward Devil's Gate. Grant in the meantime was notified by courier of company five's desperate situation and drove eastward at once with some of his wagons. They met at Greasewood Creek, sixteen miles east of Devil's Gate. Grant then led the emigrants toward Devil's Gate on November 2, where the rest of his wagons awaited them.

Grant now sized up his situation. What he saw rent his heart. Between five and six hundred exhausted and starving men, women and children, many of them sick and dying, looked to him for deliverance. His wagons contained a mere pittance to clothe and shoe so many against the freezing cold. His food supply could help, but not last long. Only about one third of the company could walk. Grant immediately dispatched Joseph Young and Abel Carr to Salt Lake City for help. Grant, of course, did not realize the immensity of relief preparations already in progress there.

As Grant ministered to the stricken company, two Mormon westbound wagon trains came upon them. These trains had also been caught in the early winter and were low on food. Twelve hundred people were now assembled there.

Leaders of the group decided to unload supplies from the handcarts onto wagons and abandon the carts. Handcart emigrants able to walk were to accompany the relief wagons; newly arrived wagons were to haul the sick. The wagon trains then proceeded along the Sweetwater River toward Devil's Gate, where freight would be stored in an abandoned fort to make room for more handcart emigrants in the wagons.

On November 6 the temperature dropped to 11° below zero Fahrenheit. Each day people died from cold and hunger; others became ill or suffered frozen extremities. No additional relief trains

The Devil's Gate area where starving and storm-battered members of stalled handcart companies four and five met vanguards of relief wagons from Salt Lake City.

had arrived, nor was there much hope any would. They were unaware of the relief trains proceeding from Salt Lake City.

Meanwhile Willie's company four and Kimball's relief wagons ploughed slowly westward through deep snow. Although the relief train gave strength and hope to many, others seemed beyond help. They were completely exhausted or mentally apathetic. Many of these unfortunates perished on the trail. John Chislett, a subcaptain, wrote in his diary of efforts to encourage them, and also of his increasingly difficult task of rounding up the many discouraged stragglers.

Willie's brigade suffered its worst hardship crossing the tortuous terrain at Rocky Ridge, twenty-five miles east of South Pass (the Continental Divide). Extreme cold and blizzards battered them. Finally the company was forced to halt for a day to gather and bury the dead. Fifteen bodies were buried in a mass grave in a simple ceremony under the open sky.

Approaching South Pass, the emigrants began to meet relief trains from Salt Lake City. After they negotiated the Pass, more relief wagons began arriving until at Fort Bridger all were able to ride in wagons. Finally on November 9, 1856, survivors of company four reached their "City of Zion." Sixty-seven remained in unmarked graves along the rugged trail.

Thus ended the epic struggle of company four. But company five was still on the trail 325 stormy, desolate miles from Salt Lake City. As they floundered westward from Devil's Gate, unbeknown to them, relief trains were ahead, but severe storms had forced these trains to halt. In fact, many in the relief trains stalled near South Pass concluded that company five must have put into a winter camp or perished. Some relief wagons even turned back; however, others waited patiently at South Pass. At this point, Ephraim Hanks, one of the greatest Mormon scouts, defied the howling storm and crossed snow-swept South Pass alone on horseback in a desperate attempt to locate beleaguered company five.

Toward evening, as the sun faded and transformed the blinding whiteness of the snow to cold blue, Hanks scanned the bleak horizon and saw the hapless emigrants making camp. Riding quickly into the camp, he distributed a quartered buffalo he had killed on the trail. What he saw appalled him. In addition to starvation, wretchedness and death, Hanks observed frozen limbs hanging useless, which it was necessary for him to remove.

Hanks dispatched messengers to alert the relief wagons at South Pass. In response, four wagons, ladened with flour, crunched eastward day and night, reaching the camp at five a.m., November 12.

With nourishing food and milder weather now strengthening and encouraging them, the emigrants again moved on. Four days later at Rocky Ridge, scene of company four's deadly ordeal, Martin's caravan met ten more relief wagons. Several days later other relief wagons arrived. By November 19 enough wagons were available so that all could ride in the comparative warmth and comfort of canvas-covered wagons, and none too soon, as more snow and freezing cold swept upon them. At Green River additional relief wagons awaited them, swelling the number of such vehicles to 104.

On November 29 the long train started winding over Big Mountain, the last mountain barrier before Salt Lake City. Here they found Joseph A. Young, his brother Brigham Jr., and several other young men keeping the mountain road open by moving animals to and fro. Finally, on the following day, from the summit the emigrants gazed at the distant valley where Salt Lake City lay. Descending into the valley, the train arrived later that day to a warm and loving welcome. However, about one

Survivors of the handcart companies parade at a Pioneer Jubilee in Salt Lake City on July 21, 1897.

fourth of the original company did not live to see this day. Between 135 to 150 men, women and children lay in graves along the trail.

This rescue mission is considered one of the most courageous, massive and selfless ever witnessed in the Old West. It undoubtedly saved companies four and five from annihilation.

The tragedy of these two handcart brigades dampened enthusiasm for this mode of travel. The problem was that these companies had left Iowa City too late in the summer to reach their destination before winter enveloped them. Church officials recognized this and continued to encourage this inexpensive means of transportation. To prevent more tragedies it was ruled that no handcart company should leave the Missouri River later than July 1, and that handcarts should be made stronger.

Two more handcart brigades came through in 1857; number six under Captain Israel Evans arrived in Salt Lake City September 11, and number seven arrived September 13. They had left Iowa City May 22 and June 13. Though experiencing the usual hardships of the first three companies, they were considered successful ventures.

Because of the so-called Mormon War, no handcart brigades ventured out in 1858. However, 1859 saw one such migration under Captain George Rowley. It too was termed a success. The following year companies nine and ten made successful journeys, the final year handcarts were used. The last three companies had a shorter trip since emigrants could now travel by railroad to Florence (Omaha), Nebraska. After 1860, Mormons brought their emigrants to Salt Lake by operating round-trip wagon trains from Salt Lake City to Florence and back. As the railroad advanced westward, this route became shorter until trains ran to Salt Lake in 1869.

Thus ended one more episode of that great American epic of westward expansion that welded together a great nation—an epic made possible by pioneers such as these staunch handcart emigrants who were willing to face extreme hardship, danger, and even death to build what they visualized as a better life for themselves and their progeny.

Stagecoach dashes for the safety of the relay station in this reproduction of painting by H. W. Hansen.

4

Traveling by Stagecoach

Six spirited horses drawing stagecoaches that pitched and rolled along the roads shared a bustling scene with smoke-belching river steamers, freight wagons and pack mules in the Old West. By the mid-1860's major stagecoach lines had spanned most of the Old West linking major cities, settlements and mining areas. In California, stagecoach travel developed early and rapidly.

Following the gold rush of 1849, many independent drivers operated short-range stage lines on irregular schedules between gold-mining camps. Early equipment was usually crude and drawn at times by half-tame mustangs, but business was brisk and profitable. Passengers willingly hazarded travel on such precarious transport for fifty cents per mile; a rate several times higher than that of a modern jet airliner per mile.

During the 1850's a few far-sighted men such as Jim Birch, Jared Crandall and Warren Hall realized that stagecoaches should run not only between a few mining camps, but also between principal towns. They realized the need for regular schedules and first-class vehicles and began forming stage lines on these bases. Soon California was crisscrossed with stage routes carrying passengers and the U.S. Mail at fares less than one quarter those charged during earlier gold-rush days. By mid-1850 these stage lines had merged into the California Stage Company, a huge transportation empire headed by Jim Birch, headquartered in Sacramento until 1857, when the company moved its office forty miles north to Marysville. During the late 1850's and early 1860's, this company operated twenty-eight stage lines for a total of one million stage miles annually.

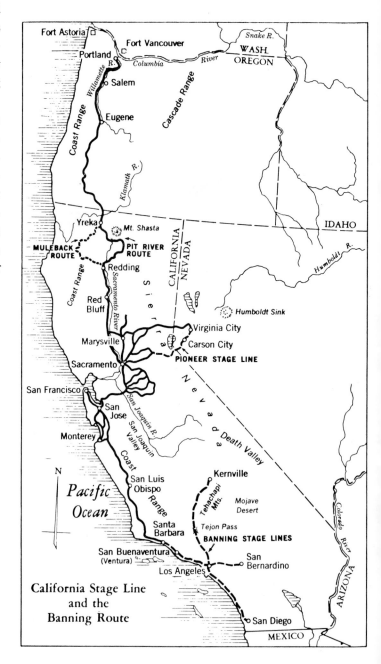

California Stage Line and the Banning Route.

In 1860 the company added seven hundred miles by extending service from Sacramento to Portland, Oregon, via Marysville, thus linking Portland to Los Angeles and San Diego by stagecoach. Actually the Santa Barbara-Los Angeles-San Diego portion was operated by the Banning and Alexander Stage Company that also ran eastward routes through the Tehachapi Mountains to Kernville, California and to San Bernardino.

Until the great transcontinental stage routes to the East were established, the California Stage Company's Portland-Sacramento-Los Angeles-San Diego line was the longest in the world. When measured by stage miles driven per year, the million miles of the California Stage Company made it an even larger operation than the transcontinental lines. Keeping these sprawling routes operating required 1,500 horses; 205 Concord coaches and wagons; and 300 agents, drivers and hostlers.

Contemporary advertisements beckoned travelers with alluring announcements promising comfortable travel in luxurious Concord coaches between Sacramento and Portland in only six days. En route, passengers spent two nights in way stations, thus affording them the opportunity to refresh themselves. During the remaining days of travel time, passengers rode day and night. However, should this prove too strenuous, travelers were granted the privilege of leaving the stage at any overnight station; they could take the next stage at no extra cost except for the night's lodging.

California Stage Company (the world's largest stage line company) ad in the MARYSVILLE DIRECTORY, 1858.

Courtesy Bancroft Library, University of California, Berkeley

California Stage Company ad in the 1854-5 CITY DIRECTORY OF SACRAMENTO.

The advertisement did not exaggerate in referring to the Concord coach as luxurious when compared to other types of contemporary horse-drawn conveyances. The Concord was used extensively on stage lines in the Old West and became a favorite for travelers. Though a trip by stagecoach was at times one of travail and danger, most Westerners admired and venerated the famous vehicle that contributed to the development of the Old West.

One feature that endeared it to travelers was the unique manner by which the body was suspended on the frame. No metal springs were used; fore and aft on each side of the frame were slung straps made of several layers of tough steer hide.

These straps, or thorough braces, sagged in the middle like a hammock. The curved bottom of the body of the coach rested snugly on these sagging but sturdy thorough braces. Only in the middle of each thorough brace was the body fastened to it; thus the front and rear body were free of restraint. Such suspension permitted the coach body to pitch fore and aft and to roll sideways, eliminating many of the severe jolts encountered on rough, rocky frontier roads. On metal spring-suspension wagons, these jolts were telegraphed to the coach's body, passengers and teams. On a Concord coach the body would pitch forward and rearward when the wheels ran over rocks or ruts, or roll sideways if wheels on one side dropped into a depression.

The resultant ride has been compared to that of a ship gently pitching and rolling over a swell, but as on a ship, this could cause motion sickness.

Not only did thorough brace suspension shield passengers from sudden jolts, it also spared teams such jolts. It has been said that without thorough braces, teams pulling stages at ten to fifteen miles per hour could not have withstood the punishment.

The well-constructed, mostly hand-built Concord was manufactured by the famous Abbot-Downing Company, at a cost of fourteen hundred dollars. The stagecoach derived its name from the company's location in Concord, New Hampshire. An example of the Concord's ruggedness was that

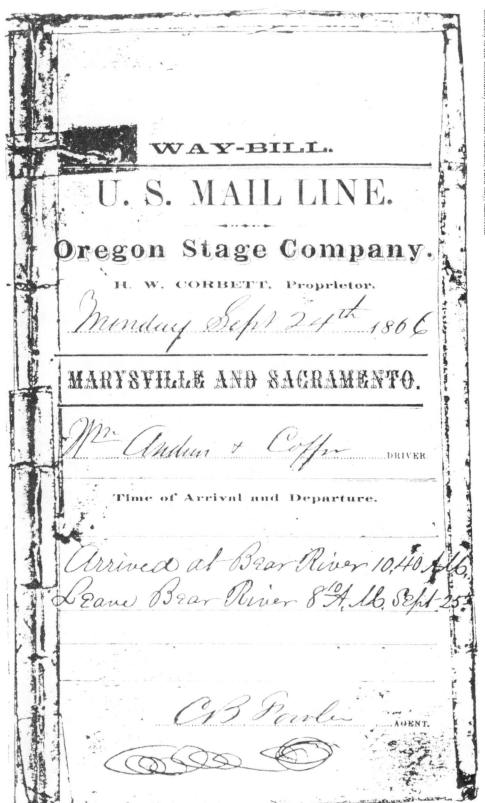

The Oregon Stage Company purchased the Sacramento-Portland stage route from the California Stage Company in 1865.

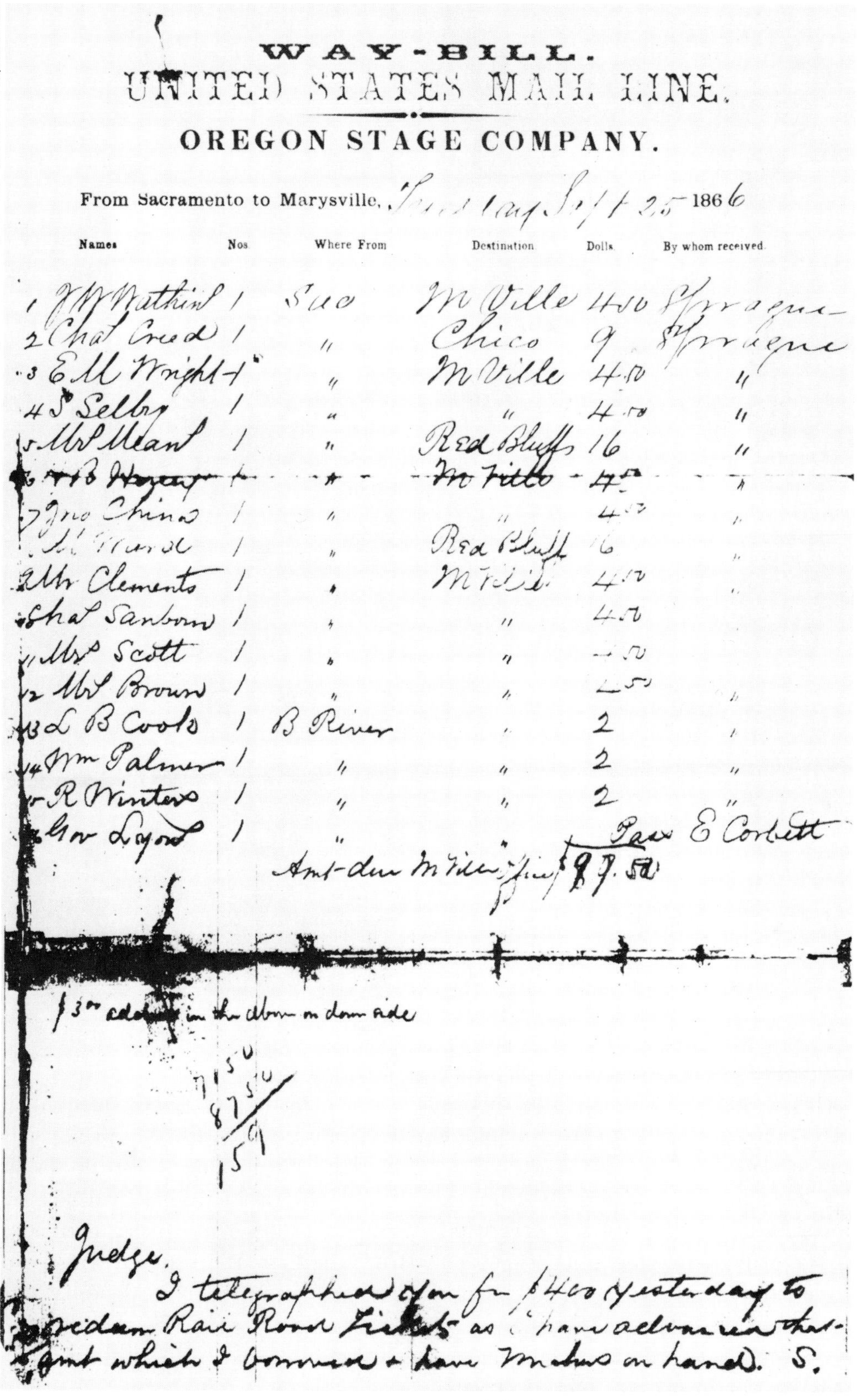

WAY-BILL.
UNITED STATES MAIL LINE.
OREGON STAGE COMPANY.

From Sacramento to Marysville, *Tuesday Sept 25* 1866

	Names	Nos	Where From	Destination	Dolls	By whom received
1	J W Watkins	1	Sac	M Ville	4.50	Sprague
2	Chas Creed	1	"	Chico	9	Sprague
3	E M Wright	1	"	M Ville	4.50	"
4	S Selby	1	"	"	4.50	"
5	Mr Mean	1	"	Red Bluff	16	"
6	~~T B Hogan~~	1	"	~~M Ville~~	~~4.50~~	"
7	Jno Chino	1	"	"	4.50	"
8	M Ward	1	"	Red Bluff	16	"
9	Mr Clements	1	"	M Ville	4.50	"
10	Chas Sanborn	1	"	"	4.50	"
11	Mrs Scott	1	"	"	4.50	"
12	Mr Brown	1	"	"	2.50	"
13	L B Cook	1	B River	"	2	"
14	Wm Palmer	1	"	"	2	"
15	R Winters	1	"	"	2	"
16	Gov Lyon	1				Pass E Corbett

Amt due M Ville $87.50

$3.00 ado in the above on down side

7.50
87.50
15.9

Judge.
I telegraphed you for $400 yesterday to
redeem Rail Road Tickets as I have advanced that
amt which I borrowed + have nothing on hand. S.

Way-bill showing names of passengers, driver, agent, including fares and destinations of the passengers.

State station built in 1850, about twelve miles south of Sacramento near Elk Grove.

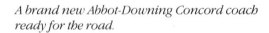

A brand new Abbot-Downing Concord coach ready for the road.

of one stowed aboard a sailing vessel that rounded the Horn. The ship sank in a storm, but when the vessel was salvaged three months later, the submerged coach was still in good condition. It was put into service in California where it ran for fifty years.

Coaches made by other builders (some imitating the Concord's suspension system) were used on western stage lines, but the Concord coach dominated the business. Another version of the Concord made by Abbot-Downing was the so-called California mud wagon. This lighter, open-sided vehicle could negotiate muddy roads, whereas the standard Concord, weighing over a ton empty, often bogged down to the axles in mud.

While adequate stagecoach transportation was developing within the Far West, establishment of overland-stage connections with the East was confronted by problems that delayed similar development there. There were two possible routes from the East. The southern route from St. Louis ran through Missouri, Oklahoma, the Texas Panhandle, New Mexico, Arizona to Fort Yuma (on the California-Mexico border) and then north to San Francisco. The other route, the central-overland, ran from either St. Joseph or Independence, Missouri, and followed the Oregon Trail through

Courtesy Museum of New Mexico

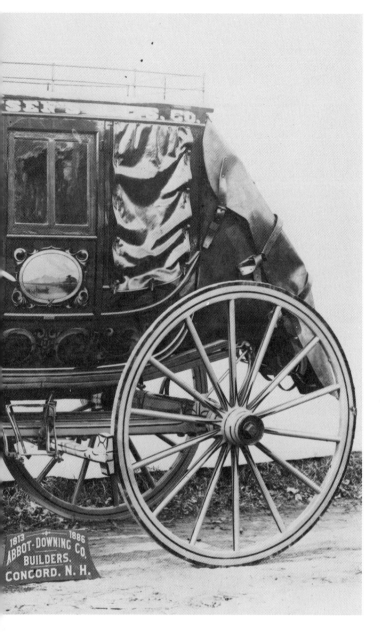

A bit battered, but still imposing, a retired Concord mudwagon stands in quiet dignity.

Nebraska, Wyoming, Utah, Nevada, and into Sacramento.

The central-overland route to California was shorter and faster but along its way rose rugged mountains, and winter blizzards and deep snows were hazards. The southern route, though 1,100 miles longer than the 1,966-mile central-overland route, was relatively free of snow and high mountains.

The southern route was supported by Southerners who dominated Congress until the Civil War. Pro-slavery interests envisioned a huge slave

empire in the lands acquired from Mexico after the Mexican War, so an excellent stage route through the area was essential in their eyes. Such disagreement between Northerners and Southerners in Congress delayed positive action until 1857. During that year astute political maneuvering by Southern sympathizers prompted Congress and the Postmaster General to authorize John Butterfield to provide semiweekly passenger and mail service over the southern route between St. Louis and San Francisco, to be named the Butterfield Overland Mail.

Meanwhile, beginning in 1850, several contracts had been let to deliver mail between Independence, Missouri, and Salt Lake City and between Salt Lake City and California. These were only halfhearted efforts by Congress; efforts that attracted only ill-equipped and ill-prepared contractors who delivered the mail or passengers

85

Butterfield Overland Mail route.

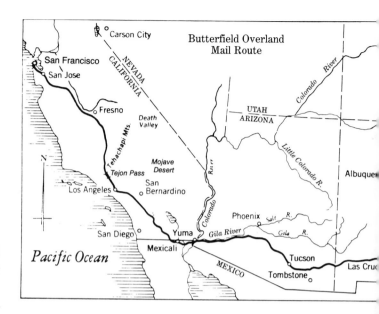

spasmodically, if at all. So until the Butterfield contract, California was practically without regular overland-mail or -passenger service to the East.

The southern route, the world's longest, extended nearly three thousand miles—bending south from St. Louis to El Paso, stretching westward to Fort Yuma, California, then turning north to Los Angeles and terminating at San Francisco.

Planning, constructing and operating the Butterfield Overland Mail route was a monumental undertaking, even when compared to today's tremendous feats. The construction and maintenance of the route was a credit to the courage, foresight and ability of those who took part. It was not for the timid nor for the weak.

Between Little Rock, Arkansas and El Paso, Texas, stretched fifteen hundred uninhabited, trackless miles over endless prairies and deserts; the last two thirds passed through Comanche country. Beyond El Paso to Fort Yuma lay what was considered the most dangerous six hundred miles in North America—dangerous because of its extreme aridity, and also because of the 160 miles of Apache territory between the Rio Grande and Tucson. The Apaches, a most menacing tribe, controlled Apache Pass over the Chericahua Mountains, scene of many Indian ambushes against stages and travelers. In this area the U.S. Army maintained widely scattered forts such as Fort Smith, Fort Belknap, Fort Cranborne and Fort Yuma. Cavalry from these forts occasionally escorted coaches and guarded way stations, but many times troops were unable to be where they were desperately needed.

Most of the route was an arid, furnace-hot desert along which water holes needed to be located or wells dug. One section between Mustang Springs (a branch of the Colorado a few miles west of the Concho) and the Pecos was absolutely waterless. Here the stage crossed seventy-five waterless miles; here lay the bleached skeletons of hundreds of wagons, animals and men. They were victims of maddening thirst and the grinding, miring sand—casualties of the thirty thousand '49ers that passed this way en route to California. When the Butterfield Overland Mail ground over this seventy-five miles of wilderness, only mules pulled the coach. No relay stations lay between Mustang Springs and the Pecos so, to spare their strength, teams pulled the stage through slowly. The team was allowed to drink its fill before starting, as were passengers and crew. Water kegs were filled and hung under the coach. A drover herded spare mules to replace jaded ones.

The mail contract specified that Butterfield run stages semiweekly each direction on a schedule not over twenty-five days. This schedule required eight coaches west while eight ran east. Maintaining this timetable required two hundred way stations and relay posts, one thousand horses, five hundred mules, eight hundred harness sets and five hundred vehicles. Of the latter, about half

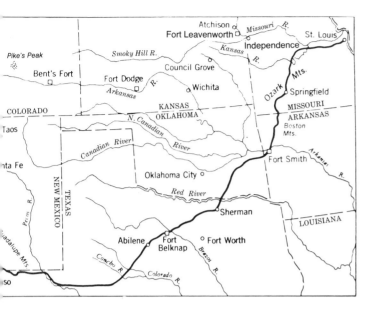

were Concord coaches and the lighter so-called California mud wagon; the rest were freight, utility, and water wagons. All this at a cost of one million dollars, a huge capital outlay in 1857. Two thousand employees were hired to operate the business.

To supply these two hundred stations was an enormous task. Each post had to be stocked with horses or mules and cattle in addition to food, harnesses, forges, household equipment, clothing, medicines, animal feed and other sundry items. Every station required one hundred tons of hay and grain a year. Even water was carted to many desert stations.

Relay posts were established on an average of every fifteen miles along the route; some only eight miles, others up to twenty-five miles and on rare exceptions even farther apart. Stages changed teams at relay posts. Rules required a post manager to keep a fresh team ready to go day or night and he was immediately to harness a team upon hearing the trumpet of an incoming stage. Teams were to be changed and under way within ten minutes. Teams were also changed at way stations scattered

Copy of a watercolor by Ogelby depicts stage station in California on Butterfield's Overland route. Note that the coaches are so-called California mudwagons.

about 120 miles apart, but here passengers could dine for seventy-five cents to a dollar (if they had not brought their own food). Here, too, a passenger could spend the night if the trip were too tiring. If he did so he might have to tarry several days, since he had to remain until a stage arrived with a vacant seat.

A through passenger, a reporter for the *New York Herald-Tribune* named J. Waterman Ormsby, described the meals:

> *The food could hardly be compared to that of the Astor House . . . consists of bread, tea, and fried steaks of bacon, venison, antelope, or mule flesh—the latter tough enough. Milk, butter, and vegetables can be met with towards the two ends of the route.*

Jerked beef, mesquite beans, corncake, black coffee and an ominous sounding dish called "slumgullion" also appeared on the menus.

Way stations were operated by a manager (sometimes with his wife) and a crew consisting of blacksmiths, herders, cooks and roustabouts. Many station employees were Mexicans and Indians. Managers were held accountable for the safety of passengers and mail and for the condition of company property. Managers and employees were armed, but if attacked by Indians they were not to use their weapons except for the protection of

lives. If Indians ran off stock, managers were to attempt by diplomacy to retrieve the stolen animals; failing in this, they were to report the loss to the nearest U.S. Army post and then take no further action.

Life for these way station and relay post employees must have been one of loneliness in the vast wilderness whose profound stillness was broken only on occasion by the mournful howl of coyotes, the unwelcome yell of warlike Indians (an ever-constant threat), or the welcome blast of the trumpet aboard an oncoming stage. Many stations sat on a prairie that swept eternally to a distant horizon for 360 degrees. At some stations, a remote hill, mound, or mesa stood silhouetted against the sky. At others, brownish-gray hills and mountains, devoid of all vegetation, lay shimmering in the desert sun. Then there was the sand, the dust and the heat.

Stage crews consisted of two, the driver and conductor. Drivers rode about sixty-five miles, disembarked and drove back the next returning stage over the same sixty-five miles. Thus drivers knew their routes intimately—helpful knowledge since they drove all night at times. The conductor was in complete charge of the coach including passengers, mail and express. His orders were to guard them with his life if necessary. Unlike drivers, conductors remained on the stage several hundred

Butterfield Overland stage leaving a relay station on a moonlit night somewhere in the Old Southwest. (Reproduction of a painting by Marjorie Reed Creese.)

miles. Both, however, were required to continue on duty if their counterparts at the end of their runs were unfit for duty for any reason. This often happened; Indians at times raided a station wounding or killing the attendants. Rising smoke on the horizon signaled to a stage crew that at best Indians merely had driven off the stock, or that at worst, all attendants were killed and all supplies and stock stolen. Then there was nothing to do but drive to the next station with a jaded team and hope to arrive safely. Conductors and drivers carried weapons, but like station attendants, they were to use them only if lives of passengers and their own were at stake or the mail was endangered. To reduce chances of robbery by road agents, coaches on the southern route carried no gold, although they hauled other express that was forwarded by Wells Fargo.

Passengers and mail began moving over the Southern Overland Mail route in September 1858. Stages rumbled along at an average of 120 miles within a twenty-four-hour day, about five miles per hour. On smooth, level prairies, coaches sped up to fifteen miles an hour. When teams strained to pull their burden up hills, or when wheels ground into sand or mired in mud, progress slowed to a monotonous three to four miles per hour. By rolling 120 miles a day, stages went through from St. Louis to San Francisco in just over twenty-four days, but a passenger rode day and night if he wished to make the through journey. This meant sleeping in the coach. Seats unfolded so that passengers could sleep stretched out. If the coach was crowded, passengers took turns sleeping; presumably those not sleeping rode outside. On hot nights some passengers slept on the roof and tied themselves to the luggage rack to prevent being rocked off. J. Waterman Ormsby wrote a realistic record of slumbering en route:

Perhaps the jolting will be found disagreeable at first, but a few nights without sleeping will soon obviate that difficulty. . . . A bounce of the wagon which makes one's head strike the top, bottom or sides will be disregarded, and 'Nature's sweet restorer' found as welcome on the hard bottom of the wagons as in the downy beds of the St. Nicholas [Hotel].

For the privilege of the adventure, a passenger paid $150 one-way between St. Louis and San Francisco; short trips were ten cents per mile. Each passenger was allowed forty pounds of luggage free of charge.

And an adventure it was. To lighten the load for the teams, passengers at times were asked to walk up hills or through deep sand or mud. Deep,

*Eastbound Butterfield Overland meets
the Westbound Overland near a relay station in
the Old Southwest.*

gushing rivers were forded; on the most treacherous crossings, a man on horseback preceded the stage, at night he carried a lantern. Some relay stations had only half-wild mustangs or unbroken mules to hitch to the coach and hours were sometimes spent in roping and hitching unwilling beasts. When hitched, they might stomp, rear, jerk, or twist, gyrating coach and passengers into a dust-swirling maelstrom. But on and on rolled the coach over miles of trackless, endless, uninhabited deserts, prairies and mountains.

Some passengers endured the hardships with little murmuring; others complained rather bitterly. Ormsby, who planned to return to New York by steamship, remarked, "Had I not just come out over the route, I would be perfectly willing to go back." Another passenger proclaimed, "I know what Hell is like. I've just had twenty-four days of it."

Ormsby's description of his arrival at San Francisco at the end of nearly twenty-four days must certainly reflect the impression of every passenger that rode the entire route:

It was just after sunrise that the city of San Francisco rose in sight over the hills, and never did the night traveller approach a distant light, or a lonely mariner descry a sail, with more joy than did I the city of San Francisco on the morning of Sunday, October 10, 1858. . . . Soon we struck the pavements, and, with a whip, crack, and bounce, shot through the streets to our destination, to the great consternation of everything in the way and the no little surprise of everybody. Swiftly we whirled up one street and down another, and round the corners, until finally we drew up at the stage office in front of the Plaza, our driver giving a shrill blast of his horn and a flourish of triumph for the arrival of the first overland mail in San Francisco from St. Louis.

In the eyes of the U.S. government and John Butterfield, bringing mail through on schedule was paramount. Butterfield's repeated admonition to each employee along the line was: "Remember, boys, nothing on God's earth must stop the United States mail!"

Even though Butterfield's Overland Express was the most famous and most important southern mail route to the Pacific, another stage company simultaneously operated a mail stage between San Antonio, Texas (via El Paso) and San Diego, California. Owned by Jim Birch, recently retired president of the mammoth California Stage Company, the San Antonio-San Diego Stage Company carried the mail on the 1,475-mile run semimonthly on a thirty-day schedule. The mail contract paid

The Butterfield Overland mail departing San Francisco for St. Louis, 1858, from HARPER'S WEEKLY, December 11, 1858.

$149,800 per annum for four years. Jim Birch received the contract for this service from Postmaster General Aaron Brown on June 22, 1857.

Historians have pondered why the U.S. Post Office would authorize this lesser mail route when the Butterfield Overland Mail Company was the main mail carrier over much of the same route. The answer apparently lies in politics and personal commitments. In 1856 and 1857, when direct-overland-mail service to the Pacific was discussed and debated in Washington, most people concerned were certain that Jim Birch, one of the founders of the California Stage Company and a millionaire at the age of twenty-nine, would certainly be awarded the mail contract. Among those thinking so was Aaron Brown, Postmaster General, who undoubtedly had made such a commitment to Jim Birch. However, John Butterfield was a close friend of President Buchanan who was determined that Butterfield should receive the mail contract. The President accordingly overruled Brown.

Brown was now in an embarrassing situation, but after some apparent horse trading with Buchanan and dexterous maneuvering through postal laws, the Postmaster General offered Birch the rather lucrative San Antonio-El Paso-San Diego mail route as a sop for not receiving the main Pacific-mail contract.

Eight days after receiving his contract Birch had the line in operation, since a wagon road was already in existence along the entire route and six military posts were scattered along the trail. This fact reduced the number of new relay stations needed to about fifteen, which were built and stocked as the first mail and passengers were being carried.

The Overland Mail crossing a stream at night, from Frank Leslie's ILLUSTRATED NEWSPAPER, October 23, 1858.

Because the Apaches and the Comanches were extremely hostile at this time in west Texas, six armed guards accompanied the coaches. At times a mule carried the mail pouch to ensure the mail's arriving on schedule. Indians raided stations and military posts on the line, but apparently the mail went through; since the *San Francisco Herald* reported that forty Apaches tried to stop the mail but "the mail travels so rapidly that the Indians have no means of making any combination to stop it." This dispatch meant that the mail pouch was fastened on a grain-fed mule, accompanied by mounted guards, and the mule when panicked could outrun the grass-fed Indian ponies. During such encounters with Indians, passengers were left behind to fend for themselves. To contend with the hazards of travel on this line, a San Diego newspaper considerately advised prospective passengers to carry:

One Sharp's rifle and a hundred cartridges; a Colts navy revolver and two pounds of balls; a knife and sheath; a pair of thick boots and woolen pants; a half dozen pairs of thick woolen socks; six undershirts; three woolen overshirts; a wide-awake hat; a cheap sack coat; a soldier's overcoat; one pair of blankets in summer and two in winter; a piece of India rubber cloth for blankets; a pair of gauntlets; a small bag of needles, pins, a sponge, hair brush, comb, soap, etc. in an oil silk bag; two pairs of thick drawers, and three or four towels.

Only mules were used on the line because they could withstand the desert heat better than could horses. Spare relay teams accompanied the stages because of the great distances between stations.

Arrival of the first Overland Mail stagecoach in San Francisco.

Courtesy California State Library

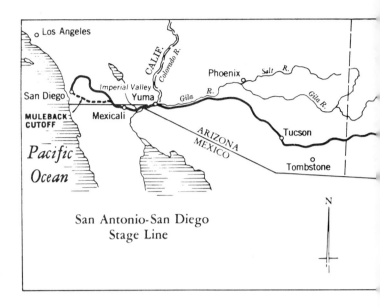

San Antonio-San Diego
Stage Line

San Antonio-San Diego stage line.

Since the only draft animals were mules, the line was referred to as the "Jackass Line" or "Jackass Mail." But other asinine conditions existed that warranted such an apt appellation. The stages served towns that could barely be called even hamlets. Aside from El Paso, the only other town en route was Tucson, with less than twenty people who could read or write. El Paso was already served by a stage line between San Antonio and Santa Fe, and the Butterfield stages ran from El Paso to within one hundred miles of San Diego. One writer referred to the Jackass Mail as going "from no place through nothing to nowhere."

Jackasses pulling the first Jackass Express Mail wagon (coaches were added later) triumphantly trotted into San Diego amidst enthusiastic shouting of the townspeople and a clanging chorus of one hundred anvils. On September 5, 1857, the *San Diego Herald* glowingly heralded the "unprecedented [fast] time across the continent of thirty-four days traveling time!!! [Actually 1,450 miles and thirty-eight days in all.] This great event for the Pacific Coast will long be remembered with just pride!" Three days later the newspaper gleefully reported that "the [Jackass] Overland Mail Company will, we learn, advertise on the first of next month, to take passengers to New Orleans for $200!!! What do you think of that, ye northern croakers against the Southern route!!!" When later in October 1857, jackasses pulling in relays hauled the mail through in only twenty-six days and twelve hours, the clanging of one hundred anvils again resounded over the hills and across San Diego Bay as citizens wildly cheered this new unprecedented speed record.

Very few passengers ever rode the route simply because very few people lived along the route. Such a small amount of mail was carried during the life of the Jackass Mail (it slowly expired until only 367 miles of it remained by 1861) that it has been estimated each letter carried cost the United States government sixty-five dollars—further evidence of the Express' asinine characteristic.

Except for Butterfield's Overland Express and the Jackass Mail, most eastern termini for stage routes rolling westward and southwestward clustered along a bend of the Missouri where the river curved northward forming the border between Missouri and Kansas. Here lay the towns of St. Joseph, Independence, Atchison and Fort Leavenworth. Freight and passengers from the East could move by train or Mississippi River steamers to St. Louis and then transfer to Missouri River steamers for the trip on that portion of the river that flowed almost due west to these towns. Important stage lines emanating from these settlements at the bend of the Missouri were those following the central-overland route (the Oregon Trail); the Santa Fe Trail; and Denver, Pike's Peak and Smoky Hill Trails.

The Santa Fe Trail (stretching from Independence, Missouri, to Santa Fe, New Mexico) was first

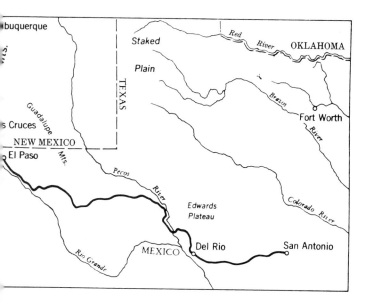

used in 1821 by traders who established a lucrative trade with the Mexicans in Santa Fe. The 860-mile trail passed through hostile Comanche and Kiowa hunting grounds. Much of the trail crossed shimmering, waterless deserts that contained few settlements between Independence and Santa Fe.

Traders on the Santa Fe Trail experienced difficulties with Indians, but were able to establish somewhat friendly relations with them until General Kearny's Army of the West passed through the area in 1846 on its way to California during the Mexican War. Kearny's army consisted of many nondescript volunteers whom their officers had difficulty controlling. These troops enraged the Indians because the Dragoons wantonly killed buffalo and considered Indians fair game. They enraged prominent Santa Fe Mexicans by violating the marriage sanctity of many señoras and the virginity of many of their daughters. With the passing of Kearny's army westward, much of the Santa Fe Trail became inflamed with hatred of all whites by Indians; a hatred that turned the trail into one of the most dangerous western routes.

Stagecoaching and mail delivery was neither as heavy nor as frequent on the Santa Fe Trail as on some other western routes. The first mail contract was let to Waldo, Hall and Company in 1850 to make monthly deliveries between Santa Fe and Independence. Each stage had two drivers and was guarded by an eight-man escort. All hands were heavily armed. Six mules pulled the coach and extra mules were herded along as relief teams. The only relay station was at Council Grove, Kansas, six hundred miles from Santa Fe.

In the summer of 1851, Alexander Majors and his freight-wagon train came upon the remains of the first Waldo, Hall coach to leave Independence. Near Wagon Mound, New Mexico, lay the burned-out coach and skeletons of ten men and numerous mules, all killed by Indians. Firepower of the drivers and guards was 136 rounds without reloading, as each man carried several repeating Colt revolvers and rifles. But this firepower proved inadequate at Wagon Mound against the Kiowas, who used only bows and arrows.

Originally the Santa Fe Trail ran westward to Great Bend and followed the Arkansas River to Bent's Fort, Colorado, then turned southward through Raton Pass in the Sangre de Cristo Mountains. A cutoff or alternate trail left the Arkansas River at Fort Dodge, Kansas, bore southwest to the Cimarron River and continued southwesterly until it met the main trail at Wagon Mound. Though the cutoff was shorter and not mountainous, it was more dangerous. On it were nearly sixty trackless, waterless, desert miles between the Arkansas and Cimarron. Anyone losing his way was doomed to die of thirst. Then too, this was the territory of the ferocious Comanche and Kiowas. Both ways were used at various times. (The chapter "Traversing the Trails by Wagon" deals more fully with the development of these branches.) Stagecoaches taking the cutoff rested their teams and soaked the wagon wheels in water before making the dash for the Cimarron.

By 1853 the mail entourage consisted of three wagons: an ambulance with spring suspension for passengers; one wagon for mail and baggage; another for feed, water and provisions. At times military escort accompanied the mail, but the stage line apparently always sent eight armed guards with each mail run. At night this small caravan formed a triangle and posted two guards for protection against Indian ambush.

Mail went through irregularly at times because of Indian attacks. In 1854, Hall, now the sole owner, asked Congress for damages incurred by Indians. Instead his compensation was increased from $10,980 per annum to $20,000. Military protection, however, was inadequate and the additional compensation failed to cover his losses by Indian attacks.

By 1858 the line was owned by Hockaday and Hall. Regular stagecoaches and mail wagons now replaced the older equipment, but no additional relay stations were built. As steel rails stretched westward across Kansas, the stage route grew shorter and shorter. By 1880 the railroad reached Santa Fe and wagon wheels stopped rolling along the colorful but dangerous Santa Fe Trail.

In the summer of 1858, activity on the central-overland route between St. Joseph, Missouri, and Sacramento increased. Mail contracts between St. Joseph and Salt Lake City, and between Salt Lake City and Sacramento had been liberalized. The men operating the two divisions of the route began establishing stations and stocking the route. Concord coaches were added to the service. Since the route had as yet fewer stations per hundred miles than did Butterfield's Overland Mail, service was slower on the central overland even though it was shorter than the southern line. The *Sacramento Union* reported on July 19, 1858, that the overland mail from St. Joseph had arrived in twenty-nine days. The report also expressed confidence that running time could be shortened considerably with the addition of more stations.

An old stagecoach relay station south of Albuquerque in present-day New Mexico.

With the Civil War imminent, the Postmaster General in March 1861 authorized daily mail service on the central overland and ordered Butterfield to abandon his southern route and establish himself on the central overland. He was given the portion from Salt Lake City to California. Before he had moved, the Confederates captured some stock and equipment on his eastern divisions, but he was able to move sufficient stock and equipment north to supply his portion of the route.

Russell, Majors and Waddell, the wagon-freighters, operated for a time the eastern section between St. Joseph and Salt Lake City under the name of the Central Overland and Pike's Peak Express Company. The Pike's Peak Express portion of the title had its origin in the Leavenworth and Pike's Peak Express Company that was organized by Russell, John S. Jones and various other stockholders early in 1859 to serve Denver and the newly discovered gold fields near Pike's Peak. In organizing this stage line, Russell had also obligated the credit of his partners, Majors and Waddell, who were actually opposed to the project.

In 1859 the first Concord coaches rolled westward from Leavenworth for Denver on a 687-mile route south of the Oregon Trail. This route to Denver paralleled the Republican River west of Junction City, Kansas. In anticipation of a gigantic gold rush near Pike's Peak, twice-a-day service on a ten-day running schedule was promised. To maintain such service required over fifty Concord coaches each drawn by four of the best mules that could be purchased in Missouri. Relay stations were built every twenty to thirty miles and elaborately stocked with hay, grain, extra teams and all the sundry items necessary to operate a first-class stage line. At certain stations along the route, overnight accommodations and meals were provided for any passengers wishing to utilize this service. Fare was $125 one-way. It has been estimated that the company spent $250,000 equipping the line. But since the Pike's Peak gold rush fizzled,

An old stagecoach relay station near Pecos in present-day New Mexico.

An old stagecoach relay station near Santa Fe in present-day New Mexico.

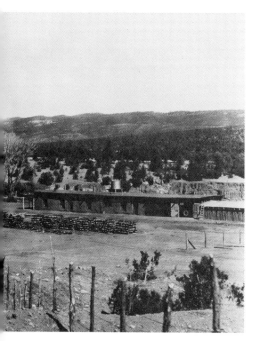

Courtesy Museum of New Mexico

99

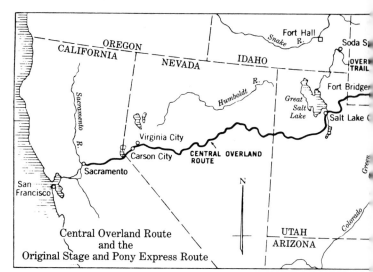

Central Overland Route
and the
Original Stage and Pony Express Route

the Leavenworth Pike's Peak Express Company carried far fewer passengers than anticipated, thereby straining the financial resources of Russell, Majors and Waddell.

When the wheels of the Leavenworth Pike's Peak Express Company began rolling between Denver and Leavenworth, Russell purchased the eastern section of the central-overland route (St. Joseph to Salt Lake City) from Hockaday and Liggett. Ultimately the eastern section mail express became known as the Central Overland and Pike's Peak Express Company. The stages on this section originally followed the Oregon Trail from St. Joseph, Missouri, but in 1861 the Central Overland switched off the Oregon Trail at Julesburg, Colorado, and followed the Cherokee Trail via Rawlins, Wyoming, to Fort Bridger, Utah, where it rejoined the Oregon Trail. In 1864 the Central Overland swung southward to include Denver and then veered northward again to the Cherokee Trail.

In March 1862, Ben Holladay, the stagecoach king, gained control of the Central Overland and Pike's Peak Express Company because of the financial difficulties of Russell, Majors and Waddell. (See the chapter "The Pony Express" for details.) In fact, Holladay acquired most major stage lines west of the Missouri (except Butterfield's Overland mail company operating between Salt Lake City and Sacramento, a company controlled by Wells Fargo). When gold was discovered in Alder Gulch at Virginia City, Montana, in 1863; in the Boise Basin of Idaho in 1862; and in Last Chance Gulch, now named Helena, Montana, Holladay seized this opportunity to add another thousand miles to his stage lines. Shortly after gold was discovered at Virginia City, a local stage outfit, Oliver and Company, began operating a lucrative stage line from Virginia City to Salt Lake City. But by drastic cut-rate tactics, Holladay soon ran this company off the route. He also secured mail contracts to run stages triweekly between Salt Lake City and Walla Walla, Washington, via Boise, Idaho; a route that was later extended to The Dalles, Oregon. The Virginia City line was also extended north to Helena and Bannack, Montana.

Service between Salt Lake City and Walla Walla began August 11, 1864. Holladay's coaches actually ran no further than Boise, for he had made a subcontract with George. F. Thomas and Company to take the mail from that point to Walla Walla and later to The Dalles. The schedule between Salt Lake City and The Dalles was sixteen days and eight hours, about half the speed of stagecoaches on the main central-overland route between St. Joseph and Sacramento. Holladay's stages to Montana mining towns and those to Walla Walla ran on a well-traveled road in good condition, but at Fort Hall the stagecoaches turned off the main overland route and from there on bounced over rough, tortuous trails to Montana and to Walla Walla that jolted stage passengers unmercifully. The trip's agony was compounded since Holladay had replaced his original luxurious Concord coaches with inferior, hard-riding conveyances after he had

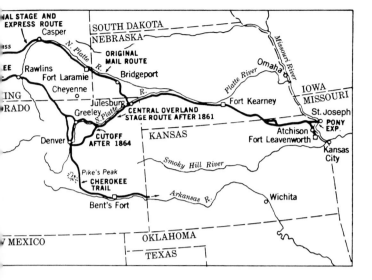

driven off his competitors. He had also increased fares manyfold. Of the trip Larry Barsness wrote in *Gold Camp*:

> *There was of course no rebate of fare to passengers who had paid for first-class travel and had to put up with any conveyance Holladay chose to thrust upon them. Nor did Holladay ever rebate any fare to the passengers who were fool enough to pay out good money to ride the coach from Salt Lake City to Virginia City in the spring, and who found that they also had to push, or at least get out in the boggiest part of the road and wade through gumbo so that the vehicle could move. These mud-bedaubed trips were so common they became a wry joke among the b'hoys who called them 'walking to Virginia City on the coach. . . .'*

To assure continuation of its virtual monopoly on express forwarding in the West, Wells Fargo had been purchasing various Western stage lines, and finally acquired all of Holladay's in 1866. Wells Fargo now controlled all major stagecoach lines west of the Missouri. The company replaced Holladay's spine-jolting, inferior vehicles with Concord coaches and also reduced fares. The romantic, golden age of Old Western stagecoaching now blossomed into its brightest hue. Gleaming red Concord coaches, with "Wells Fargo & Co. Over-

Smoky Hill Trail and the original Leavenworth & Pike's Peak Express route.

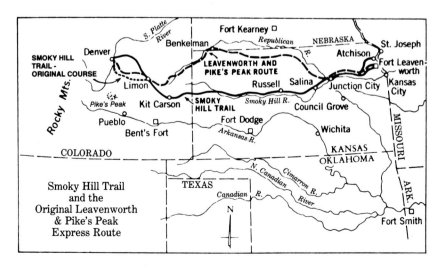

Stagecoach leaving Salt Lake City for the East, 1868.

land Stage" emblazoned in gold letters over the door and windows, pitching and rolling along dirt and sandy roads, pulled by six spirited horses, over whose heads the "popper" at the end of the driver's lash periodically snapped, were as much a part of the Old West as Indians, sagebrush, mountains and mesas.

When Butterfield moved his staging operation to the western division of the central-overland route (Salt Lake City to Sacramento) in 1861, he and other stage operators on the eastern division (St. Joseph, Missouri, to Salt Lake City) built and stocked enough relay stations to offer daily service each way between St. Joseph and Sacramento on a schedule of twenty days between these points. Stages ran day and night to maintain this schedule except for a one-night layover in Salt Lake City. Fare was $200 one-way and twelve cents per mile on shorter runs; twenty-five pounds of luggage per person was carted free of charge.

By 1862 there were about 153 stations an average of twelve and one-half miles apart on the 1,966-mile route. A typical station was a square, one-story building made of hewn logs and containing three rooms. Surrounding the station sprawled corrals and barns for stock and feed. Generally the stations were located on pasture land near water, but some necessarily lay on parched prairies where water had to be hauled in.

The central-overland route proved, however, to be more dangerous in several ways than the southern overland—dangers such as hostile Indians, deep snows and blizzards, and treacherous mountain passes. The snow and hazardous mountain passes were more readily overcome than were the Indians. Roads were improved and crews managed to clear snow most of the time. But even at their best, mountain roads were still narrow, twisting and rock-strewn. Bounding stages occasionally toppled off them into canyons.

An Overland stage leaves for the West.

Virginia City-Helena and Salt Lake City-The Dalles stage lines.

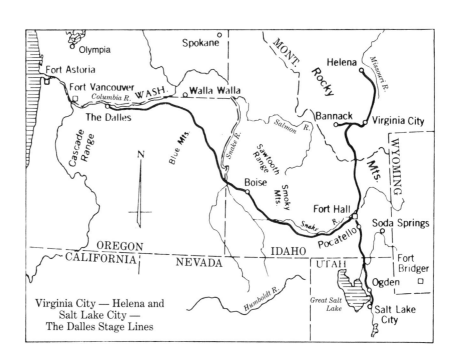

Virginia City — Helena and
Salt Lake City —
The Dalles Stage Lines

Indian troubles increased during the Civil War, since the Union, needing all available troops to fight the Confederacy, almost stripped Western forts of soldiers. The stage division east of Salt Lake experienced more Indian assaults than did the western division which was certainly dangerous on parts of its run. During this period, passengers, crews and station employees were in constant danger. Many were wounded or killed.

Hiram S. Rumfield, Overland Mail agent at Salt Lake City, gave the following report in 1863 of the first Indian attack in the western division:

An hour later ... another message informed us that the Indians had made an attack upon the stage, (going east), in the canyon 10 miles west of Deep Creek, killing the driver and mortally wounding a passenger. When the attack was made, it appears that another passenger, Judge Mott of Carson, Delegate to Congress for Nevada, was seated outside with the driver. The driver being shot dead at the first fire of the concealed foe, the venerable Judge with great presence of mind seized hold of the lines and kept the frightened horses in the road. The murderous savages with hideous yells and frantic gestures broke from their hiding places behind the jagged rocks and ran after the stage at their utmost speed; but being outdistanced in the chase, they soon gave up pursuit as unavailing. ... Judge Mott reached Deep Creek in safety. The dead driver was lying in the forward boot, where the body lodged when it fell from the seat above. Inside the stage was Mr. Liverton, the other passenger, insensible but alive. A bullet had pierced his skull and his brains were oozing from the wound. The wounded man was accompanied by his two little sons, who were unharmed. A party of soldiers ... arrived at 8 Mile Station early yesterday, (Monday) morning, and found the station buildings in ashes, the horses gone, and the two unfortunate men lying dead, naked and scalped upon the ground. ... They are doubtless Snake or Sho-sho-ne Indians, and belong to Poca-tel-la's band. ... This is the first Indian difficulty we have had upon our road since the line was started.

Road agents convincingly demand the express box.

104

A stagecoach traveling near Mt. Shasta.

*A shipment of Concord coaches riding piggyback
westward for Wells Fargo & Co.*

A runaway team on a corduroy log road, from an original by Charles Russell.

Following are affidavits of Indian raids in the eastern division in 1864, that were sent to Ben Holladay, owner at the time of that section of the central-overland route:

Affiant states that he was passing from Split Rock Station west to Three Crossing of Sweet Water with the United States mails on the said 17th day of April, A.D. 1862, in company with eight other men, all of the mail party; that they were attacked by a band of Indians numbering thirty or more, who commenced a furious fire upon them with rifles and bows and arrows; that resistance was made by said mail party for hours, when the Indians retreated. Affiant further states that six men out of the nine who composed said party were wounded, one with arrows and five with guns.

The Indians attacked a party of nine men running two coaches, and commenced a furious fire upon them, wounding six men, including this affiant, whose body was penetrated by two rifle-balls; that after a resistance of four hours the Indians captured nine head of mules, nine sets of harness, and partially destroyed two coaches.

Courtesy Wells Fargo Bank History Room, San Francisco

Rescuing passengers from an overturned stagecoach, from an original by Charles Ru

On July 29, 1865, the Overland Mail agent at Fort Laramie (Wyoming) reported:

The Indians have possession of the mail route between Virginia Dale and Sulphur Springs. We have six companies of cavalry there, but they are not sufficient to keep the route open. General Connors is sending the mail over the interrupted line in Government wagons with large escorts. He will have two regiments of cavalry soon. It is impossible to prevent an interruption of the mails with the number of troops he has. The General starts on his campaign next week, and is in hopes that interruptions to the mails and emigrants will cease with his return.

With the ending of the Civil War, additional troops were dispatched to the troubled areas and danger from Indians lessened.

In May 1869, the Pacific railroad was completed, thus ending transcontinental-stagecoach service. But for many years stagecoaches were the major mode of travel in much of the Old West. Innumerable feeder lines branched into major stage lines and to railroads as they stretched their steel rails across the West. One unusual operator of such a branch line was French nobleman Marquis de Mores, who for a time ran stagecoaches between Medora, North Dakota (on the Northern Pacific Railroad) and Deadwood, South Dakota, near the gold mines of the Black Hills — a distance of 215 miles. This colorful Marquis, who had established a feudal estate to raise cattle in western North Dakota, operated the largest *abattoir*, or slaughterhouse, in the Old West. By implication he at one time challenged Theodore Roosevelt to a duel.

Road agents robbing the night stage.

PIONEER STAGE LINE,
LOUIS McLANE & CO., PROPRIETORS.

Carrying United States Mail and Wells, Fargo & Co's Express
STAGES LEAVE VIRGINIA CITY DAILY, FOR SACRAMENTO,
Via Gold Hill, Silver City, Carson, Genoa, Lake Bigler, Strawberry Valley and Placerville;
CONNECTING AT FOLSOM WITH THE
SACRAMENTO VALLEY RAIL ROAD.
And at Sacramento with the California Steam Navigation Company's Boats for San Francisco.

Mining directory ad for Louis McLane & Company stage line.

An 1858 Wells Fargo & Co. stagecoach schedule.

*The Pioneer Stage Company ran coaches from
Sacramento to Virginia City, Nevada.*

By the early years of the twentieth century, the iron horse had largely replaced the stagecoach. Thus faded from the American scene one of the great episodes of the Old West—the radiant red Concord, ladened with treasure, express, baggage, mail and passengers, driven by the most skillful and courageous reinsmen the world has ever produced. Many drivers, or jehus and whips as they were then called, had colorful names to match their characters; names such as Hank Monk, Sage Brush Bill, Billy Carll, Cherokee Bill, and "polite, profane, tobaccer chewin', cigar smokin' One-eyed Charlie." But when they laid out One-eyed Charlie after the jehu died in 1879, they were dumfounded to discover him, or correctly her, to be a woman!

Alongside the driver sat the equally courageous "shotgun." Together they drove the endless expanses of the Old West in extremes of heat, cold, rain, or snow, in the face of danger from Indians and road agents. Almost forgotten now, these men and the builders of the stage lines deserve the honor and credit due for their important share in creating a great empire that is part of our great nation.

What was it like to ride a Concord stagecoach in the late 1850's? Time has suddenly turned backward to 1859 and you will board a stagecoach outbound from Marysville, California. Bearded miners, shopkeepers and tradesmen stroll about the Plaza. Others loiter under the shade of wooden awnings covering boardwalks. White clouds slowly drift against an azure sky. You notice stacks of merchandise piled along the levee and more being hand-trucked by stevedores unloading the *Governor Dana*, a familiar Feather River steamboat gently nudging her wharf on the Yuba River. Black smoke lazily drafts from her stacks.

Most of her freight will ultimately reach the Sierra Nevada gold diggings transported in huge freight wagons drawn by six and eight mules. One of these "mountain schooners" just now lumbers away from a commission merchant's warehouse.

111

What finally catches your eye is a large, magnificent Concord coach, her new red paint glistening in the sunlight. Her wheels are a bright yellow. Hitched to the coach are six sleek chestnut bay horses.

Under the driver's seat is a leather compartment called a "boot" that is used to stow the express box and cargo. On the rear is another leather boot, the familiar triangular-shaped one. Into this boot and on top of the stage, cargo such as mailbags, round-topped trunks and miners' packs are stowed.

You queue up with other passengers at the ticket window and purchase a ticket for Sacramento. Someone remarks, "Here is the jehu." Others refer to someone as "Charlie" or "whip."

Looking around, you realize they are referring to the stage driver.

He is typical of western stagecoach drivers. Actually they were individualistic, but most of them shared certain qualities to a greater or lesser degree. They were good drivers; they had to be. Not everyone could control six spirited horses galloping at perilous speed over rough and treacherous frontier roads, especially narrow, curving mountain roads where a miscue could hurl a coach hundreds of feet down a steep canyon.

Some drivers were swaggering, rough-spoken men, but in spite of these manners, nearly all of

California Stage Company coach.

them were courteous to their passengers, especially ladies. As Bancroft the historian wrote: "The average stage driver was above all, lord in his way, the captain of his craft, the fear of timid passengers, the admiration of stable boys, and the trusted agent of his employer." In the Old West only steamer captains were held in higher esteem.

Your driver is a tall, somewhat slender man with powerful shoulders. He wears a bright-yellow vest over a white long-sleeved cotton shirt and tie; his trousers are spotless dark blue tucked into expensive black boots. Shoved back on his head is a brown, low-crowned, round-rimmed hat under which a crop of brown hair lops over the left side of his forehead. He is clean-shaven except for a drooping mustache. His age is about thirty-five.

Your first reaction is that he is a dandy. But you soon learn that this is not so, that many drivers wear very individualistic clothes and are neatly dressed.

The driver walks slowly around the coach carefully inspecting running gear and harnesses. A loose wheel bolt, a faulty brake, a twisted trace, or a loose buckle could cause disaster. During inspection a hostler stands by the lead span (the two horses in the front) grasping the team's reins.

A California mudwagon-style Concord coach preparing to depart from a station (probably in Cloverdale, California).

The driver now draws the reins from their place, places three between the fingers of each hand (since the team has six horses), grabs a whip and in three steps is on the seat.

You board the coach. This Concord seats nine passengers. Two seats are on the ends, one facing fore, the other aft. The other is in the center. Three can sit on each seat, allowing fifteen inches per person. "Rather a tight fit, especially if the traveler is large or a lady is wearing bustles," you reflect. Six more could ride on top. Including freight, passengers and crew the coach has a capacity of four thousand pounds.

Inside, the seats and walls are covered with fine leather. Tapestry and embroidered cloth are also used for covering, but since western stages are subject to rough treatment, leather is generally used. As you enter and sit in the rear you feel a slight rocking movement, first aft and then fore. The seat is padded but not as plush as those of a modern airliner or train. You are next to a window that reaches from the ceiling to the armrest. The

coach has four such windows, next to the end seats. No glass encloses these openings; during cold weather, however, leather side curtians can be rolled down from the top. The stage has two small glass windows located on each side of the door; the door also has a glass window.

You observe last-minute preparations. Two bearded men emerge from the express office carrying a green, locked box labeled Wells Fargo Express. Both men strain to hoist the box to the driver's seat and into the boot. You wonder what valuables it contains—gold perhaps from the high Sierra Nevada on its way to San Francisco. How much you wonder—enough to lure road agents? An armed messenger (sometimes called the shotgun) mounts the seat alongside the driver. Two newly invented Colt revolvers dangle from his hips and across his lap lies a double-barreled, ten-gauge, sawed-off shotgun. The driver is similarly armed. Several male passengers also carry side arms.

One of them remarks, "In case o' trouble, we

The Marquis de Mores, a French nobleman who ran a stagecoach line from Medora, North Dakota, to Deadwood, South Dakota.

Stagecoach flees from attacking Indians. From an original by H. W. Hansen.

115

Stagecoaches traveling between Bismarck, North Dakota, and Deadwood, South Dakota. The line was operated by the Marquis de Mores, a French nobleman.

an' the jehu, an' the shotgun kin throw out a lot o' lead; shore make it hot fer any road agents what wants tuh rob the stage." You wonder just what you may be getting into.

Other passengers begin boarding the Sacramento-bound stagecoach. Among them is a well-dressed lady of about thirty years. She seems to experience difficulty boarding because of her long skirt.

Immediately the driver jumps to the ground and helps her into the stage. You wonder if a lady traveling alone in this primitive land is safe. Actually she is safer in the Old West than in many other parts of the world then or today. Ladies were rarely molested, provided of course that they were ladies

and acted like ladies. Other passengers include a middle-aged, gray-bearded miner dressed in a red wool shirt and black trousers tucked into work-scuffed boots; a stocky, well-dressed Englishman with a handlebar moustache that turns sharply upward at either end and a bowler hat resting squarely on his head; a handsome Spanish-Mexican with black intelligent eyes, a colorful blanket draped over his shoulder, and on his head, the traditional sombrero; and a genial-appearing merchant wearing a dark, wrinkled business suit.

Departure time has arrived. The driver scans the hitching gear for twisted straps or faulty fittings that he might have missed from the ground. Satisfied that all is in order, he shouts, "All aboard! Keep your feet off the seats please!" Then nodding at the hostler holding the lead span of horses, the driver gives the order, "Let 'er go, Johnny!"

The hostler drops his hands and steps aside. Now you observe the driver gently pulling the reins up until he feels the horses' mouths, then

116

suddenly loosening them and simultaneously releasing the brake, he shouts "G— long! H— up, there!"

Six horses lurch against their collars in unison, traces snap taut, metal fastenings clink and the stage leaps into motion. You feel the coach gently pitch backward and then roll forward as the Concord gets under way. The hostler waves as the coach passes him; looking backward you see the station agent and passersby wave in admiration at the beautiful departing vehicle. As if in salute, the wail of the *Governor Dana*'s whistle reverberates across the Plaza.

As the Concord rounds the corner and turns south on D Street, the miner remarks, "Thought o' takin' that 'ere steamer, but this 'ere stage is a heap safer. Hain't never heerd o' no stage explodin'. Bin too durn many of 'em blowed sky high—people gitten' kilt or scalded. O' course, a stage kin git robbed, but, on the arter hand so kin a steamer; but, in a robbery yuh got a fightin' chance, but yuh ain't got none when a biler blows up."

Eight stage drivers of the Old West are formally posed.

Turning to you, he questions, "Yo're a stranger in these parts, ain't yuh? Thought so. Ever hear 'bout whut 'lucky' and 'unlucky' means? No? Wal, it's unlucky if yuh misses yore steamer, but lucky when yuh hears it's been blowed to kingdom come." With this he slaps his knee and guffaws at his own joke and chomps off a huge bite of plug tobacco.

Gazing along D Street and across the Plaza, you notice numerous newly built brick buildings, unusual for a gold-rush town. The merchant remarks, "These buildings were built after the fire of

117

late 1853. Most of the town burned down. The fire started during a celebration upon the arrival of an emigrant train from the East. Representatives from Marysville had talked these emigrants, when they were crossing the Sierra Nevada, into settling in Marysville. It seems the celebration got a little out of hand, whiskey flowing freely, and through carelessness the town caught fire. But everybody sobered up and started to rebuild. This time they used brick."

His conversation is suddenly interrupted by the loud, hollow clop of horses' hooves on a wooden bridge. Just as suddenly you hear the deep rumble of wheels as the coach itself rolls onto the Yuba River bridge.

Reaching the south bank of the river, the stage picks up speed. The team is trotting at a smooth rhythmic gait. Each of the six horses' right front legs hits the ground simultaneously, and so do their left front legs. Their hind legs follow the same pattern. This is an excellent team, well-trained.

The road is fairly smooth; the coach gently teeters forward, and then backward, occasionally rolling sideways as the wheels on one side pass over a depression. You estimate the speed to be almost fifteen miles per hour. Dust billows skyward in the Concord's wake. Left windows frame the distant blue Sierra Nevada. The tree-lined Feather River comes into view on the right.

Suddenly the stage violently pitches forward and jerks backward. You brace your feet and clutch the armrest. But as the coach gradually steadies, you relax. The wheels have bounced over a deep rut that runs across both tracks of the road. You now realize the worth of thorough brace suspension. Without it, passengers and horses would be taking punishing jolts.

The Spanish-Mexican slowly turns his head, faces you, and softly remarks. "Ah, señor, you Americans, you are ambitious, you are hard working, you wish to get things done fast, today. Your

Hank Monk, a famous California stage driver of the 1850's-60's. Monk drove Horace Greeley on his wild ride over the Sierra Nevada to Placerville, California.

language shows this. See that River? Americans call it the Feather River. The old Spanish explorer, Don Louis Arquello, in 1821, named it el Rio de las Plumas. Don't you see? The Spanish, it is longer to be sure, but how much more beautiful to the ears. The Feather River, it means the same, but so short, so plain, like so much in a hurry." With a shrug of his arms and shoulders, he continues, "But then, much time has passed since Arquello, much change."

As the Concord stagecoach rolls along, you glance upward at the driver. He is sitting straight as a ramrod and almost as still as a statue. He holds a whip but rarely uses it and then just gently cracks the "popper" (several foot-long strands of silk cord at the end of the whip) over a horse's head to correct the animal. "How different," you think, "from TV or movie stage drivers who constantly crack their whips and continually rock forward and backward."

As the road swings nearer the Feather River, passengers notice a cloud of black smoke drifting downstream. As the stage draws closer, the outline of a white steamboat comes into focus. Now you can see her name, *Cleopatra*, on the side of the wheelhouse. She is a shallow-draft Feather River steamer on her upriver run from Sacramento to Marysville.

After observing the boat, the miner turns to you inquisitively, then turns to the window again and releases a stream of amber liquid under considerable pressure. Passengers instinctively pull away from that side, but fortunately the wind is in the right direction, carrying the amber spray away from the open windows.

The miner again looks at you. "Say," he says, "since you 'peer ter be a stranger, mebbee you haint heerd o' the steamer race 'tween the *Governor Dana* and the *R. K. Page* right on this 'ere river 'bout six years ago. No? Didn't think you had. Wal, I saw hit from a stagecoach. Them two boats hed left Marysville thet mornin' 'bout the same time. An when they gits out o' the Yuba River an onter the Feather, the race wuz on.

"We warn't too fur above Nicolaus. Them steamers wuz a runnin' side by side; black smoke an' sparks a flyin' out o' them 'ere stacks. An' the way them paddlewheels wuz a churnin' the water! Made the water look right like the bottom uva big waterfall.

"Wal, the *Dana* she finally pulls ahead o' the *Page*. An' then all at once 'way down yonder jist below Nicolaus we see fahr, smoke, steam, an' steamer parts a shootin' an' a flyin' in the air; then we heerd an' felt the blast. Most like t' of bolted the stage over; almost stampeded the hosses. The *Page* had blowed t' kingdom come. Now, thar war cartainly sumpthin' right funny 'bout hit. Only feller not to git hurt wuz the bartender. Evurbody else wuz kilt or hurt, some purty bad. An' they still ain't found the remainders o' three passengers.

"Kinda the fault o' the people on the boat though. The way we heerd 'bout hit later wuz that when the *Dana* started pullin' ahead, a passenger on the *Page* bet the *Page*'s engineer a box o' seegars thet he couldn't pass the *Dana*. Wal, yuh know how 'tis; hard ta pass up a bet like thet. So whut does thet 'ere fool engineer do but tie down the safety valve, an' then he throwed a bar'l o' oil inta the fahrbox. This heated things up a bit an' somethin' had to give, an' it shore did. But thet's racin' fer yuh. Them fellers whut owns them boats, I guess, kin do with 'em whut they wants."

As your coach gently pitches and swings along the road, punctuated by an occasional hard roll, you notice vineyards stretching away from the opposite bank of the Feather River. The merchant turns to you. "That's John Sutter's farm, called the Hock Farm. It's all he has left of his original Mexican land grant. One of his chief crops is grapes from which he makes fine wines."

The Spanish-Mexican gazes at the Hock Farm for some time and then speaks to you. "What reduced conditions! To Capitán Sutter this must perhaps seem like a prison. Capitán Sutter was the grandest of the great dons of old California. Dons, señor, owned huge ranchos—land granted by the Mexican governor of California. Señor, perhaps you do not know how much land el Capitán once had. I will tell you that this ride today will start and end within the land that once was his. From the middle part the eye could not see the end either to the north or to the south.

"Think of it, señor. Eleven square Mexican leagues, over forty-eight thousand acres were his as a grant to him by Governor Alvorado from Monterey. From the south below Sacramento, the land stretched to the north along the Sacramento River for over forty miles and then turned east to a line a few miles east of the Feather River and a few miles north of Marysville. Just exactly where is not certain. But what difference a few thousand acres when you have so many? To the Mexican government in Monterey, it made little difference. To the American government it made the big difference.

"Governor Alvorado, the Mexican governor of Alta California, wished to have el Capitán Sutter hold for the Mexican government this big Sacramento Valley. For a few years el Capitán was able to do this. He had a fort near Sacramento and a small army.

"Capitán Sutter had power of life and death over his people; his word was law. Some say he was just; others say he was not. He was very generous. To all who came to his fort el Capitán gave food, shelter, or clothes, or work; even to General Frémont's hungry and ragged soldiers. It is said he did not pay others what he owed them; perhaps he thought others to be like he was, generous.

"There was no thought of gold then, you may believe me. It was stock in those days—sheep, horses, cattle, and now that I come to hink of it, there was some wheat and other things planted in the ground. Money was scarce, but there was plenty to eat and clothes enough.

"The American government captured California in 1846, but still Capitán Sutter held the land. Then his foreman discovered gold on the American River near Coloma in January 1848. Think of it—his land was that far to the Sierra Nevada! When el Capitán heard the gold had been discovered, he was unhappy. He asked his men to keep the discovery a secret. But the secret, it could not be kept. Thousands of people came the next year looking for the gold; they moved onto Capitán Sutter's land, and el Capitán could not hold the land. Perhaps it is all for the best, who knows?

"Speaking of gold, señor, do you know of Theodor Cordua? This señor had a big rancho at the place where Marysville now stands. His land stretched far to the north. In 1842, Capitán Sutter leased him part of el Capitán's land north to Honcut Creek. Governor Alvorado granted the señor more land north of the Honcut. In all he had about thirty-one thousand acres. He raised on his rancho many of the same things that Capitán Sutter did. Cordua came from Mecklenburg, Germany, so he called his rancho New Mecklenburg.

"Now, to get back to the gold; it was also discovered on the Yuba River in the spring of 1848. The señor's peons now left to search for the gold. He could not operate his rancho. He took a partner, thinking this would help. But things did not go well, and the next year Señor Cordua sold his interest to two señors.

"But would you believe it; Cordua had three hundred pounds of gold, but no rancho, his real wealth. The señor knew this. He left this place with the tears running down his face.

"What to do with the gold? There was very little to buy, and what there was to buy was so high. He could not get to Europe. Some of the gold was stolen; some he spent. In time he was able to return to Mecklenburg, but with very little of the gold. Had he not died soon after, he perhaps would have lived in poverty."

Sometime after the Spanish-Mexican had finished his discourse, the coach rumbles to a halt in front of a small house surrounded by corrals and barns. The merchant tells you, "This is a place where teams are replaced. Teams are changed about every ten to fifteen miles."

As hostlers unhitch the team, you and the other passengers disembark to stretch your legs, as do the messenger and driver. In a very few minutes the fresh team is hitched. The driver takes the reins, calls, "All aboard!" and mounts his seat. Soon the Concord is rolling again. Shortly a stop is made at Nicolaus where two passengers leave the stage and another boards it. Mail is picked up and some dropped.

"Doesn't take long to change teams," explains the merchant. "Many stages average ten miles an hour including stops."

Someone asks the Englishman, who has been quietly watching the countryside glide by, how he likes the West. "Well, I must say things are a bit different here than in England. Most of our stage roads are now paved. We move along at a merry clip with very little dust, you know. But I find it rawther difficult to accommodate myself to your lack of classes or divisions of passengers on your stages. Everyone is mixed together, so to speak. Rawther unusual, don't you think?

"But I had a most unusual experience the other day. The stage that I was on met another stage. Those aboard each coach exchanged greetings. Now, Americans are, without a doubt, extraordinarily hearty in their salutations, but this exchange of greetings! By jove, the blasphemy! The raucous manner in which the various references each made about the other's ancestry — strange indeed! Seems as though no one had any human antecedents or legitimate birth!

"Everyone seemed good-natured, smiling and laughing, and how fortunate since they were armed. But come to think of it, confound it, you know, this good humor and blasphemy just don't seem to go together."

"They knew each other, perhaps were very good friends," interjected the merchant.

"Oh, really, how odd, rawther puzzling, what! But it's a jolly good thing there were no ladies aboard either stage."

"Had there been, the language would have been more civil," explains the merchant.

"But now since you have asked me," continues the Englishman, "I must say I do enjoy your countryside. I recall one exhilarating stage ride recently. To sit behind six spanking horses tearing along the road is a delightful experience at any time, but the mere fact of such locomotion formed only a small part of our journey that day. Oh, the atmosphere was absolutely so soft and balmy; it was a positive enjoyment to feel it brushing one's face like the finest floss silk." As he speaks, his voice rises in an excited crescendo.

Several passengers look dumfounded. One whispers to another, "Whut'd thet feller say?"

"Durn 'f I know," replies another.

The miner looks up and turns his face to the window. Remembering that he is chewing a large cud of tobacco, passengers pull away from the windows in unison. Again the wind is in the right direction.

He shifts the tobacco from one side of his mouth to the other and says, "Thet 'ere express box must have lots of gold in 'er. Notice how it took two men tuh swing it aboard?

"Speakin' o' gold reminds me o' the time a stage close to Marysville was held up some time back. Thar was a shotgun ridin' on the seat with the jehu, an' inside wuz two passengers, men. It wuz kind o' cold, so the leather side curtains wuz rolled down.

"Thet stage hed to slow down fer a curve an' right then three road agents jumps right in front o' the stage. Ulp . . ."

Suddenly the Concord violently lurches forward and with a sharp jerk pitches backward; wheels bounce over rocks and ruts; passengers are shaken and lifted from their seats. After a few seconds, the stage is again on smoother road. You look out and notice that the coach has passed over a dried stream bed.

"Durn if I didn't swaller ma tobakker, dad burn it!" resumes the miner. "Wal, I got more." He bites off a big chew and continues, "Now let's see; whar wuz I? Oh, I remember; three road agents hed stopped thet 'ere stage. They got the draw on the jehu and the shotgun all right. Then them robbers asked fer the express box, but fer some reason they didn't pay no 'tention to them two passengers. Didn't know they wuz thar, I guess. Wal, when them passengers seen what wuz up, they reached fer their newfangled Colt revolvers.

"One passenger stuck his gun just barely through the openin' in the curtain; t'other one did the same on t'other side. Each drawed a bead on a road agent and fahred together. Two robbers dropped to the ground dead. T'other rode away with a hole in his hide."

The merchant confirms the holdup attempt and begins relating another. "It was August 1856, shortly after I came out here. A stage with $100,000 worth of gold in her express box was not far out of Marysville. The driver was John Gear and the messenger, Bill Dobson. The coach was creeping up a hill when several masked and armed men appeared and ordered the stage to stop.

"Dobson immediately unloaded his shotgun at the men and pulled his two revolvers and kept firing. The driver and several passengers joined the fight. The surprised road agents fired back, but they soon rode away without the gold. Over forty shots were exchanged and unfortunately a lady passenger was killed; another passenger was hit in the leg, and the driver was shot in the arm. Some of the gang was wounded too.

"The leader of this gang was Doc Tom Bell, a real doctor. A posse of citizens from around here hunted him for months. They finally caught him and hanged him within a few hours. Justice is swift and stern out here—got to be—best way to keep law and order."

The stage stops again to change teams. After you are underway the miner suddenly tosses his head back. "Har, har, har!" he guffaws. "Har, har, har!"

"Whut's so funny?" someone asks.

"I wuz jist thinkin' 'bout that 'ere wild stage ride down the Sierra Nevada that Hank Monk give that 'ere Eastern newspaper eddyter. Whut wuz his name? Sumpthin' like Harry Creely."

"You mean Horace Greeley, the editor of the *New York Tribune*," answered the merchant. "He was in California this year. Came West on the Central Overland Stage."

"Yup, thet's him. Seems as though Mr. Greeley wuz on his way to Placerville from the top o' the Sierras. He wuz supposed tuh give a speech at Placerville thet evenin'. An' he thought mebbe he would be late. So he asks the jehu, Hank Monk, if he could go a mite faster.

"Wal, you know Hank Monk. He sez, 'Shore, Horace, I'll git you thar on time, and he let 'er rip. Thet 'ere stage bounced up an' down an' swayed 'round and 'round them sharp curves. Down an' down they roared into the canyon. Now Mr. Greeley wuz gittin' mighty uncomf'table.

"He looks out o' the winder, an' he sees whar the edge o' the road drops down hundreds o' feet. He then yells at Hank thet he really warn't in sech a big rush after all, thet he allowed he had plenty o' time. But ol' Hank tells him to jest keep his seat, thet he would git him thar on time, an' he jest kept on a drivin' them hosses as fast as they would go.

"Ol' Hank sez thet Horace wuz a bouncin' an' a yellin', an' thet his vest buttons popped off, and thet finally his head went clean through the roof o' the stage."

"It was a wild ride all right," said the merchant. "There are several versions of it, and of course, old Monk might have stretched it a bit. But then Mr. Greeley was badly shaken. When he got to Placerville, he rushed past the reception committee and ran to the barroom for something to steady his nerves."

All passengers except the Englishman enjoy a hearty laugh. He stares incredulously and exclaims, "Don't you think this chap Monk carried the thing a bit too far? After all, really!" For several minutes passengers sit in puzzled silence. The Briton unable to fathom Hank Monk, and the Americans unable to understand the Englishman.

The stage now rumbles onto the wooden bridge over the American River and is nearing Sacramento. The lady passenger remarks, "This has been a much nicer trip than one I took a few years ago from Marysville to Sacramento. The roads are some better now, and the recent rains have helped settle the dust.

"I made that other trip in the middle of the summer; it was 110 in the shade, and the stage was crowded, sixteen people on board, I believe. The heat was stifling, and the dust was so thick; it got into your eyes and nose and hair and your clothes, even your mouth. The road was so rough. Some of the wooden bridges must not have been very strong because the driver made the passengers walk across several of them. It took over six hours to make the trip."

As the stagecoach rolls to the depot in Sacramento, you look at your watch. The trip has taken about four and one-half hours.

The driver helps passengers disembark; he is especially helpful to the lady. You look at her and realize that perhaps because she was on board, not a single word of profanity was spoken on the trip.

An unidentified windjammer, her masts snapped and her sails shredded, founders at Cape Horn, a victim of screeching pamperos and williwaws.

5

Around Cape Horn to the West

Until the completion of the Pacific railroad in 1869, travelers from the East Coast had the choice of three routes to the West Coast. One was directly overland. Another was by sea to an isthmus in Central America, then across the isthmus, and by sea to the West Coast. The third route was entirely by sea around Cape Horn. With the discovery of gold in California in 1848, travel on each of these routes swelled from a trickle to a torrent.

The voyage around the Horn offered advantages. Sailing vessels and crews on the East Coast were readily available and could sail in winter, whereas the overland trails were impassable during that season. Some dangers of the overland routes were not present at sea; however, passage around Cape Horn was about seventeen thousand miles south on the stormy North Atlantic. The voyage went through the tropics, the torrid zone and Capricorn, and the frigid, howling gales of the Antarctic and then similar latitudes in reverse going north. Traveling time was uncertain, at least three months and often exceeding six months.

Many more sailing vessels rounded the Horn than did steamers. The latter usually made one trip to get the ship to the West Coast where it was put into service. Sailing vessels made repeated voyages each direction by way of the Horn. The first years following the discovery of gold they carried passengers, but windjammers were primarily freight haulers. They were the most economical and practicable means by which Eastern merchants could tap the lucrative San Francisco gold-rush trade.

As the steamer-isthmus routes developed, steamers carried the bulk of seaborne passengers between the East and West Coasts. The high cost of handling prohibited much freight from passing over these routes.

Immediately following President Polk's confirmation that gold had been discovered in California in 1848, ships were in tremendous demand. Every brig, bark, schooner and packet that was idle, and even those that were not, was requisitioned by thousands of Argonauts clamoring to speed to the gold diggings of the Sierra Nevada. Many sailing vessels were sound of timber and construction; too many others were overage, their wooden masts, ribs and planks softened by rot. But money was money and fortunes could be realized by shipping freight around the Horn to San Francisco at $60 a ton. So many a master hoisted sails and plowed southward in ships that were twisted and crushed under heavy seas and battered by screaming gales.

Even with the finest ships commanded by the most competent masters, the trip around Cape Horn was a hazardous adventure. Lieutenant Mathew F. Maury, an expert on navigating the Horn, wrote:

> The California passage is the longest and most tedious within the domains of Commerce; many are the vicissitudes that attend it. . . . It tries the patience of the navigator and taxes his energies to the very utmost. . . .

Even summer south of 52 degrees latitude can be frigid and the prevailing winds, strong westerlies, sweeping around the tip of the continent added difficulties for a sailing vessel plowing westward around the Cape. These prevailing winds could suddenly switch into twisting gales and blasting williwaws that snapped masts before sailors were able to reef or furl sails.

Captains had two alternative routes when passing from the Atlantic to the Pacific—negotiating the Straits of Magellan or rounding Cape Horn itself. In the Straits were narrow channels, capricious tides, currents and wind. The rocky, fog-shrouded hills were monotonous and forbidding. Since sailing vessels required three to six weeks to pass through the Straits, masters of windjammers generally avoided this route.

After Magellan discovered this passage in 1520, many sailing vessels navigated around the Horn, but until the early 1850's, when Lieutenant Maury made a study of the meteorology of the area and compiled this information, skippers were on their own in setting courses to pass this perilous point. They bulled into adverse currents and head-on winds that slowed passage time by days and even weeks. They considered the Horn an ordeal to contend with. It was such an ordeal for some that they foundered or were forced to put into the nearest port to repair broken masts or split seams in wooden hulls.

Following Maury's instructions, skippers sailed to a point much further east and westered their ships in calmer winds, thus avoiding the williwaws and gale-force pamperos experienced along the former offshore course. Maury discovered distinctly different winds several degrees south of Cape Horn, and he advised masters to close-haul sails and tack with these more favorable winds rather than to claw westward against head-on winds nearer the Horn. He also advised captains, when proceeding northward in the Pacific, to swing westward rather than working nearer the coastline, because further west were southeast trade winds that provided good sailing to San Francisco. These instructions shaved weeks and even months off the passage from New England or New York to California. Of course, rounding the Horn was still perilous, time consuming and required skillful navigation.

The first wind-driven ship hauling Argonauts, the *J. W. Coffin*, cleared Boston lighthouse December 7, 1848. Soon scores of ships spread sails to the wind and followed in her wake. Thousands of gold seekers, striving to reach the gold fields ahead of those planning overland trips in the summer of 1849, sought berths on these vessels during the winter of 1848-1849.

In New York and Boston, owners quickly outfitted and repaired their ships and provided passenger accommodations. As previously mentioned, some vessels were weak from age and many of necessity put into ports along the way where stranded passengers were forced to wait for other vessels. Some ships simply never made any port. William Lamson tells about an older refitted ship, the bark *James W. Paige*. "... we had at the same time much wet, drizzling weather, which soon enabled us to discover that our ship was an old and leaky thing, and that our houses, though new, had been so carelessly constructed, that the water came in freely upon us, wetting our berths and rendering our situation exceedingly uncomfortable."

Fares and freight rates were not fixed. They were determined by bid, by bargaining, or by what the traffic would bear. For instance, 113 passengers aboard the *Cheshire* paid $150 each for a ticket to San Francisco. Freight was stowed at $60 per ton. Since wind-driven ships carried one thousand to thirteen hundred tons, fortunes were to be made in shipping. Sometimes one trip paid for the vessel.

Passengers on such a journey experienced perils and adventures bordering on the epic. California was almost as remote as another planet. Mail service to and from the East was slow and irregular. There was no transcontinental telegraph. The voyage itself was uncertain, and uncertainties awaited the travelers once they reached the Far West.

Families, friends and loved ones were separated, probably never to see each other again, but such was the restlessness that characterized Americans. In search of a better life, they had left homes far across the sea. Now, within their new-found land, they again sought what they considered a better life. This restlessness, this pioneer spirit, and the vast area of the United States molded a nation whose families and loved ones were separated as in no other land. E. I. Barra, who sailed to California in 1849, vividly describes a dockside scene as a sailing ship is about to depart:

Many of the persons there had accompanied relatives from their distant homes, even as far off as New Hampshire and Vermont. Many New England mothers were there, looking every one of them a heroine that she was. They were taking leave of their darling sons for a long while at least. As I approached the group of three persons I noticed the young man clasping the hand of the young lady in his own, while her sad, tearful face was bent down to hide her grief. The elder lady spoke and said, "Cyrus, I told you a month ago, when you first told of your intention to go to California, that a steady, industrious man can win gold at home; but a good, thrifty, prudent wife he can't win every day." At this remark the young lady burst into fresh tears, which she could not keep back. The young man softly stroked her hand while he answered her mother, saying, "Mrs. Hamblin, I am not in a condition just now to do as I would like to do; but after this mining trip of two years, or perhaps less time, I hope to be able to build a nice house over in Dracut, just far enough from Lowell to make it seem like the country. Then Deborah and myself will be married and settle down in a home of our own. And I intend to have a nice gentle horse and a family carryall, and she will be able to drive over to your house every fine day and take you all around the neighborhood." At this glowing description of anticipated happiness, the young lady looked up at her lover and smiled pleasantly at his description of the joy to come.

One wonders whether the young man's "joy to come" ever arrived and if he was ever reunited with his sweetheart.

Barra then describes the colorful manner in which the ship cast off:

Now all those that were going were hurrying on board. The pilot went on board and ordered the mate to get everything ready for a start. The mate sung out to the men aloft, "Drop the bunts of the fore and main topsails." Then to the men on deck—"Sheet home!" "Now man the halyards and hoist away!" "Aye, aye, sir!" "Give us a shanter, somebody," sung out the men, at which one of the sailors struck up a hoisting song:

> "Nancy Banana she married a barber!
> Haul her away, boys! Haul her away!
>
> She married a barber who shaved without lather!
> Haul her away, boys! Haul her away!"

When the topsails were mastheaded, the pilot sung out to cast off the bow line. "Now run up your jib, Mr. Mate. Now ease away on your spring line;" and the vessel began to move from the wharf. Then the pilot sung out, "Let go your spring and stern lines!" Then the good ship began to forge ahead; and the last cord that held the ship tied to the land was cast off and she was as free as the bird that flew around her masthead. Just then a number of the passengers mounted the quarter-deck and struck up a song that was then quite in vogue in minstrel exhibitions, changing a few words of the chorus to suit the occasion. It ran thus:

> I dreamt a dream the other night when everything was still;
> I dreamt I saw Susanah, a coming down the hill.
> She had a pancake in her mouth; a tear was in her eye;
> Says I, 'O Susanah, dear, Susanah, don't you cry.'

> CHORUS

> 'O! Susanah, don't you cry for me!
> For I'm bound to California with my washbowl on my knee!

Perhaps some of these brave passengers sang with tears welling up in their eyes.

As ships put out from New England or New York, they encountered the heavy seas common to the North Atlantic, especially in winter. Then decks heaved and rolled; bulkheads creaked and groaned. At this time seasickness afflicted many passengers. Curse of sea travel, it affects some seafarers not at all and others temporarily, but the unfortunates never recover until they reach shore. A Mr. Lamson reported that "our ship . . . rolled so badly that we could not stand for a moment without clinging with both hands to our berths or some other fixture for support, and . . . nearly all of us were suffering severely with seasickness. . . ."

In the tropics, passengers could loll about the decks relaxing, talking, or perhaps just reminiscing. A passenger wrote of "a softness and a delicate blending of the different tints of purple, azure and gold. . . . Our men are lying or sitting about the decks engaged in conversation. . . . while here and there may be seen one quietly communing with his own thoughts . . . which the friends he has left three thousand miles distant suggest to him."

The oppressive heat and doldrums of the torrid zone proved uncomfortable, almost unbearable. A completely becalmed wind-driven ship just sits. No breezes move the stifling heat on or below deck. Mr. Myers on the *Sarah Elisa* wrote that "day is unbearable; night offers a little diversion in viewing the starry heavens. . . . The Southern Cross . . . probably inspires admiration in everyone."

By far the most perilous part of the journey was approaching and negotiating Cape Horn. Here severe storms, capricious currents and freezing cold awaited travelers. Raging seas battered bulkheads, smashed deckhouses and lifeboats, and washed men overboard. Sudden blasts of williwaws ripped sails asunder and snapped masts. Close-hauled ships tacking against heavy winds would find their leeward decks awash with seas constantly running over the scuppers. During these periods, sometimes lasting days, passengers

Emigrants loiter on deck as the ship carrying them to California rounds the Horn.

remained in dark staterooms and bounced and jostled as decks violently pitched and rolled. Well-cooked meals were almost impossible to prepare or to serve properly. If crewmen were ill or hurt, able-bodied passengers were pressed to man the hawsers to furl or reef sails. Some were even sent up ratlines to the yardarms to set gaskets on furled sails. Or they might be ordered to man the pumps if leaks admitted too much water in the bilges.

A passenger aboard the *Urania* described one such storm:

The sky was as black as a pall. All at once the gale struck the ship and threw her nearly on her beam ends. I never received such a shock in all my experience. The maintopsail, although nearly new and close reefed, was blown out of the boltropes as if it had been tissue paper. The spanker followed the topsail, while the forestaysail held its own. The captain ordered the helm to be put hard up, and ordered an additional man to the wheel. The ship obeyed the helm promptly and began to pay off and was soon before the wind. The forestaysail was now taken in and the ship was scudding under bare poles before the terrible hurricane. At the first blast of the gale big combers began to lift near the stern. An hour after the gale struck the ship the seas were running mountains high. We were running before a terrific southeaster, and the ship creaked and groaned in every joint and it seemed as if she could not hold together. Great combers arose near our stern, as if they were about to engulf us, but each time the ship would shoot ahead and escape. . . . All at once an ugly towering wave approached the ship from astern. It came with overwhelming force. The captain sung out, "Look out!" and the sea came over the stern and pooped the ship. It swept everything before it. The two men at the
helm were carried from their post as if they had been two wisps of straw, but the precautionary measures taken by the captain saved them, and the life lines enabled them to save themselves from injury. The lower cabin skylight was wrenched from its fastenings and the cabin was drenched with water. The starboard quarter boat was lifted from its fastenings and wedged between the bulwark and the upper cabin. The ship was waterlogged, and everything that was not well secured on the main deck was floating around, thereby endangering the lives of the men, who were hanging on to anything that was solid enough to hold on by. The upper cabin was full of water up to the first tier of berths. The steward and the cook, who had their room abaft the galley, were nearly carried overboard, but were saved by the brawny arms of the second mate, Mr. Bryson.

As the bark *James W. Paige* approached the Horn, Mr. Lamson described what he experienced:

The passengers were running to and fro in much confusion, and the voice of the captain was loudly heard in giving orders to the sailors, who were sent aloft to take in sail, for a squall had struck us. The trunks in our cabin were dashing from side to side, breaking chairs and stools and whatever else came in their way. The earthern ware in the lockers was slipping about and crashing up in a style that threatened its speedy demolition. All was noise and confusion. The winds whistled, howled and screamed, the sails flapped, the waves dashed against the sides of the vessel and over the decks, keeping a stream of water running back and forth as we rolled and pitched, and tossed over the seas. An unlucky wave, higher than the rest, stove a boat that hung at the davits.

Mr. Barra, aboard the *Urania*, explained the finesse required when a sailing vessel changed tack in a gale:

Now came the most dangerous performance that a ship can be subjected to when she has been running before the wind in a gale; that is, to bring her up to the wind without swamping her. The captain ordered all hands to man the braces, and watched his opportunity—for in the severest gale there are periods when the waves don't break so hard, for a short spell, as they do in its most furious moments. The watched for chance came. "Port your helm four spokes," said the captain. "Aye, aye, sir!" was answered by the man at the wheel. "Ease away on your starboard braces and haul in on your lee ones." It was done. The ship came up gently—she came up to the trough of the sea. Now was our greatest danger. "Hard down your helm! Slack away on your weather braces and haul in sharp on your lee ones." The ship came up sharply, and just then a sea struck her amidships and broke over the starboard side and partially filled the decks, but the ship continued to come up to the wind until she lay close to the wind, and was lying to with an easy motion.

The quality and abundance of food aboard sailing ships varied greatly from ship to ship and also from journey to journey. Since modern refrigeration was unknown and sailing vessels had little room for stowing ice, fresh meats and vegetables were limited to the first part of a journey or when the ship put in to port for supplies. Preserved foods were the main bill of fare. A seafarer could expect a diet of salt beef, salt pork, beans, rice, salted codfish or mackerel, bread, and various puddings, pies, and canned fruit for dessert. Potatoes, onions and carrots lasted less than two months. Coffee, tea, rum and wine augmented drinking water. Large ships sometimes carried cows, hogs and chickens to supply fresh meat, milk and eggs.

Galleys were quite primitive and cooks varied in ability, some excellent, some poor. One passenger wrote about "Salt meat, not soaked but half cooked, beans as hard as bullets, and duff (a pastry dessert) as heavy as lead." Then too, cooking on a sailing vessel during heavy seas was a challenge and if a gale was blowing, all hands, including cooks, might be required on deck or aloft instead of preparing meals.

Occasionally, food supplies ran low or would be of extremely poor quality; fresh water dwindled or became polluted. Mr. Myers tells of the suffering from hunger and thirst aboard the *Sarah Elisa*. "The most horrible food was consumed on the *Sarah Elisa*. . . . It was a terrible sight to sea [sic] the ravenous faces pushing greedily towards a newly opened cask from which green and yellow-tinged salt meat spread a smell of rotteness." Apparently even those unsavory victuals became scarce because he speaks of how "sad to see the people chew roots and aromatics intended for medicines. . . . one of the doctors divided licorice and sarsaparillo roots. . . ." Drinking water aboard this ship ran out. Myers wrote, "Thirst is perhaps more distressing than hunger. . . ." Water caught from frequent squalls saved the passengers and crew.

Passengers had lots of time—months of it. But ship owners made no effort to keep them amused. Travelers organized their own entertainment such as reading, card playing and dancing. Someone usually had a violin or accordion. Of dancing, one passenger noted in his journal, "I have attempted to take this kind of exercise, but in such a circumscribed space and such a rolling ballroom, I have found the amusement anything but amusing." Many passengers formed companies for common operation of gold-mining activities once they reached California. As time lapsed into months, these activities were unable to dispel boredom and depression.

Double-checking the navigator's course.

Religion occupied the minds of many passengers. One traveler said, "Divine service was arranged ... every Sunday, during which an American preacher attempted to instill new courage and hope into us." E. I. Barra recorded:

> I discovered that the passengers were imbued with true religious fervor, which, no doubt, they had inherited from their Puritan ancestors, being transmitted from the days of the landing on Plymouth Rock to the present time. They held religious meetings, in which each one related his spiritual aspirations, and delivered exhortations on the necessity of self-watchfulness to preserve each one from the commission of sin.

Some captains of sailing vessels had never carried passengers until the gold rush. They were good navigators and seamen; they ran tight ships; some ruthlessly so. Their main concern, however, had been to sail their ships and cargo safely to their destinations. Consequently, many skippers were unconcerned about the welfare and comfort of passengers they now found aboard their ships. As a result, passengers sailing with such captains suffered unnecessary hardships. One traveler complained that the captain reduced meals from three to two a day even though the holds contained ample supplies of food. Another accused his captain of refusing to supply wood for the stove in their cabin during cold weather. As Mr. Lamson complained, "We have no reason to complain of the owners of the vessel, but charge our discomforts to the surly brutality of the captain. . . ."

Garrett W. Law records some bizarre experiences in his journal when he was aboard the clipper *Washington Irving* journeying around the Horn in 1850-1851. According to Law, the captain's behavior toward his passengers was tyrannical. At the slightest complaint, the captain's typical response was that he was master of the ship and would act as he saw fit. At times he threatened to

*Rescuing the passengers and crew from the
sinking steamship SAN FRANCISCO, disabled on her
voyage from New York to San Francisco in 1853.*

throw a passenger in irons over trivial matters, but his most diabolical act involved two sisters aged eighteen and twenty. As the ship sailed through the torrid zone, the captain denied first-class passengers drinking water. On board was a condenser, a machine to distill sea water, but certain parts of it were missing rendering it inoperable. The skipper had the missing parts but refused to release them. Finally, it became clear that no water would be given the passengers unless the older sister shared the captain's cabin. The passengers, of course, vigorously remonstrated, but the captain remained adamant. Thirst became acute, but the older girl refused to submit. Ultimately the eighteen-year-old girl volunteered to substitute for her sister. Then the condenser was repaired and the passengers received drinking water.

On another ship, the *John Bartram*, the captain was very superstitious (a not unusual quirk of many early day captains or even a few latter-day ones), or he bordered on sadism. His vessel lay becalmed in the torrid doldrums. After several such days, the captain mused that there must be a "Jonah" among the passengers, thus accounting for the lack of wind. To remedy this situation, the Jonah would have to be found and tossed overboard. Lots were drawn to find the Jonah and the victim, a passenger, finally was thrown overboard. He sank, choked and regurgitated saltwater. Later he was hoisted aboard. Coincidentally, the desired wind arose and the ship got under way, convincing the skipper that throwing the Jonah overboard brought wind, and he threatened to cast another to the sea should the ship again become becalmed. Needless to say, all passengers were anxious the remainder of the journey.

Most journals and written records left by Argonauts who traveled windjammers around the Horn in the early years of the gold rush indicate the indifference and tyranny of many captains. Apparently some captains of sailing vessels had difficulty distinguishing between fare-paying passengers and salaried crewmen. Not all Captain Blighs commanded *H.M.S. Bounty*.

Some windjammers did not make San Francisco their only West Coast port of call. Sailing vessels of all sizes — schooners, barks, brigs, barkentines, brigantines and square-riggers — put in at cities along the West Coast from Puget Sound to San Diego. Some sailed to these other ports directly from the East; many others plied up and down the West Coast only. Along with other nonperishable goods, ships hauled lumber, coal and prepared fish from the Pacific Northwest to California ports and returned with food products, machinery and other commodities. The first ties for the Central Pacific Railroad were hewn from giant Douglas fir trees felled along the shores of Puget Sound, shipped to San Francisco aboard sailing vessels and then reshipped by river to Sacramento. In 1851 the first settlers of the city of Seattle were transported to Elliot Bay in Puget Sound aboard a windjammer that sailed directly around the Horn to that site.

By the early decades of the twentieth century, steam had replaced sail. On the West Coast the age of sail was rough and dangerous. Scores of hulks strewn along its shores offer mute testimony of gale winds and ponderous waves that battered ships into helpless wrecks. Countless "iron men in wooden ships" perished in these tall ships that contributed to the survival of the Far West, since for many years no railroads ran along its coast.

The CHARLES W. MORGAN, a typical windjammer plying between the East Coast and San Francisco via Cape Horn during the gold rush era.

135

Following the discovery of gold in California and the stampede of emigrants to the area, an almost insatiable demand for consumer goods developed at San Francisco. Ships that could carry freight the fastest and return to New York to reload realized the largest profits for their owners. The famous American clipper ships were developed to meet this demand for speed. These ships ultimately carried the American ensign to all parts of the world and they played an important role in delivering the much-needed merchandise to California. American clippers were the fastest windjammers ever built. The British imitated them, but American clippers, almost without exception, left competition to wallow in their wake. They were the epitome of Yankee marine skill, ingenuity and enterprise during the days of wind-driven ships.

American clippers were larger, stronger, and hoisted more sail than any previous ship. Built of the finest seasoned New England timber, they were so rugged that they could sail full-rigged in stronger winds than could other sailing vessels.

Naval architects designed the clipper so that she skimmed over the waves, thus reducing resistance. This reduction in resistance and the huge amount of sail aloft gave the clipper unsurpassed speed. She clipped off the miles, hence her name.

Her hull was graceful as well as functional. From the bowsprit to the water line, the bow curved inward and downward. From the forecastle almost to midships, the deck swayed slightly downward. From here the deck was level until just aft the quarter-deck when it curved upward to the stern.

The Boston *Atlas* wrote the following about the clipper ship *Sea Serpent* built in East Boston:

> *The Clipper Ship* Sea Serpent *— This is the second clipper on a large scale which has been built in New England this season; the Surprise, built at East Boston, was the first. The* Sea Serpent *is about 1300 tons. She is 212 feet long over all, has 39 feet 3 inches extreme breadth of beam, and 21 feet depth of hold. She is very sharp forward and beautifully proportioned aft, without being cut up like a center-board, and broadside on she looks rakish and saucy.*

View of San Francisco from Telegraph Hill in 1850.

*The LYDIA, like the CHARLES W.
MORGAN, sailed from the East Coast around the
Horn to San Francisco during the gold rush era.*

Upon her arrival in New York after her maiden run to San Francisco, the New York *Herald* described her:

> Her bow partakes of the wedge in appearance, and she is very sharp, but her lines are nearly all rounded. Her bow is tastefully ornamented with a large gilded Eagle, with outstretched wings, beautifully carved, and has a simple and very neat appearance. Her hull is entirely black, excepting a narrow yellow line which relieved the sameness and looks much smarter than the white streak, so common on other vessels.
>
> The model of the Sea Serpent *is one that the greatest grumbler would be at a loss to find the smallest fault with. Head on she has a most rakish appearance, and her lines swell along the bow into their utmost fulness, and then taper off again into the clean run; they show incontestably that 'the line of beauty' has been made the guide in her construction. They are as perfect as perfection itself.*
>
> *Her stern is most beautifully proportioned, and is tastefully decorated with two carved full length representations of the Great American Sea Serpent.*

Most clippers carried five sails on each of their towering foremasts, mainmasts and mizzenmasts; in addition, a spanker astern; a flying jib, jib and foretopmost staysail on their bowsprits; and six staysails between masts. A more picturesque maritime scene is rare indeed than an American clipper ship under full sail slicing through the whitecaps at eighteen knots, her masts set aft at a rakish angle, her close-hauled sails silhouetted against a blue sky, and the stars and stripes proudly fluttering over the vessel's churning, foamy wake.

Some famous clipper ships were the *Staghound, Challenge, Witch of the Wave, Sovereign of the Seas, Flying Cloud, Great Republic* and *Neptune's Car. Neptune's Car* was the scene of an unusual drama which will be told later.

These ships, skippered by excellent masters using Lieutenant Maury's *Sailing Directions* and his *Wind and Current Charts,* cut dramatically the running time between the East Coast and San Francisco. Runs of ninety to one hundred days were common. Races between these ships were frequent. The *Flying Cloud,* however, holds the record between New York and San Francisco of eighty-nine days, eight hours. On her maiden voyage in 1851, she made the trip in eighty-nine days and twenty-one hours.

Her maiden run was memorable. Commanded by Josiah P. Cressy, she cleared New York June 2, 1851, fully laden and, after dropping the pilot off Sandy Hook, pointed southward full-rigged. Off Cape Hatteras, gale winds ripped her main and mizzen topgallants and broke the topsail yardarm. Unperturbed, Cressy sent up new sails and a new yardarm and drove ahead under full sail. He passed other ships that were forced to reef their

The clipper ship ARCHER, which sailed between the East Coast and San Francisco during the gold rush era.

Courtesy California State Library, Sacramento

The clipper FLYING CLOUD, which holds the speed record for vessels sailing between the East Coast and San Francisco.

Courtesy California State Library, Sacramento

Famous American clipper ship SOVEREIGN OF THE SEAS made repeated trips around the Horn between New York and San Francisco. Copy of an N. Currier lithograph.

The Mariners Museum, Newport News, Virginia

topsails because of the gale. However, the following day a raging pampero gave him trouble according to his log:

Heavy Gales, Close Reefed Topsails split fore Staysail & Main Topmast Staysail at 1 p.m. Discovered Main Masthead Sprung (same time Brig in Company to Leeward lost fore & Main topmast) sent down Royal & Topmast Yards and Booms off Lower & Topsail Yard to releave [sic] the mast, very turbulent sea Running Ship Laboring hard and shipping large quantities of Water over lee Rail. Middle & latter parts hard Gales and Harder squalls. No observations.

Captain Cressy repaired his mast and pushed southward, reaching the Horn region about July 20. Following is a portion of his log from July 22 through July 27. It indicates that he swept around the Horn on July 23 at 56.04 latitude south, his southernmost position.

July 22 Lat. 54.41 Lon. 64.50 ESE SE by S E Hard Gale with Rain and sleet shipping much water bad sea Running, at 4 P M Weather fair Saw Cape St. Diego bearing SE 15 miles, wore ship at 5 P M to NE, at 6 A M wore ship to Southward at 10 saw the land South 20 miles, at meridian St. Diego W 10 miles Weather moderate & Cloudy

July 23 Lat. 56.04 Lon. 68.16 E E E Moderate all set sail passed through St. Le Marie & Cleared the Land at 6 P M, Strong tide setting to Northward Middle Rainy, Latter fair Cape Horn N 5 miles at 8 A M, the whole coast covered with snow — wild Ducks numerous

July 24 Lat. 55.43 Lon. 72.51 ENE NE NW Gentle breezes light snow squalls; middle & Latter moderate & Clear weather, all sail set.

July 25 Lat. 53.36 Lon. 78.04 N N NE Moderate breezes with Rain and snow squalls.

July 26 Lat. 50.57 Lon. 80.33 S S SW Light breezes & Cloudy Latter fine breeze & Clear weather

July 27 Lat. 47.55 Lon. 84.06 SSWS by E Light breezes & Cloudy Sent up Main topgallant & Royal Yards set all possible sail.

It was sometime after July 27 with "all possible sail" that *Flying Cloud* set a record for speed that stood for years. In a twenty-four hour period she logged 374 nautical miles — better than eighteen knots an hour. Even streamers were unable to beat this record for more than twenty years.

A voyage around the Horn on the clipper ship *Neptune's Car*, with a beautiful lady in command, unfolded an adventure stranger than fiction. The following account of the passage is based on facts reported in the *New York Times* on January 20, 1857, and reprinted in the *Sacramento Union* March 19, 1857.

This tall-masted clipper, commanded by Captain Joshua P. Patton, creaked and strained at her mooring lines on New York's waterfront in mid-August 1856. Last minute preparations were under way for her departure. Accompanying the captain on this trip was his attractive wife Mary, just turned twenty. She had made two previous voyages with him.

As the ship cast off her spring and stern lines and gently rolled into the harbor, hot sun accentuated the pungent aroma of creosote and the sea. She drifted down the Hudson past the clippers *Romance of the Seas* and *Intrepid*, also San Francisco-bound, when Patton, proud and confident of his ship, lifted his megaphone and shouted a challenge, "Ahoy, I'll beat both o' ye to San Francisco!"

The clipper ship FLYING CLOUD en route around the Horn, from an N. Currier lithograph. This famous vessel holds the record for shortest sailing time between New York and San Francisco and for the most nautical miles logged in twenty-four hours.

Clearing Sandy Hook, the *Neptune's Car* glided into the Atlantic swells, her forecastle heaved above the horizon, paused momentarily, and then dropped to the whitecaps and repeated the rhythmic motion in endless cycles. Most hands were aloft on the yardarms unfurling all her canvas that snapped before the wind.

As days numbered into weeks and the clipper plied ever southwest, Captain Patton noticed his first mate neglecting his duties. Decks were cluttered and at times sails were improperly reefed or unfurled as the wind demanded. Captain's orders were to have all sails unfurled in favorable winds.

Through foul weather and fair the clipper sailed. She crossed the placid waters of the equator, cleared Fernando Noronha at the easternmost tip of Brazil and swung southwest toward Cape Horn.

Nearing 45 degrees latitude south, the vessel encountered a strong westerly blow. "Ideal weather for making a fast run," mused the captain, yet he sensed that the ship was not taking the wind as she should. Hurrying to the quarter-deck, he glanced at the rigging. The mainsails were only partially unfurled! The chief officer, supposedly on watch, was not in sight. Angered, the captain vainly shouted for him, and, searching the ship, found him asleep.

"Why aren't the mains'ls unfurled? Order them unfurled!" Reluctantly the first mate arose and gave the order. Frequently, Patton had to rout his chief officer out of his bunk when he was supposed to be on watch. Such carelessness added needless days to the journey.

October approached and the vessel neared the Horn. While negotiating these hazardous waters, Captain Patton repeatedly found his first mate negligent. Not only did this cause delay; it now jeopardized the ship and crew. Finally Patton's patience snapped. Summoning the mate to his cabin, the captain roared, "You are relieved of your duties. I'll stand your watch in addition to my duties!"

This added burden taxed the skipper's health and he became ill with a fever. After struggling a week to manage the ship, he was forced to quit the deck for his bunk. Calling his wife to his side, he confided that he was unable to command the ship, that she must assume command. She was inexperienced with seamanship and with command, but her husband would be her teacher.

Mary was an apt pupil. In the few days before her husband became blind and delirious, she had learned the essential duties of a master and the rudiments of navigation. Each noon and evening she made observations with the sextant, determined her location and set her course.

With the captain totally incapacitated, complete operation of the ship now fell upon Mary. Since *Neptune's Car* was still in the vicinity of Cape Horn, she faced many more weeks at sea, and the command of the crew. Would they obey her, a slight, pretty girl barely twenty?

Meanwhile in the forecastle, the crew's quarters, the first mate was fomenting mutiny. "Men," he urged the crew, "the cargo is worth a fortune. We can all be rich if we take over the ship and sail her to Valparaiso." To a penniless crew that lived without hope of wealth, this suggestion was very tempting. They came to no definite decision but seriously pondered the idea.

The launch of the famous clipper FLYING CLOUD, which in 1851 made the record run from New York to San Francisco around the Horn in eighty-nine days, eight hours.

The clipper ship NEPTUNE'S CAR.
*When the vessel's captain became
ill on a trip around Cape Horn,
his young wife successfully
assumed command.*

144

Somehow Mary Patton heard of this proposed mutiny. At first fear welled up in her—near panic. Her first impulse undoubtedly was to barricade herself in the captain's quarters. But upon reflection, she remembered her promise to her husband and her obligation to the owners and underwriters of the ship and cargo.

Her situation seemed desperate. To command a tough crew was challenge enough; to quell a mutinous one was quite another matter. She could not consult her husband. Over six thousand miles stretched between *Neptune's Car* and San Francisco.

Mrs. Patton decided to act, rather than let the matter slide with the hope that the threatened mutiny would go away. She summoned the crew to the windswept quarter-deck, where this petite lady faced these hard-bitten men as the ship pitched crazily and wind screeched through the rigging. She alone stood between mutiny and the ship's security. Bravely, she shouted above the wind, "Captain Patton is seriously ill and unable to command the ship. He is blind, delirious, and is losing his hearing. He has asked me to command the ship. And, as acting captain, I ask each of you to follow my orders and those of the second mate." She made no threats, merely a candid appeal. Would the crew take advantage of the skipper's total disability? The next few moments held the answer.

As the lonely clipper twisted through the bleak sea, this solitary lady stood awaiting the answer. Each man pondered her words. Then, whether it was gallantry buried deeply in their hearts or fear of the penalty for mutiny or respect for this brave lady, each man declared his allegiance to her. From that moment, the first mate lost all influence with the crew; he was put in irons. The second mate helped command the ship.

No vessel was kept more shipshape, nor did a crew turn to their tasks with more gusto than did the crew of the *Neptune's Car* commanded by Mary Patton. She brought the ship to San Francisco, November 13, 1856, only eight days (a mere trifle for those times) behind the *Romance of the Seas*.

Several days later Mrs. Patton was called before the board of marine underwriters that had insured the ship and cargo. "Mrs. Patton," they explained, "we are deeply indebted to you. You are indeed a true heroine. Your action saved the ship and cargo whose loss would have cost the insurance companies a large sum of money. To show our appreciation, we present you this check for one thousand dollars."

During the early 1850's, windjammers hauling freight around the Horn enriched their owners. For instance, in 1851 the *Sea Serpent* made a run with 1,304 tons of freight that grossed $54,528.36 in cartage fees, an amount greater than the cost of the ship. Another clipper, *Sovereign of the Seas* with a crew of 104, carried three thousand tons of freight and twenty-one passengers. She cleared New York August 4, 1851, for San Francisco. With freight stowed at $60 a ton, the trip produced a handsome profit. Even hay grown in New England for the beasts of burden in California was shipped around the Horn and sold there for $150 a ton. Freight rates, however, dropped each year; by 1853 they were down to $30 a ton, and to $15 two years later, but even at these lower rates, trips were profitable.

Vessels sailing around Cape Horn carried the bulk of the freight to the West until the completion of the Pacific railroad in 1869. They supplied the ever-increasing demands created by the gold rush. Sailing vessels were vital in transporting material to build the Central Pacific Railroad. At times as many as thirty windjammers were at sea carting rails, locomotives and cars for the railroad. With the completion of the transcontinental railroad, sailing vessels continued plying the route for many years, but hauling less tonnage. Then their cargo to the West Coast consisted mainly of nonperishable merchandise that did not require fast transport.

Burning of the GOLDEN GATE steamer on July 27, 1862. Fewer than a third of the 337 people aboard were saved.

6

To the West by Steamship

Until the completion of the Pacific railroad in 1869, windjammers carried most of the freight and some of the passengers from the East Coast to California; steamers carried most of the people that came west by sea, express goods, and mail, but very little freight. These early day steamers left New York or New Orleans, sailed to the Isthmus of Panama and unloaded their cargo, which was then transmitted across the Isthmus. On the west side of the Isthmus, it was reloaded on steamers bound for San Francisco. Other overland crossings were attempted in Nicaragua and on the Isthmus of Tehuantepec in Mexico, but Panama became the favored, consistent overland transit.

The United States government became interested in a mail route to the Oregon Country in 1846, at which time the area had become a part of the American Republic. The Panama route was chosen as the most practical one and so on March 6, 1846, a treaty was negotiated with the New Granada (now Panama) government permitting passage of U.S. mails across the Isthmus. The Federal government then called for bids on steamer service to deliver mail on the Atlantic to Chagres, Panama, and from Panama City, Panama, on the Pacific to Astoria, Oregon, at the mouth of the Columbia River. Panama natives were contracted to carry the mail across the Isthmus.

The mail steamers were to be built for possible future use by the U.S. Navy. The Navy at this time was slowly converting to steam power and wanted steam vessels available that could be requisitioned for compensation in time of emergency. The mail contract specified that three ships be built for the Atlantic run and three for the Pacific run. Two in the Pacific were to be one thousand tons and the third not less than six hundred tons. They were to be commanded by naval officers

relieved from active duty with the Navy for three years. Many officers applied to serve on the mail steamers, since it gave them experience in steam. They realized that future commands in the Navy would go to officers with such experience. The bids further stipulated that mail be delivered semimonthly between New York and Astoria, Oregon, for a period of ten years.

George Law and several associates received the bid as carriers on the Atlantic and formed the United States Mail Steamship Company. The Pacific division bid went to William H. Aspinwall and several associates. On April 12, 1848, they organized the Pacific Mail Steamship Company.

The sea route was considered safer and more reliable for mail transit, because hostile Indians, great transcontinental distances and winter weather handicapped overland-mail service. At the end of ten years, however, with the completion of the Butterfield Overland Express stagecoach route in 1858, this overland stage company packed most of the first-class mail until the beginning of the Civil War.

Aspinwall contracted for three steamers to be built in New York in 1848: the *California, Oregon* and *Panama*. Completed first was the *California*, a 1,058-ton side-wheeler, 199 feet long, 33 1/2 feet of beam, with a hold 20 feet deep. Her engine, a side-lever type, had a piston 5 feet, 5 inches in diameter with a stroke of 8 feet that developed slightly over 200 horsepower. As with most early steamers, she mounted three masts to carry sails to augment her engines in favorable winds and for primary motive power in case her engines should fail, or she ran out of fuel, both frequent occurrences on early steamers. Soon followed *Oregon*, comparable in size to *California*; then *Panama*, slightly smaller.

California departed New York for California October 6, 1848. Prior to this date the January 1848 discovery of gold in California had been considered merely a rumor in the East. Primitive communications had delayed confirmation of the discovery. Consequently, *California* left New York with few passengers, but shortly after her departure, President Polk confirmed the bonanza strike in California. Then the stampede began. As previously mentioned, hundreds booked passage around the Horn, but many hundreds also attempted the long trek westward by way of Panama. They arrived at Chagres on Panama's east coast in barks, sloops, brigs and steamers—anything that would sail. From there these gold seekers began the slow, laborious passage over the Isthmus to Panama City.

When the *California* dropped anchor off Panama City on January 17, 1849, she found 726 stranded gold seekers clamoring to board her for San Francisco. They had sailed on various ships from the East Coast for Chagres, the eastern port of the Isthmus of Panama. After crossing the Isthmus to Panama City, they expected ships awaiting there to take them to San Francisco, but the sudden stampede to California caused confusion and disorganization in the shipping industry. There just were not enough ships to meet the demand. Especially critical was the shortage of vessels on the West Coast. Thousands of travelers waited weeks,

sometimes months, in Panama City for passage to San Francisco during the first year of the gold rush. Many of these stranded passengers had been sold through-tickets to California by unscrupulous Eastern agents.

The *California* had been built to carry only 250 passengers, and she already had on board 69 Peruvians picked up at Callao, 17 of whom were cabin passengers, the remainder in steerage. The temper of these Americans at Panama City was such that mob action might prevent *California*'s sailing, because many gold seekers felt that their through-passage tickets entitled them to space on the *California*. But Pacific Mail had not sold these through-tickets. The Americans, nevertheless, demanded that the Peruvians, being foreigners, had no right to be aboard an American ship. They demanded the Peruvians be put ashore. Agents for Pacific Mail Steam in Panama then worked out an arrangement whereby the Peruvians in staterooms would be placed in hastily constructed berths on deck. She sailed with 365 passengers and a crew of thirty-six, arriving at San Francisco, February 28, 1849. Promptly her crew deserted for the gold country with the exception of her captain and two

Pacific Mail steamship CALIFORNIA, the first steamer to arrive in San Francisco after the discovery of gold in California.

engine-room boys. Expected coal for her engine had not arrived, so she temporarily joined other deserted ships, mostly windjammers, that cluttered San Francisco Bay by the hundreds during the next few years. By May 1, however, the *California* had replenished her fuel and crew and sailed for Panama City. She thereafter remained in regular service for years.

Her sister ship, the *Oregon*, arrived at Panama City on February 23, 1849. Here she found some 1,200 persons eagerly awaiting passage for San Francisco and crowded 250 of them on board. The *Oregon's* sister ship, the *Panama*, left New York after news of the gold strike had reached the East and sailed with 81 through-passengers. At Panama City she found about 2,000 people clamoring for transportation to San Francisco, but because of her limited capacity she jammed only 209 aboard. By this time several sailing vessels rode at anchor in Panama City and were able to accommodate many of those stranded.

When the *Oregon* arrived in San Francisco Bay, her Captain dropped anchor under the guns of an American man-of-war to prevent his crew from deserting. He arrested potential deserters. Not until seamen's wages were raised from $12 to $112 a month were his crewmen again interested in manning the ship. Shortly, these three steamers were sailing regularly between Panama City and San Francisco in compliance with the mail contract. The run to Astoria, Oregon, was temporarily suspended because of the unforeseen heavy gold-rush traffic.

These ships sailed overloaded causing passengers to suffer discomforts, if not outright misery. Feeding and sanitary facilities were a problem. Pacific Mail had not sold all those fares in advance; the company overloaded their vessels to relieve an almost intolerable situation in Panama City. Many other ship owners, however, deliberately and excessively oversold their ships and falsely advertised the capacities and seaworthiness of their craft. Many steerage passengers were crammed into holds where berths were stacked two feet above each other with the top berth only two and one-half feet lower than the overhead. Food was short and poorly prepared. American troops riding the holds of transports in World Wars I and II fared better by comparison.

Taking advantage of the unforeseen, unprecedented numbers of travelers, Pacific Mail upped fares between Panama City and San Francisco. Cabin class increased from $200 to $300 and steerage from $100 to $150.

The company soon increased its fleet to meet increased business. In addition to purchasing several older vessels, two new ships were added to the route. One, the fine steamer *Golden Gate,* was 269 feet long, 40 feet wide, with a 2,067-ton cargo. She had been built specifically to meet the new conditions of the Panama route. When the vessel first put into San Francisco, the *Herald* reported:

> *Crowds of interested citizens visited her during the day, and all were filled with admiration at her immense proportions and elegant accommodations. She is the finest specimen of naval architecture on the Pacific, being the largest and swiftest steamer in our waters, and equalled by few anywhere. Her long deck forms a noble promenade, while her beautifully fitted up accommodations, and well ventilated cabins, remind one more of a drawing room than the interior of a ship.*

*The Pacific Mail Steamship Company's OREGON
was one of the original three steamers to sail
between Panama City and San Francisco.*

Until the completion of the Panama Railroad in January 1855, crossing the Isthmus of Panama presented travelers perils and problems. On the Atlantic side, passengers debarked at Chagres on the mouth of the Chagres River. Since ships were unable to dock at the town, they dropped anchor offshore. Travelers were then taken ashore in small boats operated by natives, but heavy seas and indolent boatmen sometimes created debarkation delays of days and even weeks. Chagres was a primitive, uninviting place. Historian H. H. Bancroft describes the village:

Chagres at this time (early 1849) was a town of about seven hundred inhabitants, dwelling in some fifty windowless, bamboo huts, with thatched, palm-leaf roofs, and having open entrances, and bare ground floor. The town was surrounded by heaps of filthy offal, and greasy, stagnant pools bordered with blue mud.

Emigrants rowing in from ships anchored off Chagres (CIRCA 1849).

The local population consisted of Indians and half-breeds. The only hostelry was operated by a Swede who had taken up with a native woman. He professed to maintain a good hotel such as "the convenience of the country will permit of." The conveniences consisted of only a palm-leaf building and hammocks for beds. Unscreened windows and doors invited droves of mosquitoes, rats and cockroaches. When Spain ruled the area, Chagres had seen better times—stone-paved streets and stone buildings which had now deteriorated. Mosquitoes spread malaria and the dreaded yellow fever. Cholera epidemics were an ever-present hazard. Food was of dubious quality. Fortunate were those who brought preserved food, tents, and waterproof bedding from the States.

In 1849 the Panama Railroad, organized by William Aspinwall of the Pacific Mail Steamship Company, started surveying for a railroad across Panama. Railroad officials established Yankee Chagres across the river from old Chagres. Here the company built wooden hotels, warehouses and wharves. In typical Yankee vogue, saloons, gambling houses and brothels abounded for the accommodation of railroad workers. As the railroad labor force increased to about six thousand scattered across the Isthmus, brothels multiplied in scope and numbers. Ultimately patrons could choose from a wide variety of damsels. In addition to the darker-skinned blacks and Indians or a blend of the two, Anglo-Saxon and French girls were imported from Europe. One house offered

Another well-known Pacific Mail steamer, the
GOLDEN GATE, *also sailed between San Francisco
and Panama City.*

French lasses exclusively—the establishment undoubtedly approached somewhat the standards of famed Parisian bordellos. A by-product of the thriving enterprise was venereal disease—an abundance of it. Not only were railroad workers clients of this most ancient of professions; many California gold seekers en route across the Isthmus paused at these "palaces" of pleasure. Evidence of these interludes is attested by a San Francisco doctor who ordered drugs from the East with these words: "The marconis and whoremongers of the Isthmus are sending us more patients than we can minister to."

To cross the Isthmus, travelers journeyed up the Chagres River in bungo boats—in dry season as far as Gorgona, thirty-nine and one-half miles upstream from Chagres. During the rainy season this route was extended five miles beyond Gorgona to Cruces. From Gorgona or Cruces passengers walked, or rode on donkeys or mules, over slimy, muddy trails for twenty miles to Panama City.

Bungos were hollowed out of a single log about 25 feet long and 2 to 3-1/2 feet wide. They carried two to four passengers and their baggage. Canopies protected travelers from the tropical sun. Natives poled bungos up the Chagres River through dense jungle under the watchful eyes of monkeys and exotic tropical birds that chattered incessantly. Occasionally an alligator or iguana slithered across their path. One traveler described the river as

> ... broad, and its banks low and covered with an impenetrable jungle. As night came on, the stillness and darkness of the tropical wilderness were very impressive. The boatmen chanted monotonous songs to the dip of the oars, and the wild beasts on the shore responded with savage howls.

The trip to Gorgona required three to four days if the boatmen decided not to be balky.

At first, boatmen charged four dollars for the portage. As demand for passage increased, the wily natives upped the fare. By 1851 fares had jumped to forty dollars. Passengers were advised to pay no more than half the fare at the start of the journey and the remainder upon completion of the trip. Boatmen had a tendency to stop mid-journey, refusing to proceed unless more money were paid. At night sojourners often slept in crude native huts or on board the boats, and unless they brought their own food, partook of native food of unpredictable edibility. Hotels of a sort appeared along the Chagres River. In August 1849, the Union Hotel in Cruces advertised in the *Panama Star* that the innkeeper spoke Spanish, English, French and Italian; an asset considering the various nationalities that traversed the Isthmus. Innkeepers also served as a forwarding agent for baggage, but claimed no responsibility "for robberies on the highway, fire, or flooding of rivers," hazards that prompted the Panama newspaper continually to warn emigrants never to let their baggage out of sight.

From the head of the Chagres River to Panama City, emigrants rode mules through deep sloughs or steep, treacherous, muddy trails that were especially hazardous for women, since skirts were not designed to straddle a mule. Some ladies donned men's trousers, but others refused, according to Bancroft, "preferring to die rather than to outrage modesty, shame their sex, and exhibit their ankles even to the barbarians. . . ."

Bandits, attracted by the large amount of gold shipped across the Isthmus, menaced travelers.

Comprehensive map of the United States and
Mexico shows various routes to the American West.

*Emigrants crossing the Isthmus of Panama
aboard mules and an oxcart.*

From the beginning of the gold rush, express companies preferred dispatching gold to the East by ship rather than transporting it across the continental United States. This overland route was considered too hazardous. California stagecoaches carried large shipments of gold and silver, but only from the mines to the vaults of express companies in San Francisco. Treasure was shipped over the Isthmus on pack mules owned by local freight haulers.

No law existed on the Isthmus of Panama; anarchy reigned. Almost everybody carried a gun. The New Granada government's militia and police were impotent.

The first robbery of consequence occurred in August 1850. Masked bandits robbed a Howland and Aspinwall pack train of thirty thousand dollars on the Cruces Trail. This amount was part of a consignment entrusted to Wells Fargo and Company, then in the express business as well as banking. The company's agent in Panama, Henry Tracy, wrote to his superiors in New York predicting more robberies. He asked for rifles, revolvers, bowie knives and shotguns. "I am determined that there shall be none stolen from your trains without there be funerals."

The U.S. Consul at Panama City wrote to William H. Aspinwall, president of the Panama Railroad (then under construction) and a partner in a local mule train operation, and warned him of

bandits. Pack-train operators armed themselves and moved large shipments of treasure in convoys. Despite these precautions, a mile-long string of pack mules carrying $2,600,000 in gold and accompanied by five hundred successful miners returning home from California was suddenly attacked by screaming, shooting bandidos as they slithered along the jungle trail. In the confusion, bandits stormed into the convoy seemingly from nowhere. Mules and horses reared and snorted. Several broke from the line as prospectors and guards opened fire. Four bandits were killed, but other gang members roped several gold-laden mules, transferred gold pouches onto their own horses and quickly vanished into the jungle. One hundred thousand dollars in gold disappeared with them.

Robberies increased to the point where even bungo-boat operators became infected with the desire for plunder. Occasionally, on lonely stretches of the Chagres River, boatmen would suddenly knife passengers and toss their bodies overboard. Vultures and other predators quickly picked their bones clean.

In desperation, either the Panama Railroad, the express companies, the U.S. Consul, or perhaps all three in unison, imported a mysterious Randolph Runnels from Texas to quell the robberies. Runnels was deeply religious. Reading and quoting the Bible, he moved so relentlessly against the bandidos that he correctly earned the title of "Hangman." Runnels felt his calling was a holy mission consecrated by God.

Upon Runnel's arrival, he operated a pack train as a front. This guise offered him the opportunity to watch gambling halls, saloons and brothels along the trail. His forty employees were his unofficial deputies sworn to secrecy. Then one night he and his men struck Panamanian cities — Cruces, Gorgona, Panama City. The next morning thirty-seven bodies swayed in the gentle, tropical breezes on the ends of ropes along a prominent street in Panama City. Several were well-known businessmen. This sudden, extensive utilization of hemp restored peace on the trails for some time. Runnels, of course, was acting in an extralegal, unofficial capacity, but he had done his work well.

Later, however, other bandits began robbing express companies and individual travelers. Again Runnels struck. This time forty-two bodies dangled along the avenues of Panama City. The trails again became quiet. The *Panama Star* reported in November 1854: "The Isthmus is as safe to travel on as any part of the world—thanks to the vigilance of the Runnels' Guard and the precautions adopted by them to prevent bad characters from remaining on the road." After completion of the Panama Railroad in January 1855, travelers and treasure crossed the Isthmus unmolested.

Though some travelers were cheated by unscrupulous agents and others were taken advantage of by native boatmen, not all sojourners were successfully victimized. Some resourceful Americans outmaneuvered those who attempted to take advantage of them. Julius H. Pratt and a party of his fellow travelers displayed such resourcefulness. They had engaged thirty native boatmen to transport them from Chagres to Gorgona in ten bungos for a set price. One morning the boatmen refused to proceed. They wanted more money. Mr. Pratt and his fellow Americans brandished their pistols and rifles, formed a line behind the recalcitrant natives and ordered them to row their bungos forthrightly, or else. And forthrightly they rowed with alacrity.

After arriving at Panama City, Mr. Pratt and his friends waited for passage to San Francisco. Finally they made arrangements on a small sailing vessel, the *Humboldt*. The contract made with the consignee, a Frenchman, was that passengers be limited to four hundred exclusive of a crew of forty. The fare was $200 and at full capacity the ship would have been very overcrowded.

Upon boarding the *Humboldt*, Mr. Pratt and his companions found her so overcrowded that the ship's officers could not maintain order. It would have been impossible to feed such a milling multitude or even sail the ship. About 100 Americans, including Mr. Pratt, determined that 440 passengers were on board. Obviously the consignee had oversold the ship for his own aggrandizement, ignoring the suffering of the passengers. Mr. Pratt and 100 Americans decided to call on the Frenchman. As they went ashore, other Americans remaining on board promised that the ship would not sail until they returned. Those going ashore picked a committee of five to represent them. Mr. Pratt was one of them. The Americans, including the committee, proceeded to the house of the French consignee. All were armed. On the way they were joined by other armed, irate Americans. The Frenchman's house was a three-story building with balconies on each story.

The committee pounded on his door and demanded of a servant to see the French consignee. The servant said his master was out but would they care to leave a message. The Americans stated that they knew monsieur was home and that he had better receive them in five minutes or they would enter the house and find him. Mr. Pratt relates that the number of armed Americans milling about the plaza was sufficient to take the town by force. The French consignee realized this fact and within ten minutes appeared on a balcony.

Whereupon the committee stated its grievance and demanded that the number of passengers booked be reduced. He immediately became profuse in his apologies. With eager acquiescence, he replied that the overloading was a dreadful mistake and he could not understand how such a deplorable condition came about. The committee then informed him that he appear on the ship to reduce by forty the passenger list, and as a punitive measure, he should then reduce the passenger list by another forty persons and that these eighty people be refunded their full fare. He bowed and loquaciously condescended to every demand if only they would guarantee his personal safety. The committee agreed to protect him and he dutifully met their demands.

As construction of the Panama Railroad gradually stretched westward across the forty-seven mile Isthmus, travelers in transit rode the train to the railhead. Upon the railroad's completion in January 1855, steamer departures and arrivals at the Atlantic and Pacific ports were coordinated so train travelers could debark and board Atlantic and Pacific ships the same day. Some time after 1855, the Pacific Mail Steamship Company posted the following schedule for its steamer route from New York to San Francisco via the newly completed Panama Railroad:

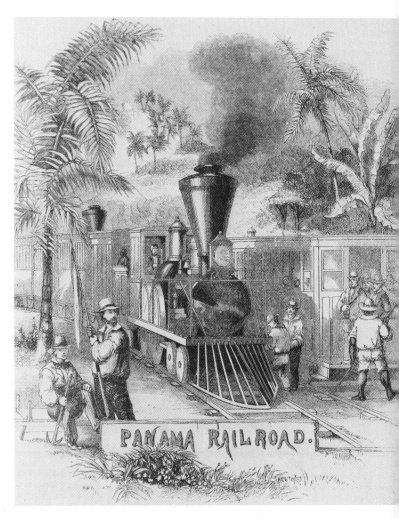

Illustration of the Panama Railroad in May 1872
HARPER'S MAGAZINE.

New York to Aspinwall	**8 days**
Aspinwall to Panama City	**4 hours**
Time for embarking	**6 hours**
Panama City to San Francisco	**12 days**

The railroad had moved its eastern port of entry from Chagres to Navy Bay on Manzanillo Island, since the latter offered deepwater port facilities. Here a new town named Aspinwall was built in honor of one of its principal founders. The government of New Granada refused to accept this name and instead designated the port Colon. For years the port went by both names depending on whether Americans or natives were referring to it; now it is officially Colon.

Construction of the Panama Railroad was a formidable undertaking. Construction was hindered by intertwining jungles, swamps, mountains, disease, and labor shortages. Mr. F. N. Otis wrote the following on-the-spot report:

The character and geographical position of the country through which the line of the road had been carried was such as might well have made the hardiest projectors shrink from attempting its construction. The first thirteen miles, beginning at Navy Bay, was through a deep morass, covered with the densest jungle, reeking with malaria, and abounding with almost every species of wild beasts, noxious reptiles, and venomous insects known in the tropics.

Laborers from Ireland, China, Jamaica and France, as well as local natives and Americans, worked at various times on the railroad. Four to six months was the average labor contract. This duration was deemed the limit a laborer could endure the tropics. In 1854 upward of six thousand men sweated and strained in the jungle. Many died of cholera and yellow fever. A cholera epidemic in 1852 halted construction for several months. Laborers, mechanics and engineers expired at an alarming rate. (It has been said that the chief export from this area at that time was corpses soaked in alcohol, packed in barrels and shipped to medical schools.) When completed, the road had cost $6,564,523 including rolling stock, land and all other expenditures — an exceedingly high price for forty-seven miles of railroad. In spite of this initial cost, the road proved to be a very profitable investment.

The Panama route was an important travel and communication link between California and the East Coast from 1848 to 1869. During this time steamers on the route remained essentially the same except that with passage of time, newer ships were larger and more elegant. With two exceptions, they were wooden and most of them walking-beam-side-wheelers.

Panama steamers were large for their times. The *Ohio* was 246 feet long with a tonnage of 2,432. The *Golden Gate* was 269 feet long with a tonnage of 2,057. Ten years later (1861) ships such as the *Golden City* were built up to 363 feet long with a tonnage of 3,374. Ships of this size approached the limit where wooden ships could be

Panama Railroad bridge over the Chagres River, Isthmus of Panama. From HARPER'S MAGAZINE, January 1859.

safely operated. These ships compared in size with the contemporary ships on cross-Atlantic runs. For example, the Cunard *Atlantic* was 284 feet long with a tonnage of 2,849; the *America* was 270 feet long with a tonnage of 1,825; the Cunard *Scotia* was 400 feet long with a tonnage of 3,871; they were all fabricated with wood. The British were beginning to build a few large iron ships, but wood still dominated ocean travel.

Panama steamers initiated the practice of installing a deckhouse the length of the ship. This house contained public rooms for passengers, officers' quarters, and staterooms. The roof of this deckhouse extended to the sides of the ship, creating a hurricane deck. This extension in turn formed a canopy for the promenade deck. On some ships, officers' quarters and a wheelhouse were built on the hurricane deck. This deck also carried lifeboats.

Passengers traveled in first, second, or steerage class. First- and second-class staterooms extended along both sides of the deckhouse and along the decks below it. On some ships dining saloons and drawing rooms were located fore and aft along the center of the deckhouse; on others they were on the deck below. Staterooms opened onto either passageways or dining and drawing rooms. Staterooms usually contained three berths, one above the other; but two- and four-berth cabins were available. For privacy, damask curtains hung along the berths. Each room was furnished with a mirror, toilet stand, washbowl and water bottles and glasses. Second-class rooms were similar only smaller; or they might be larger with more berths screened off by curtains.

Drawing rooms, dining saloons and first-class staterooms were elaborately furnished and decorated. Polished hardwood and mirrors adorned the walls. Plush carpets covered interior decks. Polished silver spittoons sat at handy locations. From the overhead swung ornate lamps. Brass fixtures gleamed everywhere.

Steamers were crowded, since many of those constructed in the late 1850's legally carried from seven to nine hundred passengers. Because most passengers rode steerage, that section must have

Pacific Mail Steamship Company ad.

TOP: *Pacific Mail steamer* SENORA *on the Panama run.* CENTER: *The* GEORGE LAW, *a steamer on the U.S. Mail Steamship Company line, ran between New York and Aspinwall, Panama.* BOTTOM: *The steamer* STAR OF THE WEST *sailed between Panama City and San Francisco.*

Courtesy Wells Fargo Bank History Room, San Francisco

The Mariners Museum, Newport News, Virginia

The Mariners Museum, Newport News, Virginia

Obtaining sufficient fuel for the boilers was difficult on Pacific Panama steamers during their first two years of operation. For instance, the *California* burned fifty-four tons of coal a day. None of these steamers stowed sufficient fuel to make the run between San Francisco and Panama City without recoaling. On the Pacific, coaling stations were installed at Panama City, San Blas, Acapulco, Manzanillo, and San Francisco. Coal had to be shipped around the Horn from Virginia and England. Later, coal was discovered in the West, thus easing the problem of supplying these stations.

Early steamers occasionally ran out of fuel. Then wood had to be substituted, usually taken from the ship, such as spars, masts, bulkheads, or berths. The ship fed on itself, so to speak. In favorable winds, sails were unfurled, but since steamers were not primarily designed as sailing vessels, wind power was not efficient.

Ventilation of early ships on the tropical Panama route was poor. To provide cooler, fresher air, later steamers included an air passage running fore and aft through which fresh air was forced by the speed of the ship. This fresh air in turn flowed into cabins and public rooms through louvered doors and vents. Larger windows also replaced portholes in cabins located on decks above the gunwales.

Unlike ships of later days, Panama steamers provided no amusement for their passengers. Patrons furnished their own. A passenger on the *California* wrote:

Plenty of fun on deck, all kinds of games going on, singing, stories, etc. ... Moonlight and plenty of singing till 11 o'clock etc. ... Lovely moonlight nights, pleasant talks of the girls, and matters and things at home, their enjoyments, and ours, the contrast etc., sitting out on the guards.

Dances were held on deck on soft tropical evenings. There was usually an accordion player among the passengers. Gambling and card playing were popular. Shipboard romances blossomed on tropical moonlit nights. As a ship bow gently swung upward and downward rhythmically through the glistening sea, and the gentle trade wind hummed through the rigging its melancholy tune, or an accordionist played sentimental airs, romance readily oveflowed in the hearts of the young in spirit. Of such enchanted evenings, a passenger wrote:

You will see as you inspect these benches, females in the close embrace of the sterner sex, their heads reclining in the most loving manner on the shoulders of their male protectors. ... They were in some cases, but a couple whose acquaintance dates back to the ship's sailing or probably a shorter time.

As could be expected, ships plying the Panama route experienced marine disasters. Vessels were wooden, their engines undependable and their lifesaving facilities inadequate. However, considering that over 700,000 passengers traveled the route both ways, accidents were surprisingly few, especially on the Pacific Mail Line. During the first twenty-four years of its operation, Pacific Mail experienced only one major disaster involving loss of life: the *Golden Gate,* that burned at sea. Two steamers were beached and broken up by the sea, but without loss of life. Ships of Vanderbilt's independent lines, on the other hand, met disaster with alarming frequency. In the Atlantic two ships on the Panama route, the *San Francisco,* owned by

Pacific Mail but chartered to another operator, and the *Central America,* owned by the United States Mail Steamship Company, were pounded to pieces at sea by ponderous waves.

In quick succession, Vanderbilt lost four of the six steamers he had in service on the Pacific: *North America* on February 27, 1852; *Pioneer* on August 17, 1852; *Independence* on February 6, 1853; and *Lewis* on April 9, 1853. These disasters left a wake of death and privation. The worst Vanderbilt disaster happened to his *Independence.* As she sailed in relatively calm seas and clear weather, the ship crashed into a reef one mile off Santa Marguerita Island. Captain Sampson backed her off but discovered the hold was leaking and taking in water faster than the pumps could handle. He headed her ashore, but water rising in the boiler room doused her fires, thereby dropping steam pressure. Consequently, the captain was unable to push his ship onto the beach, but her forward keel ran aground some distance offshore. Then crewmen fastened a line to the beach. Officers went ashore but did not return to the ship to aid passengers ashore or direct the crew in rescue operations. Soon the vessel caught fire and broke up with a loss of over three hundred lives. Some passengers bitterly condemned the captain for hitting the rocks needlessly. They testified they had warned him that rocks lay dead ahead, but that he told them to mind their own business. The *Alta California* of San Francisco reported the *Independence* was a poorly built ship. The newspaper might also have added that the *Independence* had poorly trained officers.

In another mishap, Vanderbilt's *North America* ran ashore near Acapulco on a clear night and was battered to pieces by heavy breakers. Her officers were charged with incompetence and with the most ignominious charge that could be hurled against officers and crew: that of abandoning their passengers to suffer "destitution, privation, and even death." Vanderbilt's *Pioneer* struck a rock in Talcahuano Harbor and sank. Eight months later the skipper of the S.S. *Lewis* made a navigational

The wreck of Vanderbilt's opposition steamer INDEPENDENCE.

Original sketch by Albert Scott, Santa Rosa, California

error while entering San Francisco Bay. The ship struck a rock and was beached near Bolina Bay where a mild sea broke her asunder in one day. Unaccountably, the crew delayed two hours before launching her boats, yet in spite of this puzzling delay, all passengers and baggage were saved. Thus in fourteen months, four of Vanderbilt's ships met disaster on the San Francisco-Panama City route.

Passengers escaped death more from luck than from efforts of the officers and crew aboard the Independent Line's *Union* as she ran aground near San Quentin at 3 a.m. on July 5, 1851. The crew had celebrated July 4 by consuming an abundance of whiskey and rum. By nightfall they were roaring drunk; no watch was on deck; the helmsman was too inebriated to handle the wheel. Amazingly, everyone aboard escaped death.

Between the years 1851 and 1854 there were eight wrecks of independent steamers on the Panama run in the Pacific. In six of these accidents, the officers were accused of incompetence and neglect.

Newspapers and passengers were bitter in their denunciation of Vanderbilt's steamers. The *Panama Star and Herald* wrote: "Not one of the whole Company from the Commodore down, has the slightest regard for even the most ordinary comfort of the unfortunate passengers who are forced to travel on their ships." Ernest Wiltsee said, "The Vanderbilt Line had been shockingly managed. It is difficult to understand how anyone could have traveled by this line at this time." The answer was that opposition steamers usually offered lower fares and, when they went by way of the Isthmus of Nicaragua, faster passage. Then too, many westerners resented what they considered the "monopoly" or "vested interest" of the Pacific Mail Line.

Wreck of Commodore Vanderbilt's propeller-driven S.S. LEWIS in Bolinas Bay, sixteen miles north of the Golden Gate on April 9, 1853. This steamer was one of the very few propeller-driven steamers on the Panama run.

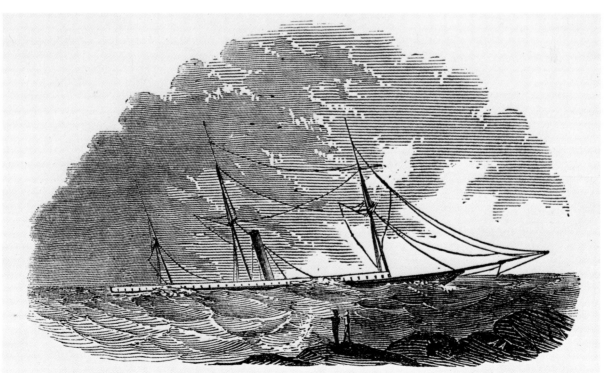

During this same period, two Pacific Mail steamers, *Winfield Scott* and *Tennessee* ran aground in dense fog. All passengers were saved and no blame was attached to officers or crew for either accident. Referring to the loss of Pacific Mail's *Winfield Scott*, the San Francisco *Alta California* on December 7, 1853, praised the captain and crew:

There was a very dense fog, so that it was impossible to see the ship's length ahead. She struck bow on, staving two holes in her bow, and then, in backing off, her stern struck, knocking away her rudder. There was a good deal of alarm manifested among the passengers, most of whom had turned in; and even after she had struck, the fog was so dense that they could see nothing before them. After the loss of her rudder, the boat drifted off a distance of about three hundred yards, and went

ashore bow on, striking a bluff. She had already commenced filling, and soon after striking for the last time sunk up to her guards. A boat was immediately sent out to find a place where the passengers could be landed. A little island separate from the main one was found, and there the passengers, mails and treasure were landed that night, and the next morning were taken on the island where they now are. The coolness and presence of mind of Capt. Blunt, under the circumstances, are spoken of in the highest terms of commendation. He remained on board until all the passengers were landed, which was nearly daylight, and during the night was busily engaged in superintending the necessary work which was in progress. We do not think that his well established reputation as a careful and skillful navigator will suffer from this unfortunate loss.

Wreck of the steamship UNION on the coast of lower California in July of 1851.

Fire aboard ships is always a danger. Since steamers on the Panama route were wooden, fire was an ever-present hazard. Boilers were fired with coal and galley stoves were heated with it. Oil lamps furnished light and many passengers smoked. Sides and bulkheads were covered with coat upon coat of highly flammable oil-base paint. Under such conditions, it is surprising that during the first twenty years of operation, only one Panama steamer burned at sea, the Pacific Mail's *Golden Gate*.

She was plying southward at dinner time on July 27, 1862, about fifteen miles west of Manzanillo, Mexico, when flames flickered upward between the forward smokestack and the cabin galley. Captain Pearson, fleet captain for Pacific Mail, happened to be aboard; the ship was commanded by Captain Hudson. Immediately Captain Pearson took charge of fire fighting, and Captain Hudson assumed command on the bridge. Hudson ordered the vessel headed toward the beach three and one-half miles away. This action, of course, fanned the flames and spread them through her ventilation system, but under the circumstances beaching the ship held the best hope of saving the 242 passengers and 96 crewmen aboard. If she hove to in deep water, most on board would have burned to death or drowned. Wooden vessels burned rapidly and ships in those days carried far too few lifeboats to accommodate all on board. Maritime law did not yet require that ships carry enough lifeboats for all on board. Not until after the *Titanic* disaster in April 1912, were ships required to carry enough lifeboats for all on board.

Captain Pearson rushed below where the crackling, roaring inferno convinced him the ship was doomed. Nevertheless, he ordered pumps and hoses into action. The crew manning the hoses bravely fought the steadily advancing, searing flames. Many crewmen were burned and though they could not quench the inferno, their rear-guard efforts delayed the fire sufficiently to save many passengers' lives. The helmsman stuck to his post until he beached the ship. In the engine room, firemen and engineers remained at their posts firing the boilers and operating the engines that kept paddle wheels churning the ship toward the beach. The brave engine room gang was finally trapped, but fortunately other heroic crewmen quickly chopped through a bulkhead, saving the trapped crew.

Running throughout the ship's passageways, Captain Pearson roused passengers, led them on deck (women and children first) and urged them forward. Here he ordered lines tied to the rails for passengers to slide down when the ship was beached. Many passengers began to panic. Both Captains attempted to calm them. Other officers managed to launch a few lifeboats into which women and children entered first.

Before *Golden Gate* reached shore, her midships became a crackling, roaring inferno from starboard to port, trapping those aft the fire. Many of those aft slid into the sea on lines tied to the taffrail located along the stern. Some jumped into the water where a few were picked up by lifeboats; many were drowned. Just as her bow began scraping bottom, about half an hour after the fire started, the upper deck collapsed and the foremast crashed to starboard. Though suffering burns, Captains Pearson and Hudson remained on board until all persons were off. Ashore officers and crew buried the dead, tended the injured and awaited rescue that did not arrive until thirty hours later. Loss of

169

life totaled 223, and $1,400,000 in gold and silver vanished. In spite of this terrible loss, officers and crew had heroically acted in the true tradition of the sea.

There was no lasting criticism of the ship nor the manner in which Pacific Mail Steam operated her. The *New York Times* did publish a scathing editorial that *Golden Gate* was not seaworthy and that her fire-protection equipment was unsatisfactory. In reply, the president of the steamship company, in a letter to the *Times*, quoted the recent *Government Inspection* report of the vessel which stated that *Golden Gate*'s hull and machinery were sound. She carried "twelve largest class lifeboats, all suspended to cranes with oars, rudders, lifelines, and water buckets. ..." On board were fifteen hundred solid-cork life preservers, two steam fire engines, "which are capable of flooding the ship." In face of this evidence, the *New York Times* printed an apology stating that the information in its editorial was incorrect. Later reports and investigations praised the crew's behavior and exonerated the Pacific Mail Steam Company. During an investigation, Captains Pearson and Hudson wept bitterly over the tragic losses.

One of two Panama-route ships pounded to pieces by the sea in the Atlantic was the *Central America*. Operated by United States Mail Steamship Company, she foundered in a howling gale off the Florida coast September 12, 1857. As happened to many contemporary steamers, her engines failed. In calm seas this failure did not present too serious a problem, but if a ship cannot make headway in heavy seas, she may slip into a trough of the ocean and risk battering by tons of turbulent seas simultaneously crashing down on her port and starboard decks. This happened to *Central America*. Why her engine stopped is unknown. Early steam engines frequently failed because they were still primitive and unreliable. At other times incompetence and carelessness were responsible.

All night towering waves battered her relentlessly. Water poured into her ports, paddle wheel shafts and upper works. She settled lower in the water. Then huge, foamy green waves thundered over her decks and broke her in pieces. Four hundred twenty-three lives were lost in addition to $8,000,000 in treasure. The *Central America's* destruction was one of the worst marine disasters of the century.

Though the 1849 mail contract with Pacific Mail Steamship Company called for steamer service to Astoria, Oregon, the company shuttled its steamers only between San Francisco and Panama City because of the thousands of gold seekers awaiting passage from Panama City to San Francisco. No regularly scheduled steamers plied the Pacific Ocean north of San Francisco until 1851 when the firm of Howland and Aspinwall (Aspinwall was also a partner in the Pacific Mail Steamship Company) put the newly built brig-rigged sidewheeler *Columbia* in operation between San Francisco and Portland. Unlike many overage hulks that followed her on the North Pacific, she was sturdily built in New York for Pacific service north of San Francisco.

In 1853 the Pacific Mail Steamship Company, having decided to extend its line to the Pacific Northwest, purchased Howland and Aspinwall's only steamer, *Columbia,* and added the sidewheeler *Fremont.* The latter was placed on regular service between San Francisco and Steilacoom, Washington Territory, then the largest town on Puget Sound.

Steamers, operating in opposition to the Pacific Mail Steamship Company, also appeared on the North Pacific run. With competition came rate wars that at times drastically cut fares. For instance, between San Francisco and Portland, Oregon, fares were lowered from $45 cabin and $25 steerage to as low as $20 and $10, and for a short time, from $10 to $3. These opposition steamers usually were inferior ships with age-weakened hulls; many ultimately met with disaster. They, and ships such as Pacific Mail's *Southerner*, were the vanguard of the many wrecks that plagued the North Pacific from San Francisco to Puget Sound and Alaska into modern times.

The wreck of the steamship CENTRAL AMERICA off
Cape Hatteras in September of 1857. The disaster
took 426 lives and more than two million
in treasure.

In 1858 gold was discovered on the Fraser River in British Columbia, an event that brought more coastal steamers to the Pacific. Pacific Mail increased its fleet and the California Steam Navigation Company, that had formerly confined its operations to San Francisco Bay and the rivers flowing into the Bay, decided to cash in on the gold rush. California Steam Navigation Company purchased two steamers from independent operators who had been running them in opposition to Pacific Mail. (These steamers, *Brother Jonathan* and *Pacific*, later met dreadful ends.) Since both companies were aware how financially depleting rate wars can be, they agreed to maintain profitable tariff rates. By 1861, Pacific Mail, having sluiced off a sizable portion of the Fraser River gold-traffic bonanza, sold its northern line to Ben Holladay, the stagecoach king. He wanted to connect his Columbia River steamers and his Overland Stage Line, both terminating at Wallulla, Washington Territory, with coastal steamers. His ocean steamers included *Cortez, Oregon, Sierra Nevada, Republic* and *Panama*. (The *Panama* and *Oregon* were two of the first three steamers to round Cape Horn in 1849 and enter the Pacific Coast service for Pacific Mail.)

Holladay's company, the California, Oregon & Mexican Steamship Company, continued the fixed-rate working agreement with California Steam. This mutually lucrative arrangement lasted until 1866 when a Yankee from Maine, named Patton, put the *Montana*, a big side-wheeler, built in the East, and the *Idaho* on the Pacific run from San Francisco to Puget Sound. To sweep him off the ocean and sink him financially, California Steam and Ben Holladay consistently lowered tariffs but Patton remained afloat. Finally, to halt such mutual financial suicide, the three companies merged into the North Pacific Transportation Company. Again rates rose to profit-making levels. By 1869, the merged company operated ten side-wheelers and six propeller-driven ships north of San Francisco.

In 1874 Holladay was in deep financial trouble caused by his devious maneuvers to control railroad building in Oregon; maneuvers that ultimately bankrupted him. Holladay still owed money on ships he had purchased from Pacific Mail Steamship Company, so Pacific Mail foreclosed to recover these ships. Pacific Mail resumed operations north of San Francisco for a year, after which time the company sold the entire northern operation to Goodall, Nelson & Perkins Steamship Company. By this time, another company, the Oregon Steamship Company, had gained control of the remaining Holladay ships, *Oriflamme, John L. Stephens, Gussie Telfair* and *Ajax*. Two years later Goodall, Nelson & Perkins reorganized their company into the Pacific Coast Steamship Company. This company dominated North Pacific shipping for more than fifty years during which time the venerable wooden side-wheeler was rapidly replaced by well-built propeller-driven, iron ships.

Meanwhile the North Pacific was the scene of many tragic shipwrecks, many of which were the result of overaged and overloaded ships and the greed of their owners. To record them all would require too much space, but a report of a few illustrates the problems of shipping along the North Pacific Coast in the early decades following the California gold rush.

Mid-nineteenth century poster advertising the steamer PANAMA.

For the Mexican Coast!

THE FAVORITE STEAMSHIP
PANAMA!

R. H. HORNER........ Commander,

will leave FOLSOM STREET WHARF,

For Ports on the Mexican Coast,
ONCE EACH MONTH.
At Nine o'clock, A. M.

For Freight or Passage, apply to

HOLLADAY & FLINT,

No. 477 Washington Street, opposite the Post Office

☞ Bills of Lading furnished to Shippers. No others will be signed.

Since the San Francisco-Panama run was Pacific Mail's primary and most profitable operation, the company tended to place its older, less seaworthy steamers on its North Pacific line, resulting in discomfort and loss of life for many passengers. The third ship Pacific Mail put in operation in this area, the *Southerner*, was one such unseaworthy vessel. Shortly after having been put in service, she was sailing north for Portland, Oregon. Off the Oregon coast, heavy swells and high winds began buffeting her. Under the strain, her aged timbers creaked and then cracked. Sea water gushed into the hold. Ordering the pumps into action, the captain attempted to cross the bar of the Columbia River but was unable to navigate across these very hazardous waters. He then set course northward for Puget Sound. Her pumps failed to keep pace with the incoming water and passengers bailed to no avail. As sea water reached the fireboxes, steam pressure dropped, so *Southerner* was able to make little headway. Now the captain abandoned his plan to enter Puget Sound and headed towards the Pacific shore southeast of Cape Flattery. With seas breaking over her decks, the crippled ship came onto the beach broadside at ebb tide. Fortunately, passengers and crew escaped. This practice of placing less seaworthy vessels on the North Pacific coastal runs was doubly unfortunate because the

The BROTHER JONATHAN broke apart in a howling gale off Crescent City, California in July 1865, with a loss of 165 lives.

seas of the Pacific Ocean north of San Francisco are much heavier and stormier than those south of San Francisco.

An earlier steamship disaster in the Pacific north of San Francisco happened to an independent ship, the *General Warren*. Late in the afternoon on January 28, 1852, she crossed the bar into the Pacific Ocean at the mouth of the Columbia. She was heavily loaded with grain and had forty persons on board. Built of wood in 1844, this side-wheeler was never meant to sail on heavy seas such as those of the North Pacific. After dropping her pilot, the aged craft wallowed southward into a heavy southerly gale. Her wooden hull creaked and groaned as ponderous gray breakers crashed over her bow. Her feeble one-cylinder engine huffed and puffed and hissed as it vainly tried to make headway. Shrieking winds broke her foretopmast. By midnight she was leaking badly. Her cargo of grain shifted and clogged her pumps. Captain Charles Thompson now eased his slowly sinking steamer back to the Columbia, arriving outside the bar in the morning. The pilot aboard the pilot schooner from Astoria did not reach the *General Warren* until late afternoon. To his horror, he found the ship unmanageable in the churning, breaking seas off the bar. The gale blew her toward Clatsop Spit and at 7 p.m. she hit the beach. Roaring breakers crashed completely over her decks sweeping away masts, funnel, and paddle boxes. Huddled below decks, the crew and terrified passengers were still alive, but it was obvious the hull had but hours to remain intact. After leaving the pilot aboard the *General Warren,* the pilot schooner, bucking headwinds, returned to Astoria, completely unaware of the *General Warren*'s fate. Captain Thompson now asked the pilot to take a small boat to Astoria for help. Many frightened passengers refused to board such a small boat in the huge breakers. With five passengers and five crewmen in the boat, the pilot miraculously sailed to Astoria, where a large whaleboat was dispatched to the wreck. When he left the sinking ship, the pilot said, "If I live, I will return." (For his heroism, he was presented a solid-gold medal inscribed with these words.) Upon returning to the scene, the pilot and other rescuers found no sign of the *General Warren* nor those on board. The sea had broken her into pieces and had completely swallowed the pieces. Later thirty bodies were found floating along the beaches of the Columbia.

On February 2, 1852, *The Oregonian* off Portland, Oregon, stated that navigating the hazardous bar of the Columbia River was not the cause of the accident, but the worthlessness of the ship; that "the vessel was not seaworthy and consequently *unfit* and *unsafe* for this and any other trade. She was one of the old tubs which have been condemned elsewhere. . . . The owners knew she was unsafe." The circumstances of her demise certainly indicate that *General Warren* was not seaworthy. Yet several weeks earlier, when *General Warren* was berthed at Portland, *The Oregonian* had praised her, "She is a fine vessel and has good accommodations for passengers. The officers are . . . good sailors which will insure a pleasant voyage. . . ."

In July 1865, Captain De Wolfe stomped down the *Brother Jonathan's* gangplank and angrily stormed into the office of California Steam Navigation Company's San Francisco freight agent. He complained bitterly that too much freight was being stowed aboard his ship. The agent replied that if the captain was too timid to sail the vessel, there were other unemployed sea captains eager to command *Brother Jonathan*. To the agent, profits outweighed human lives.

Reluctantly, Captain De Wolfe nursed the ship through Golden Gate. She staggered into a gale howling out of the northwest and was barely able to make headway. Two days later off Crescent City,

California, the gale grew so fierce that *Brother Jonathan* wallowed drunkenly out of control. The captain desperately attempted to head her into Crescent City harbor, but the reeling ship crashed into a submerged rock. Almost immediately the keel ripped off and floated away. The foremast plunged through the rotten deck and ripped the hull open. In the panic and confusion, only one lifeboat with 19 survivors got away. The side-wheeler broke apart and sank like a rock, carrying the captain and 165 persons to a watery grave. Later 75 bodies were located along the beach, but neither the other victims nor the *Brother Jonathan* were ever seen again.

Her sister ship *Pacific* (also owned by California Steam) met tragedy at night ten years later, forty miles south of Cape Flattery, the most northwestern corner of the state of Washington. With about 230 people aboard, she rammed the square-rigged ship *Orpheus*. The sturdy square-rigger, slightly damaged, backed away in the dark and was beached off Vancouver Island without loss of life; the aged *Pacific* broke asunder and sank. Several lifeboats were launched, but all foundered. Only two survivors were picked up clinging to wreckage; one of these died of exposure and shock.

The North Pacific steamers contributed to the growth and life of the Far West in its earliest years. They carried freight and passengers before stagecoaches began to operate between cities in California, Oregon and Washington in 1858. Windjammers stowed some of the freight, but passengers, for the most part, depended upon steamships for many years.

Departures and arrivals of the steamers were exciting days. Crowds milled along the wharves. Freight and baggage was carted and swung on board. Loved ones and friends, often tearfully, bade farewell to departing passengers. Bands serenaded with stirring songs. "Auld Lang Syne" brought nostalgia and tears to many as the ship drifted from her dock.

A passenger describes the *Falcon* leaving New York for San Francisco:

> *The gong sounded through the saloon and along the decks, warning ashore those who were not going.*
>
> *Then the goodbye's were hurried, warm-hearted and very hard to say. But they were all soon said, Captain Thompson appeared on deck, in his glazed cap, as manly, fine looking an officer as ever did service in our merchant marine, —he spoke a few quiet words, and made a few signals, and the steamer left her birth [sic]. Down the river we passed swiftly threading our way among the Jersey ferryboats, and all the other moving craft, —down the bay, while we watched the city receding from our view.*

Bancroft aptly describes the scene of a steamer departing:

> *At the wharf stood preeminent, sturdy miners girdled with well-filled belts, their complacent faces turned eastward. Old Californians they boasted themselves, though counting, perhaps, less than a half-year sojourn; many strutting their coarse and soiled camp attire, glorying in their rags. . . . Conspicuous by contrast were many haggard and dejected faces, stamped and broken constitutions, soured by disappointment. Others, no less unhappy, without even the means to follow them, were left behind stranded; with hope fled. . . .*

San Franciscans eagerly awaited the arrival of ships. A semaphore signal was set high atop Telegraph Hill. As vessels approached the entrance of Golden Gate, observers at Fort Point and Point Lobos signaled by semaphore to the watchman on Telegraph Hill. He in turn quickly set the arms of the signal tower to indicate the type of approaching ship. One arm up at forty-five degrees signaled a schooner; the right arm straight up indicated a brig; left arm straight up, a ship. If both arms were straight up, it meant a side-wheeler, the mail steamer, was approaching. Then excitement electrified the city. Hundreds rushed to the Embarcadero; block-long lines formed at the post office. Westerners eagerly awaited news from friends and loved ones thousands of miles away. After many hours of waiting, some, rewarded with precious letters, were joyful; others turned away, dejected after waiting vainly for a letter; still others wept over the news a letter contained. So hungry were news-seekers that Eastern newspapers sold for one dollar.

At dockside many rushed down gangplanks to happy reunions with long-separated families and friends. But an arriving steamer was not always a joyful occasion for some of those awaiting friends or loved ones. The specter of death rode on almost all ships plying the Panama route. The Isthmus of Panama was one of the worst pestholes of the tropics. Malaria, yellow fever and cholera were an ever-present scourge there and to a lesser extent on the Isthmus of Nicaragua. During transit, many passengers contracted one of the dread diseases. The medical profession became adept at diagnosing these illnesses, but had not as yet discovered their causes nor preventative measures or cures. Many of those who contracted cholera, yellow fever, or malaria on the Isthmus became ill aboard San Francisco- or New York-bound steamers. Some died en route, others on shore at the termination of the trip. Eighty-four troops died on *Golden Gate* in 1852. The *Sierra Nevada* lost 34 in July 1855. Later that year 113 died aboard her. Rare was a ship that had no deaths. Some victims were buried on islands where steamers made special burial stops. Other bodies were committed to the sea or brought to New York or San Francisco for interment. With the completion of the Panama Railroad in 1855, danger from tropical diseases lessened considerably.

It has been estimated that between 1849 and 1859 one fifth of the emigrants to the West Coast came by sea; between 1859 and 1869, one half. Except for the very early years of the gold rush, the Panama route carried many more passengers than did sailing vessels; windjammers plying around Cape Horn carried mostly heavy freight. During the 1860s, however, the Panama route began packing some heavy freight. Almost all specie ($710,753,000 in gold and silver) moved eastward by sea; the overland route was considered too hazardous to use for shipment of treasure. During the Civil War, this specie was vitally needed to support the Union. Before 1859 the steamers packed most of the mail and express. After that date, the overland stagecoaches received the mail contract. The steamers, however, carried bulk mail, second, third and fourth class matter until the completion of the Pacific railroad.

Missouri River steamer HELENA and the Northern Pacific Railroad bridge at Bismarck, North Dakota, CIRCA 1872.

7

Steamboats on the Rivers

Early in the nineteenth century the area westward from the hundredth meridian to the Pacific Ocean was a vast wilderness uninhabited except for a few fur trappers and scattered Indian tribes. This vast and remote territory—rolling prairies, parched deserts, and range after range of towering mountains—stretched into a seeming infinity so inhospitable that some Federal officials estimated it would take a thousand years, even two thousand, to fully settle it. Daniel Webster stood in the Senate in 1852 and asked, "To what use could we ever hope to put these great deserts and these endless mountain ranges?" Underestimated was the spirit of those adventurous Americans willing to utilize the resources and to settle in this rich region at a cost of sweat, toil, hardships, sorrows and death. Few times has man found such an opportunity.

To help exploit this opportunity, Americans created that colorful and legendary method of transportation, the river steamboat. A purely American innovation, this hauler of freight, animals and people was chugging and puffing, churning and drifting, even hopping and skipping over the long, intertwining rivers of the Old West soon after the 1830's. She came in all sizes from modest paddle-wheel scows to monstrous, ornate floating palaces. The wail of her steam whistle, the billowing black smoke and the glowing sparks that spewed from her towering stacks have drifted into eternity, but her memory lingers in the nostalgic heart of many Americans as a romantic symbol of the roaring, adventurous, empire-building era of their nation.

West of the Mississippi, the Old West was blessed with thousands of miles of navigable rivers. The Missouri River and its tributary, the Yellowstone, wound for many hundreds of miles into the far reaches of the West. From the Pacific Coast, the mighty Columbia and Sacramento Rivers and their tributaries floated steamers hundreds of miles eastward. They navigated the torrid Colorado River, the waters of Puget Sound in Washington Territory, and the relatively short rivers, the Snohomish and the Skagit that flowed into this inland body of saltwater.

At the gateway to the Old West, the confluence of the Missouri and the Mississippi Rivers, steamers pointed their prows into the Missouri to negotiate that stream into Dakota Territory and into Montana to the Great Falls of the Missouri, near which the American Fur Company established Fort Benton. Other steamers turned off the Missouri at the mouth of the Yellowstone and probed that stream for nearly 483 miles to within 60 miles of Yellowstone National Park.

The first steamer to sail the Missouri was *Western Engineer*, built by the government to explore the upper Missouri and Yellowstone. Bizarre appearing, she was built in the form of a huge serpent to frighten and awe the Indians. Under way, the serpent's nose snorted smoke and steam. If such a specter failed to intimidate Indians, the steamer mounted three brass cannons. Whether any Red Men fled in terror is not known. Some may have, but if they did, they rapidly vanished over the horizon never to return and admit their terror. Others merely watched the steamer, and one remarked, "White man, bad man, keep a great spirit chained and built fire to make it work boat."

The American Fur Company operated the next steamer on the Missouri River, the 130-foot *Yellowstone* in 1832. She ran from St. Louis to the mouth of the Yellowstone, where the company maintained a fort. On her first trip she returned "with a full cargo of buffalo robes, furs, and peltries, besides ten thousand pounds of buffalo tongues."

The fur company operated several Missouri River steamers but, because of treacherous navigational hazards on the upper Missouri, twenty-seven years elapsed before steamers reached Fort Benton, Montana. This head of navigation was 3,600 miles from the mouth of the Mississippi and 3,300 feet above sea level. Until the 1850's, steam navigation on the Missouri, especially the upper Missouri, was controlled solely by the American Fur Company.

Navigating the Missouri was a precarious undertaking. The channel constantly shifted, creating new sandbars overnight. Several ingenious methods evolved to enable a steamer to cross shallow shoal water. One was warping. A crewman would carry a line upstream and tie it to a tree. The other end of the line was then wrapped around a capstan on the bow, and the steamer pulled itself off the sand bar. Occasionally this procedure needed to be repeated several times to warp a boat over a wide sandbar.

If a vessel still remained mired on the shoal, it would then be "grasshoppered" with a unique engineering device that consisted of two long iron-tipped spars hanging vertically on each side of the steamer's bow. Derricks hoisted the spars and dropped them, firmly implanting their tips into the sandbar. Ropes ran through blocks atop each spar to two capstans. The capstans strained at the rope and lifted the bow almost out of the water; simultaneously full steam propelled the vessel forward. Thus the steamer literally leaped ahead; the bow plopped into the water with a splattering thud. She

Missouri River steamers FAR WEST and NELLIE PECK by the levee near Bismarck, North Dakota.

hopped like a grasshopper. The steamer *Josephine*, reconnoitering the upper Yellowstone for the U.S. Army, sailed, warped and grasshoppered up the Yellowstone River to the mouth of the Bighorn, and up the Bighorn past famous Pompey's Pillar to a spot 483 miles from the mouth of the Yellowstone and within 60 miles of the northeast corner of Yellowstone National Park.

Some Indians along the Missouri were friendly; others were not. Many steamers came under Indian arrow and rifle fire. Such attacks were most critical when the boat was warping or grasshoppering. All hands, including male passengers, were then expected to man guns.

Pilothouses were sheathed with boiler steel to deflect bullets or arrows and protect that indispensable, almost godlike potentate of river steamers, the pilot. Upon receiving his pilot's license, a pilot seemed to undergo an apotheosis. Captains spoke to their crews and sometimes to pilots, but only pilots spoke to God according to local lore. And probably rightly so, since piloting a river steamer required skills and knowledge beyond that of ordinary men. On the Mississippi, pilots had to memorize hundreds of miles of channels and landmarks (no mean feat), but on the Missouri, pilots also had to know where the channel would be, as well as where it was. It was said the Missouri was so capricious that "time after time it has gotten out of its bed in the middle of the night . . . and hunted up a new bed, all littered with forests, cornfields, brick houses. . . . Then it has suddenly taken a fancy to return to its old bed."

Snags were an ever-present, often unseen hazard. Floods and high water embedded steamers in shallow bars where a stout snag could gut the strongest hull. In fact, so perilous was Missouri steamboating that, during fifty years of boating nearly five hundred steamers were destroyed between Fort Benton and St. Louis. In spite of the peril, steamers on the Missouri produced profits; some boats netted $50,000 to $60,000 in freight and passenger revenue on a single run from St. Louis to Fort Benton.

Steamers sailing on the Missouri were unpretentious, powerful stern-wheelers built to withstand the punishment the Missouri and Yellowstone meted out. Called mountain boats, they were about 150 feet long and their spoon-shaped hulls enabled them to draw only thirty inches of water when loaded with four hundred tons of freight and two hundred passengers. Passage time between St. Louis and Fort Benton was at times nearly two months, depending on how many hours were lost waiting for thousands of buffalo to ford the river, or on how many bars had to be warped across or hopped over. Cabin fare was $300; freight, $0.125 a pound (or $250 a ton).

By the mid-1860's, the U.S. Army began shipping soldiers, supplies, ammunition, mules and horses westward on Missouri River steamers. The purpose was to subdue the increasingly hostile Sioux and other high plains tribes that were exhibiting a reluctance to remain on their ever-shrinking reservations. During one campaign in 1864, eight steamers moved four thousand soldiers and their supplies westward to the mouth of the Yellowstone. One Missouri River steamer that became famous in the Indian wars was *Far West*. In June 1876 she hauled two hundred tons of military

supplies from Fort Lincoln (across the river from Bismarck, Dakota Territory) to the Yellowstone for the troops of General Terry, under whose command General Custer's ill-fated Seventh Cavalry served. Terry's and Custer's troops had earlier marched from Fort Lincoln to the mouth of the Yellowstone. Upon the arrival of *Far West*, she became the Army headquarters. In her cabin Generals Terry, Gibbons, and Custer planned their campaign against the Sioux, who were led by Sitting Bull and Crazy Horse.

As these troops marched southward, *Far West* sailed, grasshoppered and warped herself up the Yellowstone, then into the Bighorn River and several miles up that stream to a place so narrow that cables were tied to trees on both shores to warp her upstream. As men were sweating at this task, they heard gunfire and saw smoke billowing in the sky southward. They believed that Indians were being defeated. Later that day *Far West* had been moored to an island at the mouth of the Little Bighorn. Suddenly Custer's Indian scout Curly, frantically making the peace sign to prevent being shot by the boat's guard, boarded the steamer. A Crow scout on board, who knew no English, received from Curly in Indian sign language the first report of Custer's Last Stand.

The following day couriers from General Terry confirmed the massacre of Custer and five companies of the Seventh Cavalry on the Little Bighorn. They also reported that Major Reno, in charge of seven companies of the Seventh Cavalry and Custer's second in command, had engaged the Sioux several miles from the massacre site. He

entrenched his troops high on a bluff and held off the Indians for two days until rescued by Terry's infantry. Terry ordered *Far West* to take on board Reno's fifty-two wounded troops and transport them and the dispatch of the disaster to Bismarck, Dakota Territory.

To prepare for the wounded, the steamer's doctor ordered crewmen to cut fresh grass along the shore and pile it eighteen inches deep on the open deck aft the boilers. Tarpaulins were spread over the grass, making a huge bed for the wounded. That night fires were built along the trail up the valley to guide litter bearers carrying the wounded to *Far West*. At two a.m. the long line of litters arrived with their groaning burdens. Just before *Far West* cast off, a cavalry lieutenant led on board a limping, severely wounded horse. The sleek gelding named Comanche was the mount of Captain Myles Keogh killed in the massacre. Comanche was the sole survivor of Custer's battalion. A grass-bedded stall was provided for him aboard the steamer. He was tenderly nursed back to health and cared for by the Seventh Cavalry until he died in 1891 at the age of twenty-eight. Never again ridden, Comanche trotted in every parade of the Seventh Cavalry Regiment.

The *Far West* brought to Bismarck from the mouth of the Little Bighorn the first news of the Custer disaster. Then the vessel steamed across the Missouri to Fort Lincoln to break the tragic news to the twenty-eight newly created widows living there.

Until railroads crisscrossed Kansas, Nebraska, and Montana, by the early 1880's, steamers served the area well. They transported thousands of supplies, fur traders, settlers and troops upstream; and furs, buffalo robes and gold downstream. The bonanza years of Missouri River steamboating were in the 1860's during the lusty rush for gold to Last Chance Gulch (Helena, Montana) and Alder Gulch (Virginia City, Montana). Fort Benton then grew into a sprawling gold-rush community at the head of navigation, a jumping-off place for thousands of gold seekers who rushed from there by wagons and pack animals to the gold fields.

On the West Coast, steamers began plying the rivers of Oregon and California almost simultaneously in 1850. The first steamboat sailed up the Columbia River that year, a river system second in length only to the Mississippi. Because of unnavigable obstacles, the Columbia is divided into three navigable sections: the lower, middle and upper. The lower extends from its mouth at Astoria for about 150 miles to the Cascade Mountains — through which no steamer can sail. Into this lower section flows the Willamette River from the south.

So large is this part of the Columbia that ocean-going vessels can easily sail up the lower Columbia and then up the Willamette to Portland, Oregon. On the middle section of the Columbia River east of the Cascades, other steamboats sailed to The Dalles where the Army had built a fort and where another barrier of rapids halted boats. Eastward from The Dalles, a third type of steamer navigated the upper Columbia to Wallula (now under water), a point 315 miles from the mouth of the Columbia. Wallula usually was head of navigation and from here a narrow-gauge railroad ran to Walla Walla in Washington Territory about thirty miles inland. Passengers and freight that traveled between sections of the river were transported around the rapids from one steamer to another by a crude railway pulled by mules.

A few miles north of the Washington-Oregon boundary, the Snake River runs into the Columbia. On the Snake, steamers at times sailed eastward to Lewiston, Idaho. During the mid-1860's when the gold rush (in Montana and Idaho) was at its height, thousands of passengers and thousands of tons of freight were carted into Idaho to these gold diggings. Well-known vessels that sailed the upper Columbia and Snake to Lewiston were *Yakima, Webfoot, Tenino, Nez Perce Chief, Spray* and *Okanagon.* One steamer, *Shoshone,* was built above the Snake River's Hell's Canyon and sailed to the mouth of the Boise River.

The upper Columbia vessels were utility boats unadorned by frills and luxury, but some on the lower Columbia were floating palaces. Most famous on the lower Columbia was the *Wide West,* a 236-foot side-wheeler. She boasted a cabin done "tastefully in delicate shades of lilac and the floors

185

covered with mosaic oil cloth." Her dining saloon boasted equally sumptuous fare although not served on "shades of lilac."

Before explaining in detail those devil-may-care, freewheeling days of steamboating on California's rivers of the great gold-rush era, mention should be made of steamers on the Colorado River. For about thirty-five years after 1854, steamers navigated this river that winds between rugged cliffs. Fort Yuma was the main port of call, but occasionally steamboats continued northward to Fort Mojave over two hundred miles upstream. To reach the mouth of the river, a steamer had to sail the Pacific southward around the tip of Baja California, then northward in the gulf to Port Isabel, Mexico, about fifty miles downstream from Fort Yuba. The *General Jessup* sailed to Fort Mojave in 1854. She delivered military supplies and mining equipment and returned with hides and ore. *Cocapah* later made the same torturous trip through stifling heat, swarming flies, and whining mosquitoes capable of "sucking enough blood at one bite to leave a fatal air bubble." When horses were on board, they got the shady side and an Indian boy was hired to shoo flies off the animals. From Fort Yuba the main wagon-freight lines branched over shimmering deserts to lonely military outposts, mines and ranches. At Fort Yuma, Butterfield's Overland Mail stagecoaches stopped en route between St. Louis and San Francisco. As the frontier ended about 1890, so did steamboating on the Colorado.

With the discovery of gold in California's Sierra Nevada in 1848, thousands of gold seekers stampeded westward. They came to dig their fortunes from the streams and gold-bearing strata in the foothills and remoteness of the Sierra Nevada. Until that time, California had been sparsely settled. A few huge Mexican land grants were scattered throughout California. These land grants were controlled by Dons, of whom John Sutter at Sacramento was the main mogul. Agriculture was limited; manufacture consisted of a few small blacksmith shops and hand crafts. San Francisco and Monterey were small, sleepy Mexican settlements that were suddenly awakened by the trauma of nearly one hundred thousand gold seekers bursting into the area in 1849. By the time California was admitted into the Union on September 8, 1850, its population was estimated at two hundred thousand. Few times in history have as many men converged on such a remote, lonely region in so short a time.

Supplying this vast multitude with food, clothing and hardware was an unprecedented problem of logistics. Almost all supplies had to be procured from the East. (The chapters on sea transport describe this dramatic undertaking.) Once merchandise was unloaded on San Francisco's Embarcadero, transporting goods to the gold diggings presented an almost equally baffling problem. Delivering supplies to California gold fields one hundred to two hundred miles eastward from San Francisco through unsettled, primitive, flat, hilly and mountainous country is a story of romance, of color, and of drama.

Several factors conspired to frustrate delivery. California's social and economic system of huge, feudal-like estates and the declining mission system were unable to cope with a gold rush economy. Then, as thousands of emigrants suddenly arrived, they rushed directly to the gold fields, leaving very few hands to handle and haul the freight. In addition, many miners hurried to primitive, uninhabited areas in the northern Sierra Nevada with only meager supplies, giving no thought as to how they would be replenished. Since no system of inland transport existed then except for the backs of a few mules and the bottoms of a few small boats, starvation and extreme privation at times were a specter in the Sierra Nevada during the winters of the early gold-rush years.

Fortunately, rivers flowed into San Francisco Bay whose waters were sufficient to float boats upstream about one hundred twenty miles closer

Boats such as Moon's Ferry swung on a long cable attached to a tree upstream. The cable floated on a series of pontoons. By proper angling of the ferry's rudder, the boat utilized the river current to cross the stream.

to the gold diggings. The Sacramento River followed a northeasterly course from the Bay. On the Sacramento near the mouth of the American River the town of Sacramento was established. Two rivers flowed into the Sacramento but did not converge—the San Joaquin from the south and the Feather from the north. On the Feather, Marysville was established near the confluence of the Feather and Yuba rivers, about forty-five miles north of Sacramento. The city of Stockton was located on the San Joaquin. From these three major river towns, freight was carried into the Sierra Nevada by pack mules and later by freight wagons. Boats shipped supplies to Sacramento, Marysville, and Stockton. Of the three rivers, the Feather was the least navigable, and, as will be seen, operating steamers on this stream required an abundance of determination, courage, skill and innovation.

During 1849 only whaleboats and sloops carried merchandise up these rivers. Their owners made quick fortunes by charging high cartage fees. For instance, Captain Coffin loaded a sloop with $2,500 worth of merchandise at San Francisco and charged $5,000 for hauling it to the mouth of the Yuba River near the present city of Marysville. Other boat owners purchased merchandise in San Francisco, loaded it into whaleboats and rowed up the Sacramento and Feather Rivers for exceedingly profitable ventures.

As population in the gold country exploded to over fifty thousand miners, demand for supplies at the mines was insatiable. Whaleboats and sloops proved unable to move sufficient freight. Steamboats were needed, and by December 1849 and early 1850 the first steamers began cruising the rivers. They were small and primitive; however, they stowed much needed supplies and hauled them at $160 a ton up the Feather River! A few enterprising emigrants to California had discovered that gold was to be found not only by pick and shovel.

Since California at this time lacked manufacturing facilities, these early steamers were built in the East. They were disassembled, loaded on windjammers and shipped seventeen thousand miles around the Horn to San Francisco. Here they

A broadside ad for the Feather River steamer that began sailing on the river in January 1850. The picture obviously is not of the little barge-like LINDA *that sailed the Feather. It could be a sketch of the ocean steamer* LINDA *that carried the machinery for the little Feather River steamer around the Horn to San Francisco.*

Handbill of one of several communities unsuccessfully claiming to be head of navigation on California's Feather River during the state's gold rush.

188

NICOLAUS.

HEAD OF NAVIGATION!!

DEPOT FOR ALL THE NORTHERN

MINES!

The advantages of this Town are now too manifest to be any longer denied or doubted. From actual survey on Saturday last, it was ascertained that the Bar which was last year at the mouth of Feather River had entirely disappeared, and that the only obstruction to navigation was half a mile above the mouth, where there was a narrow bar, on which was found in the most shallow passage, *three feet and two inches of water.* Between the Bar and Nicolaus *there was not found in any place less than five feet of water in the channel;* and as the river is now within six inches of its lowest stage last season, assurance is rendered "double sure" that boats drawing twice as much as the popular steamers Gov. Dana and Lawrence, can ply here constantly without the slightest obstruction.

The close proximity of Nicolaus to the rich *placeres* **on the Feather** and Yuba Rivers, Deer, Dry and Bear Creeks, and the Forks of the American, ensures its continuance *as the depot for the supplies for all the Northern Mines.*

Four lines of Stages are constantly running hence to and from Marys- ville, passing through the projected Towns of ORO, EL DORADO, PLUMAS and ELIZA.

Tri-weekly Stages run to and from Washington, distant 60 miles, Nevada City, 42 miles, Rough and Ready, 35 miles, Auburn 25 miles, Nye's Crossing on the Yuba, 32 miles, and to the American Fork, 35 miles; in addition to which, Coaches can always be obtained to transport passengers to any other point.

Teams are in readiness on the arrival of every steamer to convey freight on the most reasonable terms to any of the Towns above, or to any of the Mines.

Nicolaus is located on the tract of land for many years known as "Nicolaus' Ranche," which has always been regarded as the most healthy point in California It has never, in the recollection of the Chief of the Rancheria, been invaded by the turbulent stream which gracefully winds its devious way before the Town. That the climate is salubrious is evidenced in the fact, that, though several hundreds of persons have resided here for the last six months, none of them have been attacked with any of the diseases incident to other parts of California, and that there has been but one death in the neighborhood for several years.

To the Merchant, the Speculator, the Trader, the Mechanic and the Miner, we unhesitatingly assert that Nicolaus presents greater advantages than any other place in California. We offer the unsold Lots at original prices, and invite all who are desirous of securing comfortable homes, or acquiring rapid fortunes, to visit the Town, judge for themselves, and make their investments before the most eligible of the unsold Lots are disposed of.

CHARLES BERGHOFF, Cor. Front and Sutter Sts., Nicolaus.
JOSEPH GRANT, Tehama Block, Cor. Front and J Sts.,
Sacramento City,

Nicolaus, August 4, 1850. *Agents for the Sale of Lots.*

"Sacramento Transcript, Print."

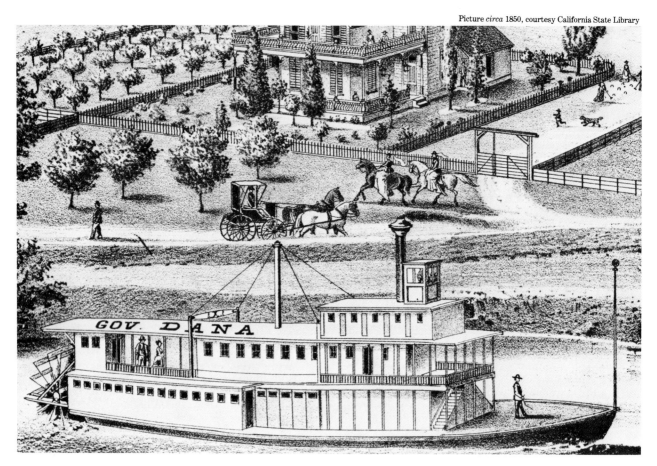

Sketch of the first of three GOVERNOR DANA's that sailed the Feather and Sacramento rivers during the 1850's and 1860's. The steamer shown was built in Maine, shipped aboard a windjammer around Cape Horn and reassembled in San Francisco.

were quickly reassembled. Usually only their machinery was shipped westward and the hulls were built in California. *Lawrence* and *Linda* were such vessels. Another early steamer was *Governor Dana*, an eighty-tonner. She was built in Maine and named after the governor of that state. By the end of 1850, enough steamers were plying the rivers to reduce freight rates to $50 per ton, but still high enough for fortunes to be made. Often one trip paid for the cost of the steamer.

Shipping the *S. B. Wheeler* around the Horn illustrated the ingenuity of her owners. Since the steamer was 120 feet long, she was too large to be stowed on the deck of a windjammer; she was also too small to sail around the Horn. To solve the dilemma, her owners purchased a larger deckless bark and sank her. Then they ran the *S. B. Wheeler* over the sunken bark, refloated the bark, rigged her with masts and sails, and sailed her laden with the steamer to San Francisco. There the bark was

demasted and sunk. The *S. B. Wheeler* floated free and was ready for service.

More steamers arrived on the rivers until by the spring of 1853 enough boats were moving sufficient freight to supply demand. Thus the specter of starvation and privation in the gold fields had been all but eliminated within a year.

Navigating the Feather River was a continuous struggle and hazard. During the dry season less than three feet of water flowed down her channel and less than that over her shoals. Steamer after steamer grounded or snagged on sunken logs. Many sank or were beached. Yet, it is a credit to the crews and boats that daily service was maintained to Marysville for nearly twenty years. A particularly hazardous year for steamers plying the Feather was 1850. No fewer than ten, including the *Governor Dana*, were sunk by grounding or snagging. Since the river was shallow, most sunken steamers could be repaired, pumped out and refloated. Other steamers, however, straddled shoals and broke in two, a total loss. Valuable cargo was lost but fortunately no lives.

Resourceful Captain Farris of the steamer *Marysville* solved the problem of shallow shoal water by a unique method. On board he kept a large supply of shovels. When his steamer began scraping bottom, he shouted, "All hands [and this meant passengers also] overboard, shovel in hand!" Overboard they went into water surging to their knees and shoveled a path through the muck and mud.

To overcome this danger to navigation, naval architects designed special shallow-draught boats. They sat so high in the water that they looked like ducks. For instance, *Gazelle* was 120 feet long and drew only twenty inches when loaded with one hundred tons. The *Pike* was 150 feet long and 26 feet of beam. Yet she drew only twelve inches of water empty and twenty-four fully loaded with over one hundred tons. One little steamer, *Yuba*, drew only ten inches of water when laden with ten tons. These low-draught steamers drew so little water they were reputed to be able to "sail on dew." Another innovation was empty steamers towing laden barges. Loaded barges drew less water than equally loaded steamers and could float over shoals only two feet deep.

Captains became skillful at maneuvering their crafts over shallow rivers. The captain of *Knight #2* with her barge hauled what must have been a record. With 9,000 sacks of wheat, 30 bales of hops and 38 hogs on board she sailed on only twenty inches of water losing neither wheat, nor hops, nor hogs!

By the mid-1850's, larger, more luxurious steamers appeared on the rivers. The *Queen City*, built in San Francisco for enterprising merchants of Marysville, was put into service in November 1854. They planned to sail her between San Francisco and Sacramento where her freight would be reloaded on smaller Feather River steamers bound for Marysville. She was described as a floating palace and a magnificent specimen of naval architecture. Designed on the lines of Mississippi steamers, her twin stacks towered forty-five feet above her hurricane deck just fore her pilothouse. She was 200 feet fore to aft and 31 feet of beam. Her nine-foot hold stowed up to five hundred tons. Running water was piped to each stateroom, rooms that were elegantly furnished and contained two berths. The ladies had their own lounge with a piano for their entertainment. Mark Twain would have been proud of her.

Early Californians relished special occasions and pulled out all stops when they celebrated one. Maiden voyages of steamers were considered special events. And the maiden trip of *Queen City* proved such a gala affair. She left San Francisco November 4, 1854, with 917 passengers. To add color, a squadron of the California Guards Flying Artillery in full uniform were aboard. They lashed artillery pieces on deck — barrels pointing through the railing, wheels resting in the scuppers. Steaming across San Francisco Bay, the *Queen* swept by an anchored French naval squadron. With true Gallic gallantry, the squadron fired her guns to honor *le magnifique Vaisseau*. The California Guards appropriately returned a roaring salvo.

As *Queen City* churned up the Sacramento River, a brass band on deck played stirring marches and gay airs. Later she nudged to the dock at Benicia, where shore batteries exchanged welcoming salvos with the *Queen's* heavy guns. Nine and one-half hours later she arrived at Sacramento where huge crowds cheered until they were hoarse. Bands played. Welcoming artillery thundered until a pall of smoke hovered over levee and docks.

Sacramento's Embarcadero in the mid-1850's.

When *Queen City* departed two days later, the *Sacramento Bee* reported that the largest crowd ever assembled in Sacramento bid her farewell. Brass bands blared; enthusiastic crowds roared. The steamer eased from her berth, but instead of heading south, she sailed north about a mile, then turned around. The *Queen* now floated past the city proudly displaying her grace and beauty before her adoring crowds. Again the heavy guns roared on land and on steamer.

Larger and more elegantly furnished river steamers were built later and made daily scheduled runs between Sacramento and San Francisco. The six-hour overnight passage was popular. Smaller steamers ran daily to Marysville, Stockton, and up the Sacramento to Red Bluff. The larger, more famous steamers included *Chrysopolis, Yosemite, Antelope, New World, Capital City* and *Senator*. Scores of other steamers made up the fleet that at various times sailed the rivers of California.

The *Chrysopolis* was truly the epitome of plush Victorian elegance. As were most river steamers, she was a side-wheeler. Her hull was 245 feet long, her beam 40 feet and her hold 10 feet deep. Despite her size, she drew only four and one-half feet of water. She weighed 1,050 tons. Her engine, with a huge five-foot piston and eleven-foot stroke, generated 1,357 horsepower—lots of horsepower for her day. The two paddle wheels measured 36 feet in diameter and mounted buckets eight feet wide. This power plant pushed the steamer at speeds of 19.8 knots per hour or 22.7 miles per hour. Her two boilers were placed on each of her guards over the paddle wheels, an innovation unique at the time. In case a boiler exploded (not uncommon in those days), this location would wreak less havoc with her one thousand passengers. Her twin stacks towered upward fore the pilothouse in true Mississippi River steamer style.

Nothing was spared to create the ultimate splendor of Victorian motif in her cabins and public rooms. Decor and furnishings included filigree moldings, plate-glass mirrors, polished hardwood panels, leaded windows of many-colored panes, marble-topped tables, and red-plush upholstery on chairs and divans. Polished brass lamps hung on walls and overheads. Other steamers approached her in elegance, but *Chrysopolis* was one of the most famous.

The increasing numbers of river steamers in 1854 led to devastating competition. Freight rates at times dropped so low that profits vanished. Passengers frequently were carried free. Operators complained that their only profits came from the liquor dispensed in the steamers' saloons (indicating the prodigious amount quaffed by westerners of the gold-rush era).

Steamboat operators finally decided to end this profitless chaos on the river. They met in San Francisco in March 1854, and formed the California Steam Navigation Company, a joint stock company capitalized at $2,500,000 with twenty-five hundred shares of stock valued at $1,000 each. Cooperating boat owners turned their steamers over to the corporation in exchange for stock equivalent to the value of their boats. Most individual boat owners and small steamer companies united with the corporation, also referred to as the Combination.

Even though the Combination did not include all inland water steamers, enough joined to control shipping, creating a virtual monopoly. Freight rates were set at $8 a ton between San Francisco and Sacramento and $15 between San Francisco and points beyond Sacramento, such as Marysville. Passengers paid $7 deck passage from San Francisco to Sacramento and $3 more to further points.

Since these rates and fares were considerably higher than those charged heretofore, opposition to the Combination was immediate, virulent and widespread. The *Sacramento Union* denounced it as a "Mammoth and Monster Steamboat Company." The *Marysville Herald* reviled it as "conceived in sin and born in iniquity." Others referred to it as a "soulless, heartless corporation." Agitation began for a transcontinental railroad to offer the Combination competition. Ironically, the same epithets that were hurled at the California Steam Navigation Company were later to be hurled at the Central Pacific Railroad.

Independent steamers did at times ply the rivers in competition to the monopoly. Rates dropped when they did, sometimes drastically, but rates doubled and even tripled when no opposition steamers ran. To combat competition, the Combination either ran their opposition out of business through rate wars or bought them off.

TOP: California Steam Navigation Company ad in the MARYSVILLE DIRECTORY, 1858. BOTTOM: Sacramento River steamer YOSEMITE tied up at Sacramento in the 1870's.

Thus many independent captains decided that "if you can't beat them, join them."

Competition engendered the dangerous sports of racing and ramming, activities that often resulted in injuries and death. Such events today would seem appalling, but old westerners were independent, freewheeling and aggressive—attitudes that were often reflected by steamer captains. The speed of a craft involved the honor of both crews and passengers. Bets were often made and passengers of opposing steamers were even known to shoot at each other during the heat of a contest. Sometimes arrests were made, but suits brought by victims resulted in few convictions or settlements, so the deadly sport continued for well over a decade. Collisions and explosions, many the result of racing and deliberate rammings, took their toll of lives and injuries with such disconcerting frequency that a current joke described the terms "lucky" and "unlucky." One was unlucky if he missed the particular steamer he wished to take; he was lucky to be safe at home when he heard that this steamer had exploded.

An early disaster involving western steamers and attributable to competitive racing occurred on August 16, 1851. When the *Fawn* and the *Gabriel Winter* left Sacramento for Marysville, a race was on. As flame and smoke spewed from her stacks, three Frenchmen on board the *Fawn* anxiously eyed the rising head of steam and retreated far astern as the safest spot should the boilers explode. Up the river they furiously raced; both engineers franticaly threw fuel in their fireboxes, building up an alarming head of steam. Suddenly the boilers of the *Fawn* shattered with a resounding roar ending the race. Several were killed and many badly injured or scalded. Among the sur-

194

Sacramento steamer CAPITAL *tied up at the foot of K Street in Sacramento,* CIRCA *1865.*

vivors were the three French passengers cowering far astern. Cause of the explosion is not clear, but it is possible the *Fawn's* engineer tied down the safety valve, a practice not uncommon during the heat of a race, or the boiler may have been made of poor material, also not uncommon on early steamers. Then too, passengers probably urged engineers to strain their boilers, for the *Sacramento Daily Union* complained that passengers all too frequently instigated racing.

On another occasion *Governor Dana* and *R. K. Page* raced to disaster on March 22, 1853. Both steamers had left Marysville together and either by coincidence or, more likely, by prearrangement, raced down the Feather, stacks billowing smoke and paddle wheels churning water. Neither had the lead until they neared Nicolaus when the *Dana*, straining her boilers, eased ahead. A passenger on board the *Page* then bet her engineer a box of cigars that he could not pass the *Dana*. With these cigars and what he considered his honor at stake, the engineer eagerly sought a way to increase steam pressure. On deck was a keg

of oil which he threw into the firebox and no doubt he fastened down the safety valve. Steam pressure went up and the boiler blew up. According to reports, only the bartender survived without injury. Several on board were killed or scalded. Three passengers completely vanished so shattering was the blast.

The most heated races occurred between the California Steam Navigation Company's steamers and opposition boats. One such race between the "monstrous Monopoly's" *Confidence* and *Queen City* almost resulted in fiery disaster in 1855, but it did provide real excitement. In those days most steamers fired with wood, but some Company steamers had started burning Philadelphia coal. Engineers on the *Confidence* had the advantage of this superior heat-producing fuel, whereas those on board *Queen City* did not. Consequently, *Confidence* gained the lead. In desperation *Queen City's* engineer forced her fires with pitch pine until tongues of flame roared from her forty-five-foot twin stacks like two enormous blowtorches piercing the night sky. Showers of burning embers settled on the deck aft the pilothouse. *Queen City's* passengers, who were mostly Marysville citizens

195

Two California river steamers, the AMERICAN EAGLE and the STOCKTON, exploded in 1853. Incompetent crewmen, weak boilers, or racing brought many steamers to violent destruction.

and faithful and true to their city's steamer, rose to the occasion by forming two groups, one to pass wood to the firemen, the other to pass buckets of water to quench possible fires caused by sparks from the fuel the first group helped stow into the fireboxes. This mighty effort was in vain. The coal burner proved too fast, and in spite of the *Queen City's* valiant but reckless effort, she dropped behind losing the race. Fortunately, after the fires had backed down the *Queen's* tall stacks and her boilers had cooled, passengers and steamer surprisingly were still intact.

Not so fortunate were passengers and crew in another race between steamers of an opposition company and the Combination. The *Enterprise* had left Marysville at 7 p.m., as had the Combination's *Pearl*, each with about one hundred passengers. After both boats had cleared the mouth of the Yuba River, about one-half mile downstream from Marysville, and entered the Feather River, the race began. Paddle wheels whirled until water surged upward in spray and foam. Side by side the steamers strained for the lead until they neared John Sutter's Hock Farm when the *Pearl* moved ahead. Undaunted, the *Enterprise* stayed in the race and both steamers churned down the Feather and into the Sacramento River. The *Pearl* approached the capital city ahead of *Enterprise*. As *Pearl* was sliding into her berth near the mouth of the American River, her horizontal boilers suddenly vibrated violently, then thundered forward like a rocket through passengers crowding the forward deck waiting to disembark, ripping into them with splinters of wood and iron and showering them with scalding steam. Sixty-seven were killed and many injured or scalded.

A coroner's inquest that included much conflicting and acrimonious testimony was held. Captain Summers of the *Enterprise* testified that the *Pearl's* engineer was incompetent. The engineer was arrested, but he was released on ten thousand dollar bail. What caused the explosion is not clear. Perhaps the engineer, prior to docking, had neglected to let off steam as he shut down his engines, a necessary process to relieve boiler steam pressure that otherwise would have gone through

the cylinders while running. Or he may have tied down the safety valve during the race to increase steam pressure. Either action alone could cause disaster, but a combination of the two almost guaranteed it. The *Marysville Herald* remarked that Atlantic states courts would "deal stern justice" in a case such as this, but how California courts would act was "more than we can predict." Words that indicate the more independent laissez faire theory held by westerners as compared with the more strict control of business attitudes of easterners.

Sometimes races took a bizarre twist such as happened between *Blair*, a Combination steamer; *Gem*; and *Defiance* in February 1861, on an upstream trip from Sacramento. *Defiance* was in the lead, *Blair* next, and *Gem* last. During the race the *Gem* attempted to pass the *Blair*, but the *Blair* refused to clear the channel and began whipping her barge in order to prevent the *Gem* from passing. Outraged passengers aboard the Gem now jumped on *Blair's* barge, cut her lines and cast the barge adrift, thus forcing *Blair* out of the race. Threats were exchanged between those on board the two steamers. The *Gem* then passed the *Defiance* and won the race.

In another race the rival steamers, *Sacramento* and *Antelope*, performed like two maddened bulls battering each other in an arena. One day in 1860 the *Sacramento* departed for San Francisco and the speedier *Antelope* followed an hour later. Upon overtaking the *Sacramento*, the *Antelope* tried to pass, but the captain of *Sacramento* determined that she would not pass. He maneuvered his boat in the narrow channel of Steamboat Slough so as to force *Antelope* onto a mud bank. Her captain refloated her and pursued *Sacramento*. Passengers aboard the *Antelope* considered such behavior by the *Sacramento* as a personal affront to their honor. They drew pistols and prepared to settle in an honorable manner, but

The Sacramento River steamer ANTELOPE carried Pony Express mail between Sacramento and San Francisco.

Captain Fouratt of the *Antelope* convinced them that he had better plans. Upon reaching a wider channel, he jammed *Antelope's* bow into *Sacramento's* starboard quarter. *Sacramento's* captain then reversed engines hoping to slide down the *Antelope's* sides in order to remove one of her paddle wheels. Instead, the *Sacramento* wound up squarely in front of the *Antelope* which bore down on her full speed and pushed her sideways down the river for several miles, an ungainly manner for a proud steamer to be under way. Captain Fouratt was arrested the next day and charged with malicious mischief, but in keeping with the spirit of the times, nothing came of the arrest nor of the incident.

Pugnacious Captain Fouratt later became the star actor of another more serious aggressive act against an opposition boat. This time he commanded the Combination's *New World*; the opposition steamer was *Washoe*. The arena was offshore at Benicia. The *New World* was drifting to the wharf for a landing, but the natives' sympathies lay with the opposition and they refused to take her lines. The opposition steamer *Washoe* was also moving in for landing and crossed the bow of *New World*. This caused Captain Fouratt's ire to rise as high as the steam in his boilers. He rang for full speed ahead, turned his rudder in the direction of *Washoe* and rammed into her side with a splintering crash. Skillfully *Washoe's* pilot maneuvered her out of deep water and onto the beach. One of *Washoe's* passengers was killed in the rending crash and the citizens of Benicia were so outraged that they were moved to mutiny. Troops were called in to protect the *New World* and those aboard from destruction.

In due time Captain Fouratt was indicted, but through legal, or perhaps more accurately, illegal maneuvering, the case was dropped. A star witness, *Washoe's* pilot, fell and broke his neck, so was unable to testify. It was also rumored that those defending Captain Fouratt managed to intoxicate members of the grand jury and the magistrate.

Blood continued to run hot between opposition steamers and those of the Combination. In fact, blood actually flowed in an affair between the Combination's *Martha White* and opposition steamer *Princess*, one soft spring evening on May 16, 1859. *Princess*, loaded with two hundred passengers and heavy freight, was plying down the Sacramento River approaching San Francisco Bay. The Combination's *Martha White* loomed up nearby and deliberately rammed the *Princess*. Pistols were drawn by some aboard the *Martha White* and shots were fired, wounding *Princess'* captain. Again the case was taken into police court, but again it was dismissed and became a civil case. Shortly *Princess* disappeared from the river; it was believed that the Combination had bought her off, perhaps at such an attractive price that the shooting incident was forgotten.

While racing, ramming and explosions were abhorred by the press and presumably by part of the public, prevailing opinion seemed to be that since steamers were the property of individuals, these individuals had a right to do with their property what they wished. Present-day concepts of responsibilities of public utilities had not as yet been accepted by these independent westerners. The following excerpt from the Marysville *Herald* of October 20, 1855, epitomizes the philosophy of the times:

> *Captains and owners of steamers have a right to run their boats into one another, or anything else they may fancy; but to do so when the lives of hundreds of passengers are entrusted to their care, shows a recklessness and foolhardiness. . . .*

Not all explosions were caused by racing. When steamers moving by themselves exploded, other causes were obvious. Sometimes engineers were drunk or incompetent, or boilers and equipment were faulty. Faulty equipment plagued *New World* as she was leaving Marysville early in June 1851. She had just cleared her moorings when the upper sheet of the steam chimney exploded, killing one man instantly, scalding fourteen others and drowning one or two more. The accident was termed unavoidable as the boat was running slowly with only a moderate head of steam.

Many on board the *Belle* met violent death or painful injuries on the Sacramento River halfway between Sacramento and Fremont in February 1856. As the steamer proceeded upstream, a passenger in the saloon huddled close to the stove with one leg on either side of it attempting to soak up warmth against the chill day. Suddenly the stove shot through the overhead and over the hurricane deck, but the startled passenger sat there unharmed. *Belle's* boilers had exploded so violently that most of her upper works were shattered. Twenty lives were lost including her captain. Among the fifty injured was Major Bidwell, an early Chico, California pioneer, who was returning to that city from San Francisco. Shortly thereafter the steamers *General Reddington* and *Governor Dana* arrived and rescued survivors. Passengers from the *Dana* erected a tent on shore, built fires and cared for the injured and dying. Later, *Cleopatra*, outbound from Marysville, returned the dead and wounded to Marysville. Repeated short blasts of her whistle as she approached the city heralded the disaster.

Cause of the explosion was a mystery. *Belle's* boilers had recently withstood 120 pounds pressure during a test. Her engineer was reputed to be a sober, careful man, and evidence indicated the boiler contained sufficient water. On the beach near the disaster, a monument was erected in honor of the *Belle's* dead. This monument still stands as a grim reminder of the disaster.

Another boat well-known on the Feather, the *McClelland*, exploded in August 1861, near Knight's Landing on the Sacramento River. Her pilothouse, including her pilot, barge driver and another crewman, rocketed upward some distance and plummeted onto the boat deck without serious injury to any of the startled three, but fifteen others were killed and eleven injured. Freight and portions of the wreck were strewn on both sides of the river. The badly damaged steamer's furnace door was flung 400 yards and part of her boiler was hurtled 350 yards. The boat turned completely around and sank in shoal water.

The Marysville *Herald* indicated that *McClelland's* fulmination was the tenth explosion of small steamers on California's inland waters and, as often as they occurred, the press had warned the public that most small steamers were instruments of destruction. Correctly alluding to their engines and boilers, the *Herald* contended that many were but "refuse stuff" sent out from the East on speculation and "fit only for old iron."

The big *Yosemite* for some unexplained reason blew up on October 12, 1865, just as she pulled away from Rio Vista. So violently did she explode that her entire forward superstructure disintegrated into flying splinters. Live steam scalded many on board. An account of the disaster the following day in the San Francisco *Alta* reflected contemporary regard for Chinese. The report listed the names of thirteen whites as being killed, then added as an afterthought, "there were twenty-nine Chinamen killed by the explosion, all of whom were buried at Rio Vista."

When the Sacramento River and its tributaries—the Feather and San Joaquin—flooded, which was frequent, river steamers performed acts of mercy. Water at times was so high on city streets that steamers were able to navigate them. The steamer *Defiance* cruised up Marysville's main street on December 9, 1861, rescuing inhabitants from second-story windows. During the same flood, *Young America* sailed down stagecoach roads performing duties normally restricted to land vehicles. *Defiance* carried needed supplies to towns and villages that were normally miles from navigable streams.

Explosions, races, rammings, snaggings and groundings continued for many years following the discovery of gold in 1848. River steamers, however, successfully moved the freight to major cities where in turn it was moved by pack animals and freight wagons to the gold mines. Without the steamers and before construction of railroads it would have been very difficult, if not impossible, to supply adequately the thousands of people living in the Sierra Nevada working at the principal industry of the time—mining gold.

With the passing of the frontier and the construction of a vast network of railroads across the West, the golden age of steamboats on western rivers passed into history. Its passing was not sudden; steamboating went down fighting, but changing technology and railroad competition ultimately prevailed. Steamboats were invaluable in their time, moving freight, people and animals to the remote areas of the Old West. Boats still sail the rivers hauling certain types of cargo adapted to river transportation, but with scows, barges and tugs propelled by screws instead of paddle wheels, powered by diesels, and equipped with discordant air horns! How prosaic compared to yesteryear's colorful side- or stern-wheelers proudly churning the water, smoke billowing from their tall stacks, their steam whistles wailing full, pleasant (though melancholy) tones.

Billy Richardson spurs his mount westward as he initiates the first run of the Pony Express on April 3, 1860 from St. Joseph to Sacramento.

8

The Pony Express

Few feats have fired the imagination or the admiration of so many as has the Pony Express. Establishing and operating a one-man, one-horse express from St. Joseph, Missouri, to Sacramento, California, was an accomplishment almost without precedent. It was a dangerous undertaking. Not only dangerous for the participants' lives, but also dangerous for the promoters' capital. The stakes were high and the promoters—Russell, Majors and Waddell—played for high stakes. The desired prize was a daily stagecoach U.S. mail contract between St. Joseph and Sacramento. No such daily mail service on this route existed in 1860 when the Pony Express was organized. The promoters of this Express hoped to prove the superiority of the central-overland route to the southern route on which mail was carried by stagecoach from St. Louis to San Francisco via Texas.

Actually, when the Pony Express began in April 1860, Russell, Majors and Waddell, operators of a gigantic freight-wagon system, were carrying passengers and mail between St. Joseph and Salt Lake City biweekly and at times weekly. But they wanted their mail contract boosted to a daily schedule. Their stage company, that carried the mail and passengers, was the Central Overland and Pike's Peak Express Company. This company had been formed in 1859 by Russell, Majors and Waddell in conjunction with minor partners. They had purchased several outfits that were operating over various sections of the central-overland route.

The tasks of purchasing supplies and animals, building and stocking stations, hiring personnel, and later operating the Pony Express were delegated to the Central Overland California and Pike's Peak Express Company. Throughout its existence the Pony Express was listed as a service of the Central Overland. Many did not know that this stage company was controlled by Russell, Majors

and Waddell, thus they did not realize the organizing genius behind the Pony Express. Much to their later financial distress, these partners also underwrote expenses incurred by the Central Overland in organizing and operating the Pony Express.

Of the partners, William H. Russell was the actual promoter of the Pony Express. The other partners, especially Waddell, were less enthusiastic. Russell was a visionary, organizer and optimist—handy characteristics to possess in order to conceive of and to originate a 1,966-mile Pony Express over prairies, mountains, and deserts and to operate it on a once-a-week, ten-day schedule between points each way. The three partners, with Russell the leader, decided upon the Pony Express early in 1860 with neither promise of a United States Mail contract, nor assurance of a future triweekly or daily mail contract for the Central Overland California and Pike's Peak Express Company. The Pony Express would have to depend on money received from its customers until subsidies from the Federal government could be obtained; unfortunately for the partners, these subsidies were never granted.

Sixty-five days prior to April 3, 1860, William H. Russell decreed that the Pony Express be organized, equipped and ready to operate by that date. While it was true that the Central Overland California and Pike's Peak Express was operating over part of the route and maintaining a few stations, organizing the Pony Express in sixty-five days was a colossal task.

Since mounts would have to be changed every twelve to fifteen miles, relay stations had to be built. At first 119 were set up and more were added later. Every seventy-five to one hundred miles a home station was located. Larger and more heavily staffed than relay stations, home stations were maintained for riders to rest in at the end of their runs. They waited there for the next mail coming from the opposite direction and then carried it back to their original home station. A few stations doubled as stage stops. Many stations were located miles from settlements, since efficiency of

*Left to right, William H. Russell, Alexander Majors
and William B. Waddell, founders of the
Pony Express.*

the route rather than beauty of environment or nearness to settlements dictated station locations. Consequently, water had to be hauled to some locations and livestock herded hundreds of miles to outlying posts. Each station was supplied initially and restocked monthly by wagon trains. Following is a typical list of supplies:

Food: hams, bacon, flour, tripe, syrup, salt, tea, coffee, dried fruits, cornmeal. Some stations kept cattle for milk and beef.

Medicine for Man and Beast: turpentine, castor oil, copperas, borax, cream of tartar.

Stable equipment: brushes, curry combs, horseshoe nails, manure forks, bridles, saddles, liniment, rope, blacksmith's tools.

Miscellaneous: nails, antelope skins, window sashes, screws, hinges, putty, well pulleys, wagon grease, monkey wrenches, rubber blankets, tin safes, twine, and most important of all—grain for the horses.

Five hundred horses were required to operate the Express. Some sources say four hundred, but either figure adds up to a lot of ponies. Only the best racers that money could buy were purchased at an average of $175 each. They had to be fast and tough because they were required to run an average of twelve and one-half miles an hour

205

nonstop between relay stations. On divisions east of Fort Kearny, Nebraska, high-grade, speedy Kentucky and Missouri stock was procured. West of that point, tough, fast and durable western mustangs were preferred. The horses averaged nine hundred pounds, fourteen hands high. Because of their importance, they were given special treatment and care. This attention and their supplemental grain diet kept them in better condition than grass-fed Indian ponies, enabling them to outrun Indian mounts when necessary.

Superior horses required superior riders. Runs averaged 55 miles in the mountains and 120 in the prairies. Routes were ridden twice a week, day and night, at an average speed of twelve and one-half miles per hour. Only skillful young horsemen (many were under twenty) tough, brave and small (most weighed under 120 pounds) were hired. The company required that they be of good moral character and not addicted to liquor. It was glamorous work that attracted hundreds of applicants from all parts of the nation. About 125 were hired. And they, along with all Pony Express employees, in fact all who worked for Russell, Majors and Waddell, signed the following oath:

> I, _____, do hereby swear, before the Great and Living God, that during my engagement, and while I am an employee of Russell, Majors and Waddell, I will under no circumstances, use profane language; that I will drink no intoxicating liquors; that I will not quarrel or fight with any other employee of the firm and that in every respect I will conduct myself honestly, be faithful to my duties, and so direct all my acts as to win the confidence of my employers. So help me God.

Almost to a man those employed were dedicated to the slogan of the Pony Express: "The mail must go through." One source indicates their pay ranged from $50 to $150 per month; another source cites $100 to $120 per month and on dangerous runs, $150 plus board and room. The wages were excellent for the times.

Riders dressed as they pleased. Most of them wore buckskin shirts, slouch hats or caps and trousers tucked into leather boots. They carried two revolvers, usually Colts, and draped a Spencer carbine over their shoulders. The carbine was later discarded as being too heavy and cumbersome. The guns were carried only for last resort protection of their lives or the mail. Their best defense against hostile Indians or road agents was the superior speed of their Express ponies.

Each relay station employed a keeper and herder; home stations, a keeper and four or five men. A keeper's duty was to have a fresh horse saddled and bridled one-half hour before the expected arrival of a rider. Only two minutes were allowed for changing mounts. Keepers detected approaching riders by dust billowing upward on the plains or by the clopping of approaching hooves in clear mountain air. At night a rider's whooping signaled his approach. As a rider galloped near the keeper holding the fresh mount, the rider flung his *mochila* (saddlebags that fit over the saddle horn) to the keeper, who plopped it over the saddle horn on the fresh mount. The rider reined in hard, dismounted in a cloud of dust, leaped astride the fresh horse, shouted a greeting such as, "All's well between here and Cottonwood," and with a clatter of hooves, sped to the next relay station. Many times this change took only fifteen seconds. The keeper then led the lathery, spent pony away to curry, feed and water him lovingly.

Station keepers were dedicated to their jobs, brave and skilled in their work. Many of them lost their lives defending their posts against Indian attacks. Station men and their assistants received $50 to $100 a month and their board and room.

Scattered at intervals of two hundred miles were division stations under the command of a division superintendent. Their pay was equal to or better than that of the best riders. Here were kept extra men, supplies and animals as a precaution against Indian attacks and desperadoes. Division superintendents were hired because of their good moral character, dedication and tough fighting qualities. Actually they were private lawmen and the only lawmen in an area where law and order was merely an abstract theory rather than a reality.

They were efficient in frustrating thieves and many a superintendent took the law into his own hands performing his duty. There were five division superintendents and a general superintendent over the entire operation. In all, four hundred employees labored in the relay, home and division stations.

Station houses came in several sizes, shapes and constructions. Building materials depended upon what was available in the countryside. If trees were at hand, houses were of logs; if not, rocks, adobe, or sod served as walls and roof. Stations in lonely areas far from civilization were crude affairs with earthen floors and they often lacked windows. In such outposts, packing boxes served as furniture. Beds were log frames against a wall with buffalo robes serving as bedding. Some stations

This building, reputed to be an original Pony Express station, was moved from the trail on the south side of the Platte River to the City of Cozad, Nebraska, where it was restored and where it now stands.

were farmhouses and trading posts and were better built and better furnished. Wives of keepers lived at a few such stations and here food was more tasty and varied. Each station had a corral for the animals and a barn for the horses.

As Russell had decreed, this entire operation was organized and ready to roll by April 3, 1860. Letters for the first run west left Washington, D.C. by train for New York on March 30, where mail was added the next day. From New York the Pony Express mail pouch traveled to St. Joseph by train.

This pouch, or mochila, was made of leather and draped over the saddle horn. It had four pouches, called *cantinas*, two on either side. Three were locked and were opened en route only at military forts and at Salt Lake City. The fourth cantina contained mail picked up en route and a time slip that recorded the arrival and departure of the rider.

The schedule for the first runs was ten days between St. Joseph and Sacramento for eight months of the year and twelve days in the winter. The summer schedule averaged ten miles an hour including all stops; the winter schedule, eight miles an hour. As soon as more relay stations were added, this schedule was lowered to eight and ten days, since with shorter distances between stations, horses could be run faster. Speed on this faster schedule averaged nearly twelve miles an hour. At first, once-a-week service was offered; later this was increased to twice a week. Letters from New York went through in twelve and one-half days at first, and ten and one-half days on the later, faster schedule.

Following is a schedule posted for the first westward runs. The hours indicate time allotted from St. Joseph to the listed stations.

Marysville, Kansas	**12 hours**
Fort Kearny (present-day Wyoming)	**34 hours**
Fort Laramie (present-day Wyoming)	**80 hours**
Fort Bridger (present-day Utah)	**108 hours**
Great Salt Lake (present-day Utah)	**124 hours**
Camp Floyd (present-day Nevada)	**128 hours**
Carson City (present-day Nevada)	**188 hours**
Placerville, California	**226 hours**
Sacramento, California	**234 hours**

On that momentous day of April 3, 1860, eighty Pony Express riders were scattered at their stations along the 1,966-mile route eagerly awaiting their chance to speed the mail along their portions of the course. Forty riders would ride eastward as forty riders galloped westward. At St. Joseph the train bearing dispatches from the East roared into the station two and one-half hours late. As a brass band played, Alexander Majors briefly orated, crowds cheered and the mochila was quickly transferred to the first rider's horse. He waved his hat, dug in his spurs, and the beautiful horse charged westward, thus opening one of the most glamorous epics of American history. The time was 7:30 p.m.

Just who rode that mount is not certain. Indications are the rider was chosen by lot. Two candidates emerge as most likely, John Frye and Johnson William Richardson. In 1923 an historian, Mrs. Louise Hauck of St. Joseph, concluded after extensive research that Richardson carried the first mochila. The *Missouri Historical Review* also picked Billy Richardson.

Richardson thundered westward attempting to make up the lost two and one-half hours. He galloped into the Troy, Kennekuk, and Kickapoo stations, changing mounts in seconds. At 11:30 p.m. he charged into Granada, his home station. He had made up three quarters of an hour of the lost time. From here Don Rising eagerly sped the mochila westward. By the time Rising reached Marysville, Kansas, the mail was only one hour late. And so went the mochila, tossed from horse to horse at relay after relay station, carried consecutively by forty riders. Over prairies, sand, mud, rivers, mountains and snow, through some of the remotest and wildest regions of the continent, sped the mail. West of the Platte, hostile Indians were a threat. At Carson City, Nevada, the terminus of a local telegraph line, the operator saw the rider thunder past and flashed word ahead to Sacramento and San Francisco. These towns then prepared tumultuous welcomes.

On April 13 Sacramentans hoisted flags, draped bunting and hung welcome signs. A cannon was rolled out. A delegation rode to Sutter's Fort to escort rider William Hamilton into town. By late afternoon crowds eagerly awaited him. About 5:30 p.m. he approached the fort in a cloud of dust and the awaiting delegation escorted him to the Express office. Along the way the surprised Hamilton was greeted by roaring crowds standing on the streets and balconies and perched on roofs. Bands blared, anvils clanged, the cannon boomed round upon round and bells rang. Pretty ladies tossed him flowers and kisses. But Hamilton's dedication to duty prevailed; with a wave of his hat, he left the ladies astern and dashed to the Express office. Here the mochila was unloaded and reloaded with letters. Immediately he and his pony boarded the Sacramento River steamer, *Antelope,* for San Francisco. The time from St. Joseph to Sacramento: nine days, twenty-three hours. The miracle had been performed!

At 12:30 a.m., as the *Antelope* drifted to her moorings at San Francisco, rockets pierced the night sky, bells pealed, anvils clanged, crowds roared, bands played. Hamilton again was overawed. A parade escorted him to the telegraph office as the band played, "See, The Conquering Hero Comes." The mochila that had so ceremoniously departed St. Joseph some ten and one-half days earlier was deposited at the Express office.

The first run eastward was made in exactly ten days between Sacramento and St. Joseph. After a ceremony in San Francisco, the mochila was carried aboard the steamer *Antelope* on horseback for the trip to Sacramento. (After the first east-west runs, Pony Express horses never again boarded the steamers; only the mochilas were transported between Sacramento and San Francisco.) At 2 a.m. the steamer docked at Sacramento where Billy Hamilton picked up the mochila and without

ceremony sloshed eastward in pouring rain and abject darkness. At Sportsman's Hall twelve miles east of Placerville, Warren Upson picked up the mail. Ahead lay what was perhaps the worst stretch of that first run. The Sierra Nevada soared upward in his path. A late spring blizzard raged, covering the trail several feet deep with snow. No team or pack train had passed over it for three days. Howling winds drove the freezing cold into Upson. At times he was forced to break trail for his mustang, but he struggled over the summit and rode into Carson City eighty-five miles from Sportsman's Hall. Warren Upson's courage, stamina and determination carried him through. From Carson City, thirty-eight riders in turn carried the mochila eastward, repeating in reverse the westward run. On April 13, 1860, Billy Richardson galloped into St. Joseph to a rousing welcome.

Hoof beats of the Pony Express reverberated around the world. Most of the civilized world knew of it, talked about it and admired it. The British and European governments took notice and used the Express to forward their Far Eastern dispatches to and from their European capitals — to New York by ship, to St. Joseph by train, to San Francisco by Pony Express, and to the Orient by ship.

Curiosity of British recipients of American mail stamped "via Pony Express" became so widespread that the *London Illustrated News* sent a correspondent to St. Joseph to cover the details. He introduced his highly informative dispatch with the following:

> *Some of our readers may possibly be puzzled, when reading American news, to find most important intelligence from California, Oregon, British Columbia and the Pacific side of North America contained in a short paragraph headed "By Pony Express"; and the question naturally arises, what is meant by a Pony Express? Where does it come from? Where does it go? and why is it a Pony Express and not a horse, or a stagecoach, or a railway*

A Pony Express rider is pursued by Indians.

express? For the purpose of giving some information on this point, our correspondent has taken the trouble to visit the locale of the Pony Express, to see it arrive and depart at its Eastern terminus, and also to get a view of it en route on the plains.

French and German periodicals published articles and pictures of the colorful Pony Express rider dashing across the vast wilderness pursued by Indians. These articles were widely read. The romance of the great adventure had gained international interest. The dashing saddlemen had become worldwide heroes.

In spite of its widespread popularity and admiration, patronage of the Pony Express did not nearly pay operating expenses. Russell spent fruitless months in Washington attempting to secure a mail contract for the Pony Express. The three partners poured hundreds of thousands of dollars into the enterprise. They obtained loans from their friend and business associate, Ben Holladay, an operator of extensive freight lines. In return for his loans, he acquired mortgages on the Central Overland and Pike's Peak Express Company.

Letters sent via Pony Express cost $5 each half ounce, and on July 1, 1861, this price was reduced to $1. In addition, all letters had to bear a ten-cent U.S. government postage stamp. In July 1861 Wells Fargo acted as agent for the Pony Express but did not operate it.

Letters were wrapped in oiled silk to protect them from wetness caused by rain, snow, fording rivers, or sweat from man and beast. To obtain the most writing for their five dollars, patrons wrote letters on tissue paper. Some newspapers in New York, Boston, Chicago, St. Louis and San Francisco occasionally printed limited editions on thin paper and sped them along the Pony Express. Businessmen in Portland, Oregon; San Francisco; Sacramento; and Oakland, as well as many in the East, used the Express. Government officials in Washington, D.C. and California communicated via the Pony Express. This communication proved invaluable during the crises prior to the Civil War and during the hectic days following the opening of hostilities. Riders carried an average of fifteen and as much as twenty pounds of mail in their mochilas, but even these heavy loads failed to produce sufficient revenue to meet operating expenses.

Ten weeks after the first run of the Pony Express, on June 16, 1860, Congress passed a bill authorizing construction of an overland telegraph between Carson City, Nevada and St. Joseph. (A telegraph was already in existence between Carson City and San Francisco.) Construction began at both ends, one crew worked west, the other east. The Pony Express carried telegrams between the termini of the ever-lengthening telegraph lines. As the gap between the east and west termini grew shorter, so did the life of the Pony Express.

Soon after the Express began operating, it met serious problems. One was hostile Indian uprisings in Utah Territory (present-day Nevada). These uprisings, known as the Paiute War, spread terror, destruction and death along the route of the Pony Express.

For reasons undetermined by historians, a war party of Paiutes crept up on Williams Station near the Humboldt Sink on May 7, 1860. Without warning, they killed David and Oscar Williams, brothers of the keeper, as they stood outside the station. Three other men who were stopping there were killed; one as he fled for his life; the other

A letter sent via Pony Express from General Vallejo to his son attending college in New York.

two died in the flames of the station that the Indians set afire. After driving off the animals, the Indians vanished. J. D. Williams, the keeper, escaped death because he was absent during the raid. Seeing the tragedy upon his return, he rode off spreading word of the massacre.

This news kindled seething hatred of the Indians into flames of revenge. One hundred and five volunteers from various Nevada settlements set out to punish the Paiutes. These volunteers lost forty-six men in the catastrophic battle of Pyramid Lake. Next, an army of 150 U.S. soldiers and 650 volunteers under overall command of Colonel John C. Hayes defeated and scattered the Indians near the previous battlefield. The war was technically over, but peace was not established. What followed was guerrilla warfare and terrorism against the Pony Express that suspended operation for several weeks. Stations, isolated and manned by only a few men, were easy, tempting targets for war parties. Station after station was attacked; keepers were massacred while valiantly defending their posts. Riders were ambushed; one killed outright carrying the mail, several mortally wounded in the line of duty. But only one mochila was lost, the one carried by the slain rider.

About May 11 Indians attacked Cold Springs Station killing the keeper, burning the station and driving off the horses. Within the next three weeks Cold Creek, Dry Creek, and Roberts Creek Stations met similar fates. At Dry Creek two men lived to tell what happened, but keeper Ralph Rozier was mortally wounded outside the station (he was later mutilated — scalped), and his assistant was so badly wounded that he put a revolver to his head and killed himself. The two survivors put up a battle and were able to escape to the next station ten miles away. One ran the distance without shoes.

The William Creek Station was successfully defended against thirty Indians by keeper Peter Neece and rider Elijah Wilson. Seven Indians burst in on Neece and demanded a twenty-five pound sack of flour for each Indian. Neece refused. The angry Indians on the way out filled an old cow full of arrows. Outraged, Neece shot two of them. Knowing that more Indians lurked in the nearby hills and that they would attempt to avenge the shooting, Neece and Wilson prepared to defend themselves. Instead of barricading themselves in the station, they lay outside in the sagebrush. Near dusk, thirty Indians stormed the station. Neece and Wilson fired, jumped to another spot and fired. These tactics so bewildered the Indians that they fired only a few shots, gave up and rode away.

On May 24 a rider from the west arrived in Salt Lake City without the mochila. He reported to the agent there that the rider carrying it had been killed and that the Paiutes had taken the mailbag. The agent at Salt Lake City then sent the following dispatch east: "May 24 — Rider just in. The Indians have chased all men from stations between Diamond Springs and Carson Valley. The mochila has been lost."

Mochilas from the East were now held at Salt Lake City until Division Superintendent Howard Eagan took them west on June 6 with an expedition of ninety soldiers, along with men, riders and supplies to rebuild ravaged stations. Eastbound riders west of Nevada had been grounded since June 3. On June 9, Bolivar Roberts, a division superintendent from the west, moved eastward with about twenty men, stock and provisions. On June 16, these two relief expeditions met at Roberts Creek Station. Bolivar Roberts then returned westward with the mochilas from the East and Eagan returned to Salt Lake City with the mailbags from the West. Service was finally restored on July 7 after an interruption of over four weeks.

These men of the Pony Express had faced abject terror in the wilderness of Nevada. But their devotion to duty, courage, toughness and stamina overcame this terrifying and seemingly hopeless situation. With very few exceptions, riders rode when ordered, and stalwart station attendants defended their stations and rebuilt demolished ones under constant threat of attack.

With the reopening of service on July 7, the mochilas began going through on schedule. Indian raids continued into the autumn. One such attempted raid resulted in a movie-like drama that ended with the U.S. cavalry charging over the hill, driving off the Indians and saving the fort at the last moment. Early in October 1860, Mike Holt and a rider named Wilson were at Eagan's Station. Eighty whooping and screaming warriors swooped down on the station. Holt and Wilson fired at them through windows and chinks in the wall until their ammunition ran out. Then the Indians broke down the door and demanded bread of the frightened men. The Indians took all available loaves and demanded more, pointing to the flour sacks. Holt and Wilson baked bread until the flour dwindled. At sundown the Indians drove a wagon tongue into the ground and tied the two men to it. Instead of more bread being baked, the men were to be.

Ceremoniously sagebrush was laid at Holt's and Wilson's feet. Indians danced around them howling and gesticulating. Unbeknown to the Indians, rider William Dennis was due from the West late that afternoon. Dennis was late, however, and the two men feared that the Indians had killed him. Finally he galloped toward the station, saw what was happening, and unseen by the Indians, quickly

reined around and sped to a column of sixty U.S. cavalrymen under Colonel E. J. Steptoe that Dennis had passed a few miles back. The Colonel ordered the bugler to play charge and the cavalry roared into the station yard shooting as they came. The Indians fled with a loss of twenty warriors and sixty horses. Holt and Wilson were rescued unscathed (or rather unsinged) except for badly shaken nerves.

The severe winter of 1860-61 also slowed delivery of Pony Express mail. This delay was partially solved by running pack mules over the trail to keep the snow packed down.

With such dangers along the route, it was inevitable that riders would perform many extraordinary examples of endurance and courage. For instance, one day at Midway Station, between Denver and the Missouri River, Jim Moore picked up the westbound mochila and galloped off. One hundred forty miles later he pounded into Julesburg, his home station. Here he learned that the rider who was to have delivered the eastbound mail had been killed the day before. The rider from the West had just arrived with the eastbound mail. In his mochila were important messages from California for Washington, D.C. Moore volunteered to carry the mochila and ten minutes after he had arrived at Julesburg, he was speeding eastward with the dispatches. (Normally he should have rested several hours.) Fourteen hours and forty-five minutes after he had left Midway Station, he returned there. Moore had ridden the round trip of 280 miles at an average of nearly eighteen miles an hour!

Other even longer rides are recorded. A young horseman of nineteen or twenty, Jack Keetley, apparently on a wager, carried his mochila eastward from Big Sandy Station in Nebraska Territory to Edwood, Kansas. Then he immediately rode westward toting the mail to Seneca, Kansas. Except when briefly changing horses at relay stations, he was continuously in the saddle thirty-one hours and rode 340 miles.

Robert (Pony Bob) Haslan, famous Pony Express rider. Picture taken around the turn of the century.

Courtesy Pony Express History and Art Gallery, San Rafael, California

Another outstanding feat of distance and endurance, with the added danger of Indian attack, was chalked up by Robert "Pony Bob" Haslan in May 1860. This ride was made during the initial phases of the Paiute Indian War previously related. His home station was Friday Station at the southern tip of Lake Tahoe. Pony Bob had picked up the eastbound mochila and was headed for Buckland's Station, his eastern home station seventy-five miles away when he learned of Indian massacres and attacks on relay stations.

He arrived safely at Buckland's Station, but here the eastbound rider refused to ride because of the Indian raids. Haslan agreed to take his place. So without rest he pounded eastward, changing horses at Sand Springs and at Cold Springs. At Smith's Creek, ninety-nine miles east of Buckland's Station, Jay Kelley relieved Haslan. Haslan had ridden 190 miles through hostile Indian-infested territory without rest. After a rest of nine hours, Pony Bob again jumped in the saddle and galloped westward with the westbound mochila. Arriving at Cold Springs relay station, he discovered that Indians had stolen the horses and killed the attendants. Here he fed and watered his somewhat spent mount and pushed westward. After he arrived at Buckland's Station, he changed horses and at once retraced his own run back to Friday Station on Lake Tahoe. In all, Haslan had ridden 380 miles through Indian country with only nine hours rest. The mail had been delayed but a few hours.

Other riders also made outstanding rides. Some have undoubtedly expanded with the telling and retelling, but even this does not detract from the courage, endurance and sense of duty of these men. The three rides described above have been confirmed as accurate.

After the Pony Express became thoroughly organized, it operated with almost clocklike precision. Except for the Paiute Indian raids that disrupted service in May and June 1860, and the severe winter of 1860-1861 that temporarily slowed the schedule, the ponies carried the mochilas on schedule. At first ten-day, then eight-day schedules between St. Joseph and Sacramento were maintained. In July 1860, the number of trips each way was increased from one a week to two a week.

Two through runs were spectacular, actually heroic. During the uncertain days of December 1860, when southern states threatened secession, a presidential message deemed important sped through to Sacramento in eight days in spite of heavy snows. Lincoln's inaugural address of March 4, 1861, was considered so important for Californians at that critical time of our country that Pony Express officials asked for an extra-speedy run. Keepers at relay stations led their horses two to three miles out to meet oncoming riders. And an extra-speedy run it was! The inaugural address came through in seven days and seventeen hours, an average of 10.6 miles per hour including all stops! On that particular trip, Pony Bob Haslan logged the fastest single ride. He thundered from Smith's Creek Station to Fort Churchill, 120 miles, in eight hours and ten minutes, an average of 14.7 miles per hour.

During its short life of eighteen months, the Pony Express carried 37,753 letters. It made 154 through runs each way (a total of 308) and logged 616,000 miles. With the completion of the transcontinental telegraph at Salt Lake City on October 20, 1861, the Pony Express reined to a halt.

The following editorial in the Sacramento *Daily Bee* on October 26, 1861, expressed contemporary nostalgia over the demise of the Pony Express:

FAREWELL PONY

Our little friend, the Pony, is to run no more. "Stop it" is the order that has been issued by those in authority. Farewell and forever, thou staunch, wilderness-over-coming, swift-footed messenger. For the good thou hast done we praise thee; and, having run thy race, and accomplished all that was hoped for and expected, we can part with thy services without regret, because, and only because, in the progress of the age, in the advance of science and by the enterprise of capital, thou hast been superseded by a more subtle, active, but no more faithful, public servant. Thou wert the pioneer of a continent in the rapid transmission of intelligence between its peoples, and have dragged in your train the lightning itself, which, in good time, will be followed by steam communication by rail. Rest upon your honors; be satisfied with them, your destiny has been fulfilled — a new and higher power has superseded you. Nothing that has blood and sinews was able to overcome your energy and ardor; but a senseless, soulless thing that eats not, sleeps not, tires not — a thing that cannot distinguish space — that knows not the difference between a rod of ground and the circumference of the globe itself, has encompassed, overthrown and routed you. This is no disgrace, for flesh and blood cannot always war against the elements. Rest, then in peace; for thou hast run thy race, thou hast followed thy course, thou hast done the work that was given thee to do.

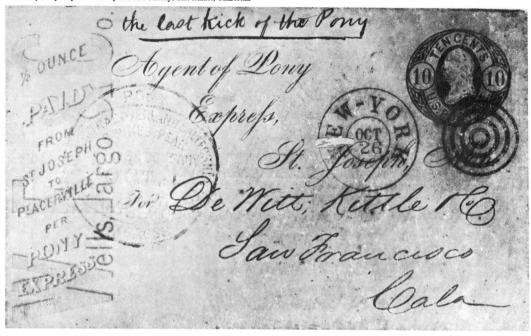

Last letter sent via the Pony Express.

A fitting epitaph to the riders appears in *The Story of the Pony Express* by Waddell Smith, great-grandson of William B. Waddell:

Many of these men were rough and unlettered. Many died deaths of violence. The bones of many lie in unknown graves. Some doubtless lie unburied somewhere in the great West, in the winning of which their lives were lost. Yet be it always remembered, that in the history of the American nation they played an important part. They were bold-hearted citizen knights to whom is due the honors of uncrowned kings.

What had this great venture gained for its promoters aside from renown? Bankruptcy. Neither mail contract nor subsidy for the Pony Express was forthcoming from Washington. Receipts from mail fell far short of meeting operating expenses. Some estimate Russell, Majors and Waddell lost $200,000, other estimates run as high as $500,000. The Paiute Indian War alone cost them $75,000. Ben Holladay had advanced the partners money to operate the Pony Express. As security he had taken a mortgage on the Central Overland California and Pike's Peak Express Company, owned by the three partners. By autumn of 1861 the three partners were in financial difficulty and in March 1862, Holladay, in order to recover his loans, took ownership of the Central Overland and Pike's Peak Express.

Because of the impending Civil War, Congress, in March 1861, granted a mail contract to the Central Overland to carry the mail six days a week from St. Joseph to Salt Lake City. Butterfield's Overland Stage on the southern route had been closed down because southern secessionists had captured some of his stock and equipment. The Federal government then asked him to transfer his remaining stock and equipment north to operate a daily stage and mail line between Sacramento and Salt Lake City on the central-overland route. But Russell, Majors and Waddell ironically lost the lucrative contract to carry mail on a daily basis between St. Joseph and Salt Lake City. This was the contract they originally wanted, and one reason the Pony Express was organized: to prove the feasibility of daily mail service on the central-overland route.

What had the Pony Express accomplished for the United States? It offered fast communication between Washington, D.C. and California during the uncertainties prior to the Civil War and during the hectic months after opening of hostilities. Three eighths of all Californians were sympathetic with the South, and devious efforts were made in California and in the South to bring California into the Confederacy. If California were lost to the Union, so would be Oregon, Nevada Territory and Washington Territory. Also the great wealth of gold and silver of California and Nevada were invaluable to the Federal government, as they would have been for the Confederacy.

During the interim after service on the southern route of Butterfield's Overland Stage was discontinued and before daily mail service on the central-overland route was established, the Pony Express offered a tenuous thread of communication between Washington, D.C. and California. It was the fastest means of communication, since mail by sea took about twenty-five days and the then existing stage schedule of Central Overland required at least that many days. Historians, including Bancroft, credit the Pony Express with greatly helping to retain California in the Union by rapidly delivering vital messages between Washington, D.C. and California.

If Russell, Majors and Waddell had been disturbed from their eternal rest by the worldwide excitement on July 20, 1969, when two Americans landed on the moon, perhaps a listener might have heard the following words from Waddell or Majors spoken to William Russell, "Bill, the Americans have just landed two men on the moon."

"Two Americans on the moon, you say? Now, boys, that doesn't surprise me one bit. What can't we Americans do?" That response would have been typical of Russell, the dreamer, promoter, organizer and optimist. His two enterprising partners would have nodded in agreement.

Chinese laborers, using handcarts, construct a dirt fill to replace a temporary wooden trestle of the Central Pacific Railroad in the Sierra Nevada.

9
Linking the West by Rail

By the beginning of the Civil War in the spring of 1861, the Far West was developing into an important economic empire. Two states (California, 1850 and Oregon, 1859) had been admitted to the Union; Washington was a territory. Mining, agriculture and logging were flourishing industries. The Comstock Lode, virtually a mountain of silver, had been discovered in 1859 in Nevada near the California border. Miners were toiling to disgorge from the earth this vast store of precious metal; nearby, lustful, bustling Virginia City mushroomed into a roaring mining camp of twenty thousand, where thousands of dollars changed hands at the flip of a card, or where a shooting fray hardly rated news on page three. In the Pacific Northwest stood millions upon millions of board feet of giant Douglas firs; in California redwoods towered and seemed to pierce the very sky—enough big and tall trees to stagger even the mind of Paul Bunyan. Gold continued to flow from the Sierra Nevada. Millions of acres of rich farmland in the Far West and the Middle West awaited the plow. The Great American Desert (so-called in the mid-1800's) stretched across the continent over a thousand miles with grasses thick enough and rich enough to nourish numberless cattle.

But as yet no steel rails bound the vast Western America to the more highly developed and more heavily populated East. Nearly two thousand miles of sparsely inhabited territory lay between the outposts of Eastern civilization along the Missouri River—St. Joseph, Independence, or Council Bluffs—and Sacramento, the traversing of which still depended on oxen, horses, or mules, grunting and tugging at rumbling wagons and stagecoaches. Steamers and tall ships were moving tons of freight and many thousands of settlers around the Horn or across the Isthmus of Panama. These beasts and the men who drove them, as well as the men who sailed ships, were doing their jobs well. But for the West to become well populated, economically balanced and socially more cultured required railroads connecting East and West.

Successful builders of railroads were men of extraordinary vision; they were bold, shrewd, grasping and they possessed a certain doggedness and perseverance not seen in lesser men. Some were dishonest; others considered the seemingly unlimited natural resources in the West as wealth to be exploited for personal gain. Yet many came to realize that the great wealth they created should be used to benefit the common man. Railroad men willingly took great risks to obtain their goals. For some these risks resulted in bankruptcy; others amassed and held on to great wealth. They were perhaps the strongest men in an age of rugged individualism and stupendous accomplishments by both entrepreneurs and laborers.

Since the early nineteenth century when steam was first harnessed to cars rolling on steel rails, men had dreamed of a railroad stretching from the Atlantic to the Pacific. With the discovery of gold in California in 1849 and the surge of people to the Far West, the fulfillment of this dream became urgent. But, as with the transcontinental stage lines, the location of a Pacific railroad became a political football delaying the laying of rails westward. Southerners favored a southerly route to California and Northerners desired northerly routes. St. Louis interests wished the railroad to run west on the 35th parallel; Kansas backed the 39th parallel; Chicago, the 42nd; other proponents projected a route along the 47th parallel connecting Lake Superior with Puget Sound. With the advent of the Civil War, an event that broke Southern power in Congress, the 42nd parallel was chosen with the blessings of President Lincoln and the rejoicing of Chicago and Omaha, cities that had much to gain from such a rail location. Accordingly, the Pacific Railroad Act was passed in 1862. This act authorized the Union Pacific to build westward from Omaha, and the Central Pacific eastward from Sacramento—their railheads to meet somewhere in the West at a place to be determined later.

The Central Pacific was big in size, big in accomplishments and big in leadership. Its builders, known as the Big Four, were inexperienced at railroad construction, but they were exceptionally capable men with a willingness to take great chances with their own limited capital. Regardless of the ruthless manner in which they may have operated their transportation empire after it was built, the construction of the Central Pacific stands as a monument to men willing to attain great goals against great odds.

The Central Pacific Railroad consumed more time and capital and overcame more formidable engineering obstacles than construction of any other early western transport system. Overwhelming obstacles of finance, competition, supply, logistics and labor plagued the builders. Nature was a formidable foe. The towering granite-walled fastness of the Sierra Nevada, whose lowest point above sea level is over seven thousand feet, stood as a barricade defying subjection.

The Big Four were Mark Hopkins, Collis P. Huntington, Charles Crocker and Leland Stanford. Originally there were five, including Theodore Judah. Stanford, thirty-eight, was a successful grocer and also governor of California. He attended

The Big Four and the man whose dream of a transcontinental railway they made reality: Top left and right, Mark Hopkins and Collis P. Huntington; center, Theodore D. Judah; bottom left and right, Leland Stanford and Charles Crocker.

California State Library, Sacramento

to political problems as they affected the Central Pacific in California. According to the shrewd Huntington, Stanford was the least capable of the partners. Huntington, forty-one, was in the hardware business with Hopkins. Huntington was the shrewdest businessman and financier of the Big Four. He also excelled at weaving through the political intricacies of Washington, D.C. It was he who raised the necessary millions to build the railroad. He was also its purchasing agent in the East. Hopkins at forty-nine was the oldest of the four. An accountant, office manager so to speak, he watched the shop while the others were off attending to sundry tasks. Hopkins was also more conservative than his three associates, a trait that acted as a balance against the impetuosity of his partners. Charles Crocker at forty was a big (over 250 pounds), hale, well-met extrovert, possessed of tremendous energy and drive. Some say he was a bully. In his own way he could be tough and shrewd. He oversaw construction of the railroad. The Big Four were men of differing temperaments, but in spite of these diversities which tended occasionally to set them at odds, they worked as a formidable, unbeatable team.

Although they were successful businessmen and modestly wealthy, they possessed only a mere fraction of the capital it would take to build a great railroad. They had connections, however, into areas of wealth and influence. And for these reasons, Theodore Judah, aged thirty-six, contacted the Big Four. Judah was a civil engineer who had engineered the Niagara Gorge Railroad and the Sacramento Valley Railroad. He possessed a fervent passion to build a transcontinental railroad. In 1861 he had discovered and made a preliminary survey of a practical railroad route over the Sierra Nevada and presented his plans to the partners.

The Sierra Nevada had seemed insurmountable to many potential railroad builders, but not to Judah, or to the Big Four after he had instilled them with his enthusiasm. History has given the glory to the Big Four, but the credit of initially inspiring and starting the great enterprise belongs to Judah. In 1863, for reasons that will be discussed later, he broke with the Big Four and left the Central Pacific.

The Central Pacific Railroad was organized June 28, 1861. At that time Leland Stanford was elected President; C. P. Huntington, Vice-President; Mark Hopkins, Secretary and Treasurer; and Theodore Judah, Chief Engineer.

To obtain financing for the railroad, Theodore Judah left in October 1861 for Washington. The Central Pacific could not have sent a more capable man. Judah knew his business, exuded enthusiasm and confidence, and could speak eloquently. Needless to say, he impressed congressmen. So much so that a special Congressional Pacific Railroad Committee appointed him its secretary. His first task was to convince the committee and Congress that financing the enormous job of constructing the Pacific railroad was too big for private enterprise. Most congressmen agreed with him and began hammering out the Pacific Railroad Act. To aid Judah and the committee to write the bill, Huntington joined Judah in the spring of 1862.

By June the bill was on President Lincoln's desk and signed into law. The act stated that the Central Pacific was to build eastward from Sacramento and that the Union Pacific was to build westward from Omaha. Each railroad was to get a 400-foot right of way and 6,400 acres for each mile constructed. The acres were to be on alternate sides of the right of way every other mile. To help finance construction, the government would loan the railroads $16,000 per mile on flatlands; $32,000 per mile on high, barren land; and $48,000 per mile in mountains. This advance was to be in the form of government bonds. The railroads in turn would have to sell these bonds (often at a discount) in order to raise cash. Interest of six per cent to purchasers of the bonds would be paid by the government. After thirty years, the railroads would have to repay the government the face value of these bonds plus six per cent interest. The bonds constituted a first mortgage on railroad property. To obtain these bonds, forty miles of flatland track had to be laid; in barren hills and mountains, twenty miles. Before the bonds could be issued, a team of government inspectors would have to inspect the tracks. In addition, the Central Pacific had to build fifty miles during the first two years and fifty miles each year thereafter or the government could confiscate the railroad.

Judah estimated that the first fifty miles would cost $3,221,496 or $60,450 per mile. Government loans to the Central Pacific amounted to only $16,000, or $32,000, or $48,000 per mile depending upon the terrain over which the right of way was built. To make up the difference between the actual costs of construction and government loans, the Big Four had to resort to additional means of raising capital. They issued Central Pacific bonds, but since they were a second mortgage on the railroad, these bonds sold at a fraction of their face value. The railroad also issued stock, but again, this security was extremely difficult to sell since financiers felt it highly improbable that track could be laid over the Sierra Nevada. So for much of their financing the Big Four used their own limited capital and borrowed on their personal credit, thus risking personal financial ruin.

Financing was not the only monumental problem facing the Central Pacific. Procurement of materials, most of which had to be purchased in the East and shipped to California, presented formidable problems. With the onset of the Civil War, Federal armies required prodigious amounts of ordnance. To move these supplies and the armies required locomotives and rolling stock. Ordnance required huge amounts of iron. C. P. Huntington

had to compete with Federal military demands as he procured locomotives, rails, rolling stock and all the sundry items needed for railroad construction. As he ordered materials for the first fifty miles of railroad, he found that inflation was rapidly rending askew his first cost estimates. And the Central Pacific faced continuous inflation during its years of construction. For instance, rails that cost $55 a ton in 1862 spiraled upward to $260 a few years later.

Sailing vessels carted locomotives and iron over 17,000 miles of perilous seas southward on the Atlantic, around storm-riven Cape Horn and northward to San Francisco. Freight rates were high; the *Young America* hauled the first locomotive, the *Governor Stanford,* around the Horn for $2,287, about 15 per cent of her cost. Insurance was also high and kept soaring as the war progressed because Confederate raiders roamed the high seas sinking Yankee ships with alarming regularity. The Central Pacific, however, never lost a cargo even though on occasion thirty vessels stowing railroad equipment were plying the high seas simultaneously.

Windjammers made the run from the East Coast to San Francisco on an average of 150 days. The fastest trip was 90 days; the slowest, 270. Usually six months elapsed from the time an eastern manufacturer finished a locomotive until it was placed in service in the Far West. Locomotives could be shipped by steamship to the Isthmus of Panama, across the Isthmus by railroad, and then by steamer to San Francisco in thirty days, but

The Central Pacific's GOVERNOR STANFORD. Note her head lamp had not yet been installed.

at exorbitant rates. Two urgently needed locomotives once took this route at a freight tariff of $37,000 each.

On January 8, 1863, the Central Pacific broke ground along the levee in Sacramento. Champagne bubbled and Governor Stanford orated. On this occasion the champagne bubbled for hours, much longer than politician Stanford's speech. The gaiety and hilarity generated mainly by the champagne numbed the minds of the attending multitude to the momentousness of the occasion. The Central Pacific was thus launched on a construction job over the most rugged mountain range yet to be conquered by rail. By October 1, eighteen miles had been graded, but until that time no rails, locomotives, or other supplies had arrived from the East. Five days later the *Governor Stanford*

arrived; and a few days later, rails and other supplies.

The Big Four, ever in need of money, looked forward to obtaining the $48,000 per mile for mountain construction, so the Central Pacific engaged experts to determine just where the flatland ended and the Sierra Nevada range began. A geologist, J. N. Whitney, determined that at Arcade Creek (which runs north and south seven miles east of Sacramento) the Sierra Nevada began. Although for many miles eastward from Arcade

224

Central Pacific Railroad yard in Sacramento in the 1870's.

Creek the terrain appears flat, from this point eastward a slight rise can be measured with instruments and the structure of the terrain is different on the east bank from that of the west bank. This decision was agreed to by E. F. Beale, the U.S. Survey General, and by J. F. Houghton, the California Survey General. Congress approved it and so did President Lincoln, although with tongue in cheek. But the Central Pacific was within its legal rights. Now it could claim $48,000 a mile eastward from Arcade Creek, but as a loan that was ulti-

mately repaid. And the rails first had to be laid to get the loan. Because the flatland east of Arcade Creek was declared part of the Sierra Nevada, the Big Four was accused sardonically of moving mountains—the Sierra Nevada—westward by several miles.

Labor shortages confronted the Central Pacific at the beginning and plagued it until near the end. Men preferred to work in the newly discovered silver mines of Nevada. Many went to work on the railroad to get a small stake or a free pass to the railhead and then proceeded to the Nevada diggings.

By the end of 1863, eighteen miles had been graded, four miles of track laid and a 192-foot-long bridge built over the American River. Expenditures were $705,000 for construction and equipment.

225

The four miles of track was a woefully long way from the forty required for receiving the government loans.

In the meantime a quarrel between Theodore Judah and the Big Four had erupted over the Central Pacific's proposed construction of a wagon toll road over the Sierra Nevada. This road was to connect Dutch Flat, a future Central Pacific station sixty-five miles east of Sacramento, with Carson City, Nevada. From Carson City lucrative trade with Virginia City could be tapped. This road would be shorter with cheaper freight rates for shippers than could be offered by the competitive Sacramento Valley Railroad.

The Big Four reasoned that their wagon road would bring in much needed revenue; but Theodore Judah believed that the Big Four were not really planning a transcontinental railroad, but merely a local line to serve Virginia City. Subsequent events proved him wrong, but to this visionary with his zeal for a Pacific railroad, practical measures such as a toll road seemed to him as detracting from the main goal. Then too, Judah was skeptical of Crocker's ability to oversee construction. Finally, Huntington gave Judah an ultimatum: either he was to buy out the Big Four or they would buy him out. He failed to raise the necessary funds, so the Big Four bought him out for $81,000 in Central Pacific Stock. With this stock and about $15,000 in cash, Judah and his wife left California in October 1863 for New York by steamer. Crossing the Isthmus of Panama, he contracted yellow fever and died a week after arriving in New York. He was succeeded as chief engineer by his twenty-eight-year-old assistant, Samuel S. Montague. Montague proved to be a gifted engineer and helped complete the dream that Theodore Judah had so desperately dreamed.

Courtesy Bancroft Library, University of California, Berkeley

Bloomer Cut on the Central Pacific just beyond Newcastle in the Sierra Nevada. This cut, eight hundred feet long and sixty-five feet deep, was dug by men drilling holes with hammers and chisels, filling the holes with black powder, blowing the powder and shoveling the debris by hand into wheelbarrows.

Construction in 1864 moved at a snail's pace because capital flow slowed to a trickle and construction of cuts and fills proved to be arduous. By the end of June 1864, thirty-one miles of track had been laid to Newcastle, but just beyond lay a wall of conglomerate rocks hard as concrete blocking the right of way. Going around it was impossible; cutting through it was slow, laborious work. Men drilled holes with hammers and chisels, filled the holes with black powder, blasted and shoveled the debris into wheelbarrows or one-horse dump carts, then more drilling, more blasting and more carting away, until finally a narrow cut 65 feet deep and 800 feet long sliced through the hill. Known as Bloomer Cut, it became famous for a while as a wonder of the world. Ahead of the cut lay a canyon 60 feet deep and 1,000 feet long that needed to be filled.

In July 1864 a financial crisis hit the Central Pacific. During one period of seventeen days, the company treasury had not one penny in it. Laborers were released and work almost stopped during the fall and winter of 1864. Costs were running higher than estimates. Then too, during the dark days of the Civil War, speculators raised the price of gold so that it took 285 greenback dollars to buy $100 in gold (about thirty-five cents on the dollar), and gold was the only medium of exchange in California. Government aid bonds also had to be discounted when converted to gold. This problem continually plagued the Central Pacific, but it was exceptionally troublesome in 1864. During the years of construction, the Central Pacific lost $7,000,000 converting paper securities to gold.

To help alleviate the railroad's precarious finances, Congress passed an amendment to the Pacific Railroad Act in 1864 that allowed the Central Pacific to issue its own bonds as first-mortgage bonds. (The original act had designated the government aid bonds as first-mortgage bonds; now they were second-mortgage bonds.) But again the railroad would have to sell its bonds at thirty-five cents on the dollar. Central Pacific stock at this time was almost worthless. Since government aid bonds could not be issued until a Federal-inspection team had approved the completed right of way, the Central Pacific received no government aid bonds in 1864. Probably because of pressures of the War, Lincoln delayed several months after completion of right of way before he appointed an inspection team.

The Big Four had borrowed on their personal credit to keep construction going. The following statement given by Crocker to one of historian Bancroft's reporters illuminates their problem:

We could not borrow a dollar of money on the faith of the company. Mr. Stanford, Mr. Huntington, Mr. Hopkins, and myself had to give our personal obligations for the money necessary to carry us from month to month. There was not a bank that would lend the company a cent. They had no faith in it.

We bought the first fifty miles of iron on our own personal obligations. We procured from D. O. Mills, who was personally known to each of us, a paper testifying to our responsibility and our honor, as men and as merchants, and that whatever we agreed to do, he believed that we would faithfully adhere to. That stands to Mr. Mills' credit in the early history of the railroad. Mr. Huntington bought the iron and gave our personal obligations for it and put up the bonds of the company besides as security, and we entered into an agreement that we would personally be responsible for ten years, to pay the interest of those bonds, as individuals.

Those were the responsibilities we took, and if we had not done it, there would have been no railroad.

On another occasion Mr. Crocker made the following remark about this period: "I owed everybody that would trust me and would have been very glad to have had them forgive my debts, and take everything I had, even to the furniture of my family, and to have gone into the world and have started anew."

In spite of their sharp personal differences, the Big Four rarely bickered; they cooperated and trusted each other and did what they could to keep the railroad moving. As one of them said, "We were all ambitious and each one dropped into his place and filled it."

Regardless of government aid loans and other means of raising capital, the Central Pacific could have failed had costs mounted to intolerable heights. The Sierra Nevada had yet to be conquered and unknown difficulties in laying track over the summit were ahead. Other large enterprises of the time had failed including those of Russell, Majors and Waddell and even Ben Holladay's, the stagecoach king. Failure for the Big Four, of course, would have meant personal financial ruin for each of them.

Not all was dark, however, the Central Pacific had now begun running passenger trains over its completed sections. The wagon toll road over the summit to Carson City had also been completed. These operations brought revenue from passenger and freight business. Of course, this income was not sufficient to solve the railroad's financial crisis. To help keep construction under way, Sacramento and Placer Counties had subscribed a total of $425,000 worth of bonds, but this money was rapidly used up. San Francisco County in April had agreed to pay the interest for twenty years at seven per cent on Central Pacific bonds. This gesture made them readily salable at par, but an enemy of the railroad obtained a court injunction forbidding San Francisco County to guarantee the interest. Finally, the problem was settled in January 1865 when the courts of San Francisco made an outright gift of $400,000 to the Central Pacific, but the railroad had already spent $100,000 in litigation fees.

The amended Pacific Railroad Act of 1864 doubled the amount of public land given the railroad. Instead of 6,400 acres per mile, 12,800 acres were donated and now the mineral rights were included for the railroad.

Early in 1865 the government had inspected Central Pacific's completed track and issued $1,250,000 worth of government aid bonds to the railroad. The bonds, however, were worth only $953,030 in gold. But this amount plus the $400,000 from San Francisco put life-blood into the company and construction started in earnest.

Charles Crocker, who superintended construction, had put J. H. Strobridge in command of construction. At thirty-seven Strobridge was tough and arrogant, a hard worker and a hard driver. Well over six feet tall, he gruffly enforced his orders by shouts — or by fists if necessary. He once said that "you couldn't talk to workers like a gentleman because workers weren't gentlemen; they were as near to brutes as you could get."

Crocker now called for five thousand workers, but three months after his order he had only eight hundred. After each payday this force dwindled by one or two hundred. Some got drunk, others drifted to the mines. Crocker now began thinking of hiring Chinese; he reasoned that since their ancestors had built the Great Wall of China, their descendents just might be able to lay his rails over the wall of the Sierra Nevada. Strobridge at first objected furiously, so did his Irish workers, but fifty Chinese were hired on a trial basis. Since many were five feet or under, small-boned, and lightweight, Strobridge thought that they would not be able to stand up to heavy labor, but he and Crocker were pleasantly surprised. Although the Chinese took smaller shovelfuls and pulled lighter loads on their carts, at the end of the day they had moved more dirt than their Irish counterparts.

The Chinese proved more docile, with less inclination to fight and argue than did Irish laborers; they drank tea, but no whiskey. When white foremen were absent, they did not goldbrick. Furthermore, they would work steadily twelve hours a day and not murmur about it. Crocker now began recruiting all available Chinese laborers in California. Then he contracted with a labor contractor to import more from the Canton region of China. By the end of 1865, five thousand men labored on the Central Pacific.

At first the Irish rebelled and attempted to run the Chinese off by force. Crocker then issued an ultimatum: either the Irish learn to work with the Chinese or the Irish would be replaced entirely by Chinese. This stratagem worked. The Irish stayed on and ignored the Chinese laborers.

Even Stanford learned to tolerate the men of China. As governor in 1862, he had delivered a speech in which he declared that the Chinese were the scum of the earth. However, being a good politician, he was able to change his mind when it became expedient for him to do so.

Labor contractors advanced passage money to the Chinese recruited in China — $40 by steamer, $25-$35 by sailing vessel. This fare had to be repaid out of wages at five per cent interest per month. Families or friends in China of each recruit underwrote those terms. Laborers from China were densely packed board the ships — some even on deck. Vessels sailed loaded 25 to 35 per cent over their passenger capacity. Many came on Pacific Mail Steamship Company ships that sailed from China to

Central Pacific Railroad Chinese construction crew camp somewhere in Nevada, CIRCA 1868.

California in thirty-five to forty days. Among the Chinese were a scattering of interpreters.

For feeding and housing, the Chinese formed themselves into gangs of twelve with a number-one man in charge. He collected their wages in a lump sum, deducted what was owed the labor contractor, distributed the rest and kept records. Each cook was paid by the Central Pacific, but the Chinese paid for their food, imported mainly from China. Their fresh meat consisted of pigs and chickens which they slaughtered on Sunday. They were paid $30 per month. Other arrangements at various times may have been made. Some sources mention that the Chinese paid for their cook, but received $35 per month. The Irish were paid $35 plus their board and room.

So prejudiced were many Californians against Chinese that upon landing in San Francisco, the Chinese were subjected to brutalities. Rowdies from the streets would beat them, or pull their braided hair as the Chinese marched to their quarters. These toughs were brave enough and able enough for this kind of harassment, but they were apparently reluctant to expend their energy working on the railroad.

After the Chinese were unloaded in San Francisco, they were taken under the wing of San Francisco Chinatown's Six Companies that controlled Chinese industry, business and social life. These Six Companies oriented the newly arrived laborers to the ways of the white world they were now entering.

Chinese laborers learned their work readily, generally from their number-one man. Others learned by observation and soon they knew enough English to understand elementary orders. They were diligent, steady and clean. Daily sponge baths were a habit with them as well as clean-laundered clothes. They endeared themselves even to gruff Charles Crocker, and they affectionately called him Cholly Clocka.

They had some vices, gambling being one. Another was smoking opium. At first the railroad officials tried to stop this practice, but later they apparently looked the other way if it did not affect construction. The Chinese reserved Saturday nights to go to what Strobridge referred to as "their seventh heaven."

The law allowed only the immigration of Chinese men, not women. To accommodate the Chinese laborers, wives and "sing-song" girls were smuggled into California by way of Vancouver, British Columbia and the port towns of the Olympic Peninsula. The Central Pacific, however, had nothing to do with the smuggling.

A Grass Valley newspaper ran an interview with one "HiKi" who was a supplier of girls for the Chinese laborers. He complained that he had to pay $550 in gold for one girl. This was too high he whined, because the girls generally died of consumption or mountain fever within a year. Even if they did survive longer, their "upkeep was oh, so very high." At the rate he paid for his girls plus their upkeep, "HiKi" must have kept them quite busy in order to eke out a living for himself!

With thousands of Chinese now swelling his labor force, Crocker concentrated on blasting out a roadbed alongside the perpendicular granite promontory known as Cape Horn rising fourteen

Southern Pacific Photo X632 by official Central Pacific photographer Alfred A. Hart, Sacramento

hundred feet above the American River. Chinese were placed in wicker baskets and swung down its side from the top with rope. Here, dangling over thirteen hundred feet above the river, they chiseled holes in the hard granite. After the holes were about eight inches deep, they were filled with black powder, packed and fused. The fuses were lit, signals shouted to hoist and up went the workman. Before a ridge suitable for a right of way was blasted, several hapless Chinese dropped into the abyss below — a broken wicker basket or conical hat floating on the river as mute evidence that something went amiss.

Beyond Cape Horn, Long Ravine had to be spanned with a bridge 120 feet high. The longest covered trestle in the world was erected as an approach to this bridge.

In spite of thousands of workers, work progressed slowly. By the end of October 1865, rails had been laid to Colfax only fifty-five miles from Sacramento. The hard granite and deep ravines of the Sierra Nevada were proving difficult, but barriers even more formidable lay ahead. Thirteen tunnels had to be blasted through the hardest granite encountered by man. Seven of these were clustered on a two-mile stretch along the top of the Sierra Nevada, and the longest at the Donner Summit was 1,659 feet long. Each tunnel would accommodate double tracks. Work on Summit tunnel began in October 1865. Freight wagons carted supplies beyond the railhead at Colfax to the Summit tunnel site. It was anticipated that one and one-half years would be required to bore the tunnel.

Working in three 8-hour shifts, Chinese labor gangs attacked the tunnel at each end. The granite was so hard that their chisels bounced off it and black powder at times merely rocketed an explosion out of the hole, but broke no granite. Each gang blasted only eight inches of tunnel a day.

Meanwhile, Crocker and Strobridge cried for more and more workers. By the spring of 1866, ten thousand Chinese and twelve hundred horses and mules worked at pushing the railroad over the Sierra Nevada. Four hundred kegs of black powder a day were exploded. Dislodging huge tree stumps on the right of way required two to ten kegs. This mighty army kept every machine shop, foundry, wagon maker, blacksmith shop, harness shop and sawmill busy within a radius of dozens of miles.

Meanwhile, to speed up work in Summit tunnel, a hole was bored from the top to track level. Chinese crews were lowered to the bottom and began working both ways. A steam engine, placed on top, hoisted debris. All winter they chiseled. As snows drifted twenty to forty feet deep, the intrepid Chinese dug tunnels to their work. Many crews rarely saw daylight.

During the winter, three thousand men worked and lived under the snow. Gangs burrowed to the bottom of drifts to lay foundations for trestles, bridges and retaining walls. So heavy and

As the Central Pacific—greatly in need of public and political support—inched its way into the High Sierra, it was a common practice to run excursion trains to various locations as the work advanced. Here excursionists are viewing the American River from Green Bluffs, seventy-one miles from Sacramento, shortly after the line was completed to this point in 1866.

Southern Pacific Photo X397 by official Central Pacific photographer Alfred A. Hart, Sacramento

deep were snow and ice on the right of way that forty-five hundred men were needed to keep the tracks cleared so that work trains could roll to the front, as the railhead was called. Work went on twenty-four hours a day on many projects—bonfires and lamps giving light to night workers.

During these winters, danger from avalanches was ever-present. With a sudden roar, tons of snow inundated and swept gangs, even camps, hundreds of feet down a mountainside. The thaws of the following spring exposed the dead, many still clutching their shovels or picks.

By late fall 1866, track had been laid only to Cisco, twelve miles short of the summit. Progress was so painfully slow and laborious that the Big Four became deeply concerned. At this time the Union Pacific was speeding across Nebraska and boasted that its tracks would reach the California border before the Central Pacific's. If both railroads had continued their current rates of construction, this could very well have happened. And if it did, the Central Pacific would be relegated to an extremely short, costly road with limited markets. The lucrative market of Salt Lake valley must be tapped and the easy, low-cost miles across Nevada and Utah must be covered if the Central Pacific were to be a financial success. So the Big Four stressed rapid construction regardless of cost.

Since Summit tunnel and other high-elevation construction required so much time, the Big Four decided to send crews over the summit by wagon and begin construction beyond the summit to the Truckee River. Trainloads of supplies for this project clattered to the railhead at Cisco. Late in November 1866, wagons, carts and sleds started the precarious transfer of materials over the

East portal of the Summit Tunnel which proved to be such a formidable construction obstacle for the Central Pacific in the Sierra Nevada.

233

Central Pacific teamsters hauling supplies to construction forces over the Dutch Flat and Donner Lake Wagon Road in 1867. This road built by the Big Four later became the highway to Reno.

snow-covered summit. Carts carrying nitroglycerin and powder went first, a mile ahead of the rest. Then three locomotives were loaded on three mighty sleds and hundreds of Chinese strained and tugged to pull them over the summit to the work area. Rails for fifty miles of track and forty railroad cars were carted by wagon. It was a prodigious undertaking in cold and snow, but it worked. On the eastern slopes of the Sierra Nevada, one thousand Chinese now hacked at the mountainside in blizzards and sub-zero cold to build a right of way.

But during 1866 ten thousand men and twelve hundred horses and mules were able to build only thirty-nine miles of track at a cost of $8,000,000. That year the Central Pacific received $1,600,000 in government aid bonds that brought only $1,100,000 in gold. The Big Four was plunging deeper into debt. By the end of 1866, huge costs forced them to spend $4,000,000 more than they would get in government bonds for some time to come. As the cost of building increased in the Sierra Nevada, the miles constructed diminished because of construction difficulties. And, ironically, government aid also diminished.

Of this period Huntington said, "I have gone to sleep at night in New York when I had a million and a half to be paid by three o'clock the following day, without knowing where the money was coming from. . . ."

The fall and winter of 1866 to 1867 was the wettest in years. So thick was the muck and mire that carts and wagons supplying crews working beyond the summit sank to their axles. Finally wagons and carts were abandoned and hundreds of pack animals carried powder, machinery, tools and food. An ever-present hazard was tons of mud that would suddenly slosh down hillsides burying the right of way, equipment and men.

Twelve thousand workers were now hacking at cuts and tunnels above Donner Lake. The seven miles between the Summit tunnel and the completed railroad to the east proved to be extremely arduous. In spite of the manpower thrown into these two years of labor, the seven miles were not completed by the end of 1867. This meant that

Pacific railroad construction supervisor stands on roadbed awaiting steel rails in the Great Plains.

235

Track-laying crew at work on the Pacific railroad in the late 1860's.

crews working to the east of the summit would again have to be supplied by wagon road during the winter.

Summit tunnel was bored through in September 1867 and the debris cleaned out by the end of the year, eighteen months after work had started on it. Black powder had proven so ineffective on the hard granite that the newly invented nitroglycerin was used. Few men realized how unstable this explosive was; many were injured and killed by premature explosions. Summit tunnel was the last hand-driven tunnel. Steam-power-driven drills were offered to the Central Pacific, but unfortunately, Crocker and Strobridge rejected them.

Meanwhile, the Union Pacific, after a slow and bungling start in 1863 and 1864, began laying track in 1866 west from Omaha, Nebraska Territory. The Union Pacific's rails were to follow the Platte River to Cheyenne in present-day Wyoming, veer about fifty miles northward at Laramie, then run westward in Wyoming through Rock Springs and Granger, and over the Wasatch Mountains to Ogden, Utah Territory, with the California border or

236

beyond as its goal. Under the direction of General Grenville M. Dodge, who became chief engineer for the railroad in 1866, construction gangs had laid 180 miles of track by September (an average of one mile per day). Dodge, one of the ablest engineers in the world and one who knew the trails of the West, was in complete charge of construction and surveying, a position of power he held in spite of occasional inner company wranglings with Union Pacific Vice President Thomas C. Durant.

Much of the Union Pacific's track was laid under the supervision of two of Dodge's lieutenants, the Casement brothers, David and General Jack. These brothers have been characterized as being small but tough, ruthless but genial, but above all competent. They knew their job and carried it out efficiently and expediently. Their work gangs were composed of ex-Union and ex-Confederate soldiers, hundreds of Irishmen, ex-convicts, sprinkled with a few muleskinners and mountain men.

General Casement developed one of the most efficient construction methods known to railroading. It was an assembly line on wheels variously based in Omaha, Chicago, and points further east where millions of dollars worth of material for the railroad was collected. Trains continually rushed supplies to the front. Here the dormitory train, consisting of many bunk and mess cars, stood on the furthest extension of the tracks. Next came strings of flatcars loaded with ties, rails, spikes and sundry hardware that were dumped along the grade. For the workmen it was hard, sweaty and dangerous work. But America was built by the sweat, sore muscles and calloused hands of such men working long hours under the burning sun of summer or in the bitter cold of winter. To expend such energy required huge amounts of food. Pitchers of steaming coffee, bowls of soup, plates piled high with roast meat, fried steaks, vegetables and potatoes burdened mess-car tables. Ravishingly hungry men sat devouring prodigious portions in a crude, primitive feast. There was no talk; men were there to eat. Sleep was no problem; they slept the deep, heavy slumber of physically exhausted men untroubled by the woes of civilization.

Union Pacific's Engine No. 1, the wood-burning GENERAL SHERMAN *was the granddaddy of all motive power in use on the Union Pacific Railroad. It was built by Danforth & Cooke of Paterson, New Jersey in 1864-65 and brought to Omaha by steamboat in June 1865.*

Courtesy Bancroft Library, University of California, Berkeley

Workmen were tough and hardy, but they loved whiskey, gambling and females (the harpy type preferred), the latter having set up shop near the work camps along with crooked gamblers and dispensers of whiskey. In Julesburg, Colorado, this sordid mixture of vice took over the town and seriously interfered with track laying. To solve the problem, Dodge ordered General Casement to clean up Julesburg. Three weeks later Dodge asked Casement if the gamblers were "quiet and behaving." Casement replied, "You bet they are, General. They are quiet and behaving out there in the graveyard." Presumably, the ladies of the night maintained a low profile—at least for a while. But the distractions of night life featured by hastily built railroad towns constantly attracted tough railroad laborers. Construction efficiency was disrupted by hangovers and injuries, or worse, suffered in endless barroom brawls. It was written, "They counted that day lost whose descending sun, saw no man killed or other mischief done."

Aware that the railroad which laid the most track would be the most profitable, General Dodge constantly reminded his crews, "Boys, I want you to do just what Jack Casement tells you to do. We've got to beat that Central Pacific crowd." The battle to lay the most track was on.

Union Pacific work train used during construction of the Pacific Railroad.

Plains Indians proved to be a constant menace for the Union Pacific. Most construction and survey gangs were Civil War veterans and were armed with rifles and sidearms. Many times they were forced to drop their shovels, picks, or instruments and take up firearms to fend off Indian attacks. General Dodge himself at times led survey gangs or construction crews to do battle with Indians. The United States Army furnished troops to protect workers, but their numbers were insufficient for protection at all times. If a company of troops were only a mile away from the scene of attack, the troops were ineffective because the skirmish would have ended by the time the soldiers arrived. Troops and workers alike suffered casualties. At one time Indian ambushes almost halted construction. Wyoming was a particularly dangerous area. Here a band of Indians swooped on a train and captured it, an act that precipitated twenty months of bitter and continuous warfare. The government then finally sent in more troops since, as U.S. Army General George Crook satirically remarked, "It was rather difficult to surround three Indians with one soldier."

Bear River City, Wyoming Territory, a hastily built construction town along the Union Pacific line. Such towns were notorious for violence, drinking, gambling and prostitution.

While the Central Pacific experienced tremendous difficulties battling the tough granite of the Sierra Nevada, it had little trouble with Indians. California Indians were docile, but not the Paiutes and Shoshones of Nevada. To make peace, Collis Huntington made a unique treaty with them. "We gave the old chiefs a pass each, good on the passenger cars, and we told our men to let the common Indians ride on the freight cars. ..." This arrangement worked much to the satisfaction of the Big Four, to the regalement of the Indians, and later to the amusement or consternation of Eastern passengers.

While the Union Pacific tracks were extended westward at the rate of a mile a day in 1867, by the

239

end of that year the Central Pacific tracks extended only forty miles further east from Sacramento. Twenty-five of these miles lay east of the troublesome uncompleted seven miles along Donner Summit. During the winter of 1867 to 1868, three thousand men were deployed on this seven-mile gap attempting to finish it.

That winter was as severe as the 1866-67 winter. Men again lived and worked under huge snowdrifts. Snow blocked twenty-three miles of track. The mountains shook as blasting powder blew huge hunks of ice and snow skyward off the right of way. Two thousand Chinese shoveled what snow and ice remained. Snow drifting fifteen to twenty feet deep over tracks in the Sierra Nevada had not been anticipated by Theodore Judah, nor by the Big Four. Unless this problem was solved, the Central Pacific would be blocked during most of the winter months. Snowsheds offered the only solution. To build them, loggers chopped down trees; sawmills ripped timbers. Hundreds of men feverishly worked on the sheds in 1867 and 1868. They erected seventeen miles of sheds west of Summit tunnel and ten miles beyond it. These sheds were effective but cost $2,000,000 an expenditure the Big Four had not foreseen.

By the spring of 1868 the Sierra Nevada was conquered and 146 miles of rail gleamed from Sacramento eastward at a cost of $23,000,000 in greenbacks or about $14,000,000 in gold. Government aid loans amounted to $48,000 per mile over mountains, but the actual cost was nearly $157,540 per mile.

California State Library, Sacramento

California State Library, Sacra

TOP: Interior of a snowshed on the Central Pacific Railroad high in the Sierra Nevada. BOTTOM: Central Pacific snowshed in the Sierra Nevada.

240

*Central Pacific snowsheds high in the Sierra
Nevada. From HARPER'S MAGAZINE, May 1872.*

Construction picked up speed in 1868 as crews moved into Nevada. Central Pacific survey parties had been previously staking out right of way across Nevada and Utah as the great track-laying race between the Central Pacific and the Union Pacific reached its climax. The latter railroad's survey parties were staking right of way across Utah westward into Nevada parallel to that of the Central Pacific.

The Big Four looked forward to hundreds of miles of comparatively easy track laying at much lower costs per mile, thereby offsetting their previous tremendously high costs per mile. Charles Crocker's New Year's resolution on January 1, 1868, was to lay a mile a day on an average in 1868.

This was one New Year's resolution that was kept. Ten thousand whites and Chinese pushed construction across the deserts of Nevada at a slightly better rate than a mile per day. At times they laid several miles per day; so did the Union Pacific moving westward across Wyoming and Utah.

In 1869 the Union Pacific laid eight and one-half miles in a single day. The Crocker forces, not to be outdone, prepared to lay ten miles in a day. To accomplish such a feat, required five 16-car supply trains, one train for each two miles of right of way. Crocker organized and sent the trains to the front. Strobridge marshaled his forces. On April 28, 1869, shortly after daybreak, horse-drawn wagons dropped ties on the graded right of way

Southern Pacific Photo X160 by official Central Pacific photographer Alfred A. Hart, Sacramento

and crews set them in place. Eight Irish track layers laid the track. Four men to a rail (rails that were 30 feet long weighing 540 pounds each), the track layers picked up their rails and carried them on the double from the special rail car and set them on the ties. Gaugers, spikers and fitters moved in. Track layers repeated their operation. Then hundreds of men with lifting rods and shovels leveled and ballasted the track. At seven in the evening, ten miles and fifty-eight feet of track had been added to the Central Pacific. The eight track layers and their two relief men had carried 1,970,000 pounds of rails. Before nightfall a locomotive was run over the track to test it and found the track to be sound.

Meanwhile, the Central Pacific's and the Union Pacific's graders were grading parallel to each other for miles in Utah. The Irish of the Union Pacific and the Chinese of the Central Pacific hated each other. Their mutual hatred often erupted into violence. The Central Pacific grade was on higher ground than the Union Pacific's. Occasionally huge rocks were rolled down on Union Pacific graders. The Union Pacific's Irish powdermen sometimes bored tunnels and set powder beneath the Central Pacific's graders. In the ensuing explosion, carts, horses and Chinese catapulted skyward. Central Pacific burial parties were kept busy. These games ended when Chinese powdermen undermined a group of Irish graders, an operation that gave Union Pacific burial parties some work.

"Camp Victory" as it appeared on April 28, 1869. The camp was appropriately named, for on that day eight brawny Irishmen, backed by a small army of Chinese and other experienced track builders, laid more than ten miles of rail to establish an all-time track construction record and win a $10,000 wager for their boss, General Construction Superintendent Charles Crocker. The job was directed by Construction Superintendent J. H. Strobridge, standing to the left on a flatcar.

Grading crews with supply wagons labor on the Pacific Railroad in the late 1860's (probably in Nevada or Utah).

243

This murderous and wasteful parallel grading was halted in early April 1869, when Congress and the two railroads established Promontory, Utah, as the meeting place for the two railroads. On May 10, 1869, the well-heralded laying of the golden spike ended the saga of building a transcontinental railroad. With the locomotives of the Union Pacific and Central Pacific almost nudging each other snout to snout, officials of both railroads and of the government stood by. Governor Stanford stood poised with a silver sledge ready to drive the last spike (a solid gold one) as a minister concluded his prayer. The hushed silence was broken as a

With locomotives of the Central and Union Pacific Railroads almost nudging, a crowd celebrates the completion of the Pacific railroad at Promontory, Utah on May 10, 1869.

all ready in the East." Every city in the nation heard the message, "Hats off!" Governor Stanford drove the golden spike into a polished laurel tie, touching an electric wire attached to the spike which sent a signal heard wherever telegraph wires reached throughout the land and where thousands

Getting ready to drive the last spike.

telegraph key clattered a message, "We have got done praying," and a reply clattered back, "We are of people had gathered to await the signal. The great Pacific railroad was completed. Celebrations erupted across the nation. A hundred guns were fired in Omaha, a four-mile-long parade wound through Chicago's streets, business in San Francisco was suspended for a day and bells clanged and whistles shrieked. Bunting was draped over ships and buildings. In Sacramento, headquarters of the Central Pacific, twenty-three locomotives lined the Embarcadero; twenty-three engineers simultaneously tied down twenty-three whistles for fifteen minutes.

The Big Four had won their stakes against great odds. Those easy miles of track laying across Nevada and Utah had appreciably lowered the overall cost per mile of the 690 total miles of the Central Pacific. Then too, the Central Pacific could tap the lucrative transportation business available in the Salt Lake valley. Without these advantages, the Central Pacific would have been extremely hard pressed financially; it perhaps would have

245

gone bankrupt as had many other ambitious transport systems, but it was not an easy victory for the Big Four. They overcame almost insurmountable obstacles to win their goal.

Amidst the jubilation, those faithful, hard-working Chinese laborers were not forgotten, at least not by a few. Shortly after the celebration at Promontory, Charles Crocker made the following remarks: "In the midst of our rejoicing, I wish to call to mind that early completion of this railroad we have built has been in a great measure due to that poor, destitute class of laborers called the Chinese—to the fidelity and industry they have shown...."

In May 1869 the *San Francisco Times* ran the following comments that were repeated in other California newspapers:

It is a significant fact that in the laying of the last rail on the Pacific Railroad, John Chinaman occupied a prominent position. He it was who commenced, and he it was who finished the great work; and but for his skill and industry the Central Pacific Railroad might not now have been carried eastward of the Sierras.

However, these words of praise were as voices in a wilderness of hate and prejudice. The Chinese in California were to be maligned and persecuted for many years to come.

An Atchison, Topeka and Santa Fe construction train in New Mexico.

Strangely missing amidst the enthusiastic celebration at Promontory during the wedding of the rails was any praise or even mention of Theodore Judah, the engineer whose inspiration and zeal initiated the building of the Pacific railroad. But even more strange is a painting of the Golden Spike ceremony that hangs in the California State Capitol at Sacramento. On this picture appears Theodore Judah who had died nearly six years earlier. Perhaps a twinge of conscience prompted one of the Big Four or someone else to ask the artist to include Judah as a physical participant in the ceremony, since he certainly must have been there in spirit.

Shortly after completion of the Pacific railroad, several other railroads began laying track westward to the Pacific. The Atchison, Topeka and Santa Fe obtained a land grant in 1869, and by 1872 had built from Topeka across Kansas to the Colorado border and then on to Pueblo, Colorado. Here the road turned south through Raton Pass. By 1880 its tracks reached Santa Fe. By 1884, after overcoming opposition by Jay Gould and Collis Huntington, this railroad reached San Diego and later Los Angeles.

The Kansas Pacific, led by one of the nation's most competent engineers, General William J. Palmer, obtained a Federal land grant and began laying track westward from Kansas City to Denver,

Locomotive at Gloria depot in present-day New Mexico. Photograph CIRCA 1880.

Courtesy Museum of New Mexico

arriving at that city in 1870. This railroad was incorporated into the Union Pacific as its eastern division, thus giving Kansas City and Denver direct access to the Pacific via a short line to Cheyenne, Wyoming, on the Union Pacific main line.

After completing the Kansas Pacific in 1870, General Palmer built one of the most scenic railroads in the world, the Denver and Rio Grande. He laid track south of Denver to Pueblo at a time when not enough people lived in southern Colorado to support a railroad. Palmer, however, was a man of vision; he foresaw the time when gold and silver would be mined in the Rockies and a railroad would be vital to these future mines. The Denver and Rio Grande was built without government subsidies.

Palmer proceeded to lay track through the Grand Cañon of Ar ansas to Leadville. He fought legal, and his construction crews fought pitched battles for this road with the Santa Fe Railroad. The road towered five thousand rocky feet upward from the river and at places was a mere thirty feet wide. Both railroads armed their construction crewmen and both built forts. After some exchanges of gunfire and a little bloodshed, the right to use the Cañon was decided legally in favor of Palmer. He was a man who could say, "The decision is made, gentlemen. It's going to be done!" and knew what he was talking about when his engineers said that building a pass over the Rockies via the Grand Cañon of Arkansas was impossible. His laborers loved him. They were will-

The portals of Grand River Canyon on the scenic Denver and Rio Grande Railroad.

ing to dangle over precipitous cliffs by ropes to blast footholds in the solid perpendicular rocks. The Denver and Rio Grande made large profits serving Leadville, one of the world's greatest bonanza silver camps. Over $2,000,000,000 worth of precious metal was shipped out of Leadville. Palmer built several branches to the mining area, and in the early 1880's laid track to Salt Lake City, thereby giving Denver yet another outlet to the Pacific via the Central Pacific.

The Pacific Northwest was connected with the East by steel rails upon the completion in 1883 of the Northern Pacific Railway that ran from Chicago through Wisconsin to St. Paul, Minnesota; through central North Dakota, Montana, Idaho and Washington. At first the line ran down the Columbia River to Portland and northward to Tacoma. Later Seattle was its terminus with a route over the Cascades to Spokane. In 1884, the Union Pacific completed its tracks to Portland, Oregon; via Boise, Idaho; from Ogden, Utah.

The Central Pacific, meanwhile, was not content to stop with its line from Sacramento to Promontory. It began buying short lines in California including the California Pacific that ran from Sacramento to San Francisco Bay; the Western Pacific that ran from San Jose eastward to the San Joaquin Valley; and the San Francisco-San Jose Railroad running between these two cities. The Central Pacific also completed its California-Oregon line north to Portland, Oregon, and built southward to

Los Angeles. Its Western Pacific line was extended to meet Central Pacific tracks being laid southward in the San Joaquin Valley, thus connecting San Francisco with Los Angeles. The Big Four also built another line east, the Southern Pacific, on a route eastward from Los Angeles to Yuma and Phoenix, Arizona, to El Paso, Texas, terminating at New Orleans. The Southern Pacific was originally organized by San Franciscans in the 1860's. These citizens believed (and so did Collis P. Huntington) that a southern route to New York would be more practical and more economical to operate than the Central Pacific's route for two reasons (1) winter snows and (2) the higher altitudes of the Northern Sierras and Rockies up which pulling trains would be more costly. Therefore the Big Four quietly purchased the Southern Pacific in 1868. Congress had given the Southern Pacific and the Texas and Pacific, led by Tom Scott, land grants to build a southern east-west railroad. A battle now was joined between the two lines. Quickly the Southern Pacific built down the San Joaquin Valley to Los Angeles without a land grant, but on the hope Congress would grant one (which it did in 1880). The Texas and Pacific was backed by San Diego and the Southern Pacific by Los Angeles. Each city offered land to interest the railroads. But Los Angeles offered the Southern Pacific a large amount of money and the port at Wilmington.

The two railroads fought each other in court, in Congress and in construction. If the Southern Pacific could lay more track eastward than Scott could westward, the advantage would be with the company that had laid the most track. The Texas and Pacific was troubled financially and asked

249

Congress to guarantee interest on Texas and Pacific's bonds. The Southern Pacific fought this proposal with the result that neither company had its bond interest guaranteed. Southern Pacific readily raised enough capital while Scott could not, so he was unable to build west of Texas. After the Southern Pacific reached and bridged the Colorado River, Congress allowed it to complete its line to New Orleans, which it did in 1883. The Central Pacific now had a monopoly in California rail traffic and, except for the Santa Fe, controlled most traffic eastward.

By the mid-1880's, most of the West was linked by rail to the East, and also within itself by rails to the north and to the south. True, other transcontinental railroads traversed the nation later, such as the Great Northern and the Pacific-coast extension of the Chicago, Milwaukee and St. Paul. Numerous smaller lines and branch lines crisscrossed the West. By 1885 most of the Old West had been linked by rail.

Two kinds of old western railroads stand out as unique—logging trains and mining trains. Without them, western lumbering and mining industries could not have moved their products to market in such huge quantities. Most logging railroads were owned and operated by lumber companies. Main-liner crews with their good equipment, regular schedules and fast speeds scorned the logging pikes as beneath the dignity of railroading. Nevertheless, the early, lowly "bush" lines required skill and plain intestinal fortitude to operate. Tracks were hastily laid over unballasted ground; their grades of over four per cent (twice) those on regular lines) would fill a regular engineer with disconcertion. Logging engines were geared which enabled them to slowly growl, chug, pant and puff up the timbered mountains on rails that soared above the clouds at times, and across tall trestles that squeaked and swayed over gaping canyons. When steam proved too weak to pull a log-laden consist over cloud-shrouded grades,

cables hooked to donkey engines tugged on the hissing locomotive. Downgrade, braking required great skill matched by great courage. Ends of huge logs rested on two 4-wheeled trucks thus forming a logging car. This type of equipment precluded the use of air breaks, so brakemen wearing caulk-shod boots scrambled over swaying logs setting temperamental hand brakes. They skillfully braked their consist of logs down steep hills and around sharp curves. Since automatic safety couplers will not work on this equipment, the primitive lock-and-pin couplings on these trains added to the danger of those early day logging crews. Engineers on the scheduled commercial runs drove their locomotives, but not so with engineers on the logging trains; they nursed their engines and consists with rare skill over every mile of tortuous logging rails. In later years, logging railroads developed larger and better equipment, but just as they supplanted the bull teams and skids in old western lumber operations, so did modern logging trucks replace most of the logging railroads until today few remain.

Mining operations began hauling ore in rail cars early in the Old West and still haul it today. Since mining was a substantial enterprise in the Old West, it was an important impetus for creation of such trunk lines as the Union Pacific, Central Pacific, the Denver and Rio Grande and the many short-haul railroads (such as famous, now-extinct Virginia & Truckee) that serviced rollicking Virginia City, Nevada, and the mountain of silver standing nearby. Also created were railroads such as the Bullfrog & Bently; Globe and Northern; and Eureka & Palisade that chugged and puffed their "hour upon the stage and then are heard no more." Extinct mining railroads pulled their consists ladened with ore from such exotically named ghost-mining towns as Rhyolite, Cripple Creek, Curay, Lizard Head Pass, Goldfield, Pioche, Tonopah, and Silver Bow. The impact these logging and mining roads made on the economy of the Old West and the color and romance of these old trains still lingers.

The transcontinental railroads helped build the West into a great empire. They brought the East and the West nearer together in time. New York was now only seven days from San Francisco. Easterners and westerners could now more freely mingle and exchange ideas; products of the East such as cookstoves, safety lamps for miners, alarm clocks, derby hats, flush toilets, gang plows, coal-oil lamps, sewing machines, stylish ladies' and men's clothing, and numerous other marvels of the machine age now became more readily available in the West. From the West, railroads shipped to eastern markets lumber, precious minerals, beef cattle, farm produce and products from the Orient. The railroad linked the East and the West in closer bonds that tended to make each section more similar socially and economically; the West ultimately ceased being a backward province of the nation.

Railroads spurred emigration westward. Many roads possessed thousands of acres of Federal land grants that they wished to sell to settlers. Then too, in order to be more profitable, railroads needed towns dispersed along their routes. To settle their lands and build towns, the railroads carried out elaborate proselytizing campaigns in the East and also in Europe. The West was portrayed as the land

The Union Pacific Railroad urges farmers to purchase low-cost railroad land in Nebraska.

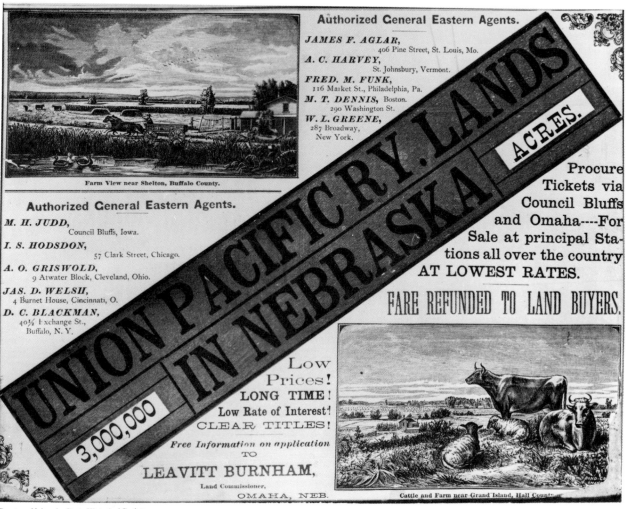

THE

UNION PACIFIC RAILROAD COMPANY

Proclaims to

FARMERS

Who have spent years grubbing stumps or picking stones, or who pay annually as much rent
as will purchase a farm in Nebraska; to

Mechanics

Who find it hard work to make both ends meet at the end of a year's toil, and to EVERYBODY
wishing a comfortable home in a healthy, fertile State:

NEBRASKA!

Is destined to be one of the leading Agricultural States in the Union, and greatest beyond the
Mississippi; Because,

1st. The land does not have to be cleared of stumps and stones, but is ready for the plow,
and yields a crop the first year.

2d. The soil is a deep loam of inexhausible fertility.

3d. Water is abundant, clear and pure.

4th. The productions are those common to the Eastern and Middle States.

5th. Fruits, both wild and cultivated, do remarkably well.

6th, Stock Raising is extensively carried on and is very profitable.

7th Market facilities are the best in the West. The great mining regions of Wyoming,
Colorado, Utah and Nevada are supplied by farmers of Nebraska.

8th. Coal of excellent quality is found in vast quantities on the line of the road in Wyoming,
and is furnished to settlers at cheap rates.

9th. Timber is found on all streams and grows rapidly.

10th. No fencing is required by law.

11th. The climate is mild and healthful; malarial diseases are unknown.

12th. Education is Free.

TICKETS By way of Columbus and Chicago and St. Louis will be furnished at reduced
rates for persons desiring to prospect and select lands in Nebraska.

☞ To those who purchase 160 Acres of the Company on Cash or Five Years' Terms, a
rebate not to exceed Twenty Dollars, will be allwoed on price paid for Ticket.

FREIGHT: Reduced Rates given on Household Goods, Live Stock, Farming Tools,
Trees and Shrubbery, in Car Loads, for Settlers' use.

LEAVITT BURNHAM, Land Commissioner U. P. R. R.

The Union Pacific Railroad and Branches.

**Best Equipped, Most Direct and Popular Route to the Rich Mineral Districts,
Grazing and Farming Regions and to the Famous Pleasure Resorts and
Hunting Grounds of the Rocky Mountain Country.**

THE COLORADO CITIES AND RESORTS are best reached via the UNION PACIFIC
RAILROAD, Colorado Division. By far the most direct, pleasant and popular route to
Ft. Collins, Estes Park, Boulder, Golden, Denver, Central, Georgetown, Idaho Springs and
Leadville. Best Hunting, Fishing and Pleasure Resorts in sight of the Union Pacific.

THE BLACK HILLS.—The Sidney Stage Line, in connection with the Union Pacific Railroad, affords the shortest, quickest, and the only safe and pleasant stage journey to Rapid
City, Custer, Rochford, Deadwood, Crook City, and other prominent points in the Hills,
being the only line passing along the entire length of the Hills.

UTAH, IDAHO AND MONTANA.—The UNION PACIFIC, connecting with the UTAH
CENTRAL at Ogden, for Salt Lake City, Frisco, Leeds, and all points in Utah, and with the
UTAH & NORTHERN, for the Snake and Salmon River Mines, as well as Helena, Deer
Lodge, Virginia, Butte City, Glendale, Bozeman, and all the best mining and Agricultural
regions in Montana.

CALIFORNIA, ARIZONA, OREGON AND WASHINGTON.—The UNION and CENTRAL PACIFIC RAILROADS form the only line across the continent, to all points in
Nevada, California, Oregon, Washington; and in connection with the Southern Pacific,
affords a through rail route to the heart of Arizona; or in connection with the finest Steamship lines, to China, Japan and India.

For information concerning the Resources, Climate, and other attractions of the Great West,
address **THOS. L. KIMBALL**, General Passenger and Ticket Agent U. P. R. R., Omaha, Neb.

RIGHT: Railway shipment ad for cattle, 1877.   LEFT: Union Pacific Railroad offers farmers and others low-cost railroad-owned land in Nebraska.

CATTLE MEN READ THIS!
Great Inducements to those who wish to
Ship Cattle on the U. P. Railroad !!

Having entered into special arrangements with the U. P. R. R. Company, by which I can ship Cattle East at greatly reduced rates, and having selected a point between Carter and Church Buttes Stations some ten miles East of the former place, near the junction of the Big and Little Muddies, and having Constructed Commodious Lots and Extensive Enclosures, and the Company having put in a Switch capable of holding 40 Cars, I will be Prepared to Commence Shipping on or before the 15th of the Present Month, and will be able to promptly ship any Number of cattle that may be Offered.

Persons driving Cattle from Montana and Idaho, and passing by Soda Springs and the Bear Lake Settlements, will cross over from Bear River to the head of Little Muddy and follow down that stream, over a good road, to within a mile and a half of the junction of the Little with the Big Muddy, where they will cross a bridge and find a rich pasture, extending many miles; good water & perfect security for their stock, within convenient distance of the stock yards.

The cattle yards are in an enclosure of some 400 acres, and stock scales and all conveniences for shipping will be furnished. If parties do not wish to ship themselves, I will purchase, at good prices, all shipping cattle that may be offered. As cattle are now bearing excellent prices East, it would be well for persons to bring their Cattle forward as soon as possible.

For further particulars, address

W. A. CARTER,
Fort Bridger, Wyo. Ter.

Fort Bridger, July 2, 1877.

W. G. Ay
Clerk, Operating Dept
Ogden, Utah.

of opportunity; farmland was cheap and fertile; jobs were plentiful. Much of this advertising was true; however, many emigrants were to find disappointment in the West. The railroads offered attractive fares to emigrants. For a small fee, a whole boxcar could be rented. To meet the demand for cheap travel to the West, "Zulu" cars were placed on slow trains. These cars had berths, but no bedding. Emigrants could cook their meals on a cookstove located at one end of the car. On the other end was a primitive washroom. Thousands upon thousands of emigrants rolled westward in these cars. New towns sprouted along the railroad lines; cities grew. Some existing towns, however, were not blessed, but blighted by the railroads because the rails bypassed them for one reason or another—in most cases because the towns or

cities refused to subsidize a railroad with money or land. Even ministers of the gospel and their congregations were induced by railroad companies to move westward and establish new homes somewhere in the West.

Between the years 1870 and 1895, the population of the United States increased by 31,000,000. Of these, one third were foreign immigrants. Many came from Europe with Germans comprising the largest ethnic group by far. It is not known how many of these people the railroad brought to the West, but it was in the millions. It is known that in the area served by the Burlington Railroad, mainly Iowa and Nebraska, over 3,000,000 people of foreign birth lived there. Thus the make-up of the continental United States was reshaped by the iron horse.

A Central Pacific train rounds Cape Horn high above the American River in the Sierra Nevada. It was here that Chinese laborers hung over cliffs in baskets to hack out the right-of-way. From Frank Leslie's ILLUSTRATED NEWSPAPER, *August 27, 1878.*

10

Early Western Trains

With the completion of the Pacific railroad, passengers could now travel the nearly three thousand miles between New York and Sacramento in seven days—much faster and much more comfortably than jolting and pitching for twenty days and nights on the Central Overland Stage between St. Joseph and Sacramento. And travel by railroad was much freer from diseases that plagued the twenty-four-day steamer voyage via the Isthmus of Panama.

Not only was passenger travel time to the Far West reduced; shipment of freight from the East Coast to Sacramento and San Francisco was reduced to ten days as compared with the three months or more required for freight shipped around Cape Horn, the route that had carried the bulk of the Far West-bound freight prior to 1869. The Pacific Railroad also shipped freight across the continent in less than half the time required by the Panama steamship route and at considerably less expense. Gold shipments now moved east by rail from the bank vaults in San Francisco, as did express and first-class mail. Panama steamers, however, still continued to carry passengers, some freight, and second- and third-class mail; much slow freight still continued around the Horn aboard sailing vessels.

The volume of passenger and freight traffic over the Central Pacific proved disappointing to the Big Four. They had anticipated a large freight and passenger business to the Orient—business that would originate in Europe, cross the Atlantic, be transshipped across the United States by rail to San Francisco, and there be reloaded on ships bound for the Orient. On the other hand, with the completion of the Suez Canal in 1869, much of this anticipated business was shunted to the Far East by way of this man-made waterway. In addition, the population of the West Coast at this time was just not sufficient to create large volumes of business for a transcontinental railroad. For these reasons, the Big Four began buying potentially competitive railroads in California in order to monopolize what business there was in that state.

Immediately after the last spike had been driven at Promontory, two passenger trains, one

MARYSVILLE, YUBA CITY, COLUSA DIRECTORY, 1870.

eastward and one westward, were put into service between Omaha and Oakland. The Pacific Express rolled westward; the Atlantic Express, eastward.

These trains were pulled by colorful and ornate locomotives, their bluish-black boilers trimmed with gleaming strips of brass; their polished brass bells, sandboxes and domes glinting in the sun. Driver wheels were fire-engine red. Gold, red, or green filigree embellished large oil headlights. Smoke billowed from towering diamond-shaped smokestacks. Along the sides of the tenders blazed locomotives' exotic names in gold letters: *Goliath, Samson, Blue Bird, Hercules, Sultan, Juno,* or *Flyer.* The consist included baggage, express and mail cars, passenger coaches, smokers, diners, and sleeping cars, all painted bright yellow. Thus across prairies and mountains leisurely swayed, clattered, puffed and whistled what must be one of the most ornate forms of transportation ever—the Old Western express train—a

257

fusion of resplendent colors and mellifluous sounds.

Four days and seven hours after boarding an eastbound train in Sacramento, passengers arrived at Omaha; a day later at Chicago; and two days later at New York. Trains averaged eighteen to twenty miles per hour including stops. A special express train hauling Charles Crocker, the hard-driving construction genius of the Big Four, made a run from Sacramento to Promontory in a record time of thirty-three hours and forty-five minutes averaging nearly twenty-one miles per hour. But then, Charles Crocker was aboard, a fact that probably motivated the engineer to strain his boilers. Mark Twain reckoned time and distance between Sacramento and New York differently—to him it was equal to 211 games of euchre, 173 drinks and 117 cigars.

Passengers traveling westward boarded the Pacific Express at Omaha. If they paid extra fare, they could ride in Pullman Palace Sleeping Cars. The latest in luxury, their interiors were upholstered in plush silk velvet. Velvet curtains with braid and tassels draped the windows. Ornate silver lamps hung from the ceiling. Floors were carpeted with large floral designs in rich primary colors. To furnish heat, water pipes connected to a boiler on a stove at the end of the car ran under the seats the length of this deluxe coach. This system of heating with hot water pipes was more efficient and much more comfortable than merely a stove at one end of the car as most railroad cars were then heated.

On the sleeping cars, colored attendants every evening converted seats into upper and lower berths. Damask curtains hung along the aisles to

provide privacy. Men's lavatories were located at one end of the coach; women's at the other. Filtered, iced drinking water was stored in a tank near the lavatory and all aboard used a common drinking cup suspended from the tank. Some sleeping cars had kitchens and food was served on tables inserted between the seats. Other cars were constructed solely as diners, but day-coach passengers bolted down their meals at station restaurants while the locomotive took on fuel and water. Only half an hour or less was allotted to order, eat and reboard the train. Some passengers brought their own food and ate in the coaches.

Ad for the grand opening of the Union Pacific's Platte Valley route.

The bill of fare on some diners, especially those east of Promontory on the Union Pacific, was quite elaborate. W. F. Ray, a contemporary Englishman riding on the Pacific railroad in 1870, described his selection of dishes:

The choice is by no means small. Five different kinds of bread, four sorts of meat, six hot dishes, to say nothing of eggs cooked in seven different ways and all the seasonable vegetables and fruits, form a variety from which the most dainty eater might easily find something to tickle his palate and the ravenous to satisfy his appetite. The meal is served on a table temporarily fixed to the side of the car and removed when no longer required. To breakfast, dine, and sup in this style while the train is speeding at the rate of nearly thirty miles an hour is a sensation of which the novelty is not greater than the comfort. An additional zest is given to the good things by the thought that the passengers in the other cars must rush out when the refreshment station is reached and hastily swallow an ill-cooked meal.

Although passenger coaches were much more comfortable than stagecoaches, a railroad passenger today would consider them substandard unless he were a railroad buff riding on a special excursion for novelty and nostalgia. Mr. Ray was impressed with the coaches, but not with the roadbed:

In America the ingenuity of the directors seems to be exerted for the comfort of the poorest classes. The carriages are large and well ventilated, with stoves for wintry weather and venetian blinds and sun shades at every window in Summer. The seats are roomy and well cushioned. For parcels or small packages there are plenty of pegs and wire racks, and there is a barrel of filtered water, iced in Summer, at one end of the car. Notwithstand-

259

Interior view of a Pullman Palace Sleeping Car used on the Pacific railroad during the 1870's. This car was converted into a diner during the day.

Interior of an old Pullman dining car, CIRCA 1870. The car was used for dining during the day and sleeping at night.

ing all this, there is room for improvement. The jumping and jolting on many of the lines is terrible. The rails are laid upon big wooden sleepers which seem often of needless irregularity in level. Great is the dust and glare in hot weather and the draft in cold weather. Except in the larger towns and at the hotel stations the depots are generally very plain wooden structures, with few fixings and at night cheerless and ill lighted.

The excitement and adventure of the long journey across lonely prairies and vast mountains to the Far West began at Omaha as passengers boarded the Union Pacific trains and the conductor shouted, "All aboard!" Then several long, sobbing wails of the whistle echoed across the plains and brake fittings squeaked as brakemen released them. (Air brakes had not yet been installed on trains.) The locomotive lurched forward and as the slack of the primitive couplings snapped taut in jolting sequence, each car in turn was severely jarred so that passengers at times were pitched from their seats. As the Pacific Express swayed westward, wheels clicked over rail joints in rhythmic cadence and dust welled upward from the roadbed during the dry season, since crushed rock was not yet in general use as ballast. In winter, prairies stretched to the horizon under a white blanket, or wind-driven snow blurred the countryside. On the Great Plains, sunsets are unsurpassed. The western sky aglow with rich reds gradually turns to deep crimson. Telegraph poles and distant hills form black silhouettes against the flaming heavens. Occasionally, awesome prairie fires reddened the night sky. At eventide, passengers gathered around an organ installed in some Pullmans and sang the sentimental songs of

*Pullman Palace dining cars on the Central
Pacific, CIRCA 1870.*

*Interior of a Pullman Palace Car on the Pacific
railroad. From HARPER'S MAGAZINE, January 1859.*

Stephen Foster or favorite hymns. As the express rolled westward through the night, passengers retired to the privacy of their berths, each with his own reverie about the exotic miles of prairies, mountains and deserts that lay ahead, and with the wail of the locomotive whistle, the puffing of steam and the rhythmic clattering of the wheels to lull them asleep.

When deer and antelope scampered near the right of way, coach windows banged upward as male passengers drew pistols and fired at the animals, but hitting a deer or antelope with a pistol from a moving train was difficult. On occasion, however, trains did halt to load venison for the diner. Buffalo still roamed the West. Occasionally huge herds thundered across the tracks and stalled trains for hours, presenting hunters with an opportunity to add buffalo meat to the menu.

Mr. Ray, the English traveler, as did many others, found the trip adventuresome:

To nearly everyone the journey is a new one partaking of the character of a daring enterprise. Four miles from Omaha the first stop is made. The journey is now fairly begun and everyone is on the lookout for new scenery and strange adventures. The first real sensation is obtained at Jackson, a small station a hundred miles from Omaha. Here many of the passengers see genuine Indians for the first time. They are Pawnees and we are told that they are friendly Indians, being supported by the United States Government. They may be friendly at heart but they are bloodthirsty in appearance. At Grand Island station the train stops and the passengers are allowed a half hour for supper. On leaving this place the traveler is told to keep his eye peeled for buffalo. The event of the succeeding morning was halting at Cheyenne for breakfast which was a plain but wholesome meal and has the charm of novelty in the shape of antelope steaks.

Interior of a day coach on the Pacific railroad, CIRCA 1870.

Frank Leslie's ILLUSTRATED NEWSPAPER illustrates the discomforts of travel in 1878.

Passengers aiming guns from car platforms and windows hope to supply this early Pacific railroad train's diner with fresh buffalo meat.

Two days and eight hours after leaving Omaha, the Pacific Express rolled into Promontory, Utah, where the Union Pacific ended and the Central Pacific began. In this crude hamlet in a wilderness of sage-covered hills hundreds of miles from civilization, passengers changed trains. Westbound travelers riding plush Pullman Palace cars of the Union Pacific transferred to Central Pacific's almost equally plush Silver Palace sleeping cars. (Except for special occasions, Pullmans did not run on the Central Pacific until 1883.)

The Central Pacific's sleepers also offered the latest in finery—deep-red velvet coverings, bevel-edged mirrors, Turkish carpets, walls of polished walnut and bird's-eye maple. Silver oil lamps attached to the ceiling emitted a yellowish glow at night. Each berth also was equipped with a small oil lamp. Unlike the hot-water heating system on some deluxe Pullmans, the Silver Palace sleeper was heated like most railroad cars of the day by coal and wood stoves located at the end of the car. In winter passengers seated near the heaters roasted while those seated away from them froze.

The changing of trains at Promontory was a unique experience, if not an outright adventure. For some the switch literally changed their lives; for others it was an education of a sort. Railroad officials warned passengers to change trains quickly, but for some the warning served only to whet their appetites to savor the allurements of Promontory.

Upon this planet no place was ever like Promontory, neither before nor after Promontory. Even ancient Sodom and Gomorrah would have had little chance competing with Promontory for the dubious distinction as the foremost den of iniquity. A Nevada newspaper, the *Independent*, of Elko, itself a place known for vice, printed this about Promontory, "Sodom had its few, particular besetting sins, Promontory presents a full catalogue, with all modern improvements, clips, angles, and variations. The low, desperate, hungry, brazen-faced thieves there congregated would contaminate the convicts of any penitentiary in the land." Its notoriety was far out of proportion to its

Promontory, Utah, the raucous town where the golden spike commemorating the completion of the first transcontinental railroad was driven on May 10, 1869, and where passengers changed trains between the Central Pacific and Union Pacific Railroads in the 1870's.

Rear view of eastbound Central Pacific train leaving Oakland in the 1870's. Note the old-fashioned link-and-pin coupler and hand brake on this Silver Palace Car.

diminutive size. Some of its four hundred inhabitants were honest and hard working; many others may have been hard working, but honest and moral they were not.

The place was nine miles from water; but what it lacked in water, it made up in an abundance of one-dollar-a-gallon whiskey—whiskey hailed to be the strongest in the West. And Western whiskey was heralded as the most powerful in the world. Promontory offered such diversions as drinking, gambling and prizefighting. Bawdy houses, stocked with adequate bevies of women, stood ready for business. Crude wooden buildings and tents housed the moral and the immoral. Prizefighters fought in tents with seats reserved for ladies. In other tents the maids of illicit love proffered their services.

With only an hour between trains, the hustlers

of wickedness became proficient in the hard sell—time was of the essence. High-pressure selling combined with high-powered whiskey brought to disaster many a naïve novice. Crooked gamblers fleeced neophytes in record time. It has been said that a spark of goodness resides in the worst of men and even the gamblers of Promontory were no exception. After they had dutifully plucked a greenhorn clean, gamblers tossed him a five dollar gold piece so he could eat until he reached his destination.

Promontory offered a condensed education to those uninitiated to the West. One can only wonder at the incredulity of a genteel Easterner or a well-bred Englishman upon being suddenly thrust into the sordid atmosphere of this pause between trains.

As the Express swayed westward from Prom-

Interior view of the Central Pacific's COSMOPOLITAN, *a dining car used on the Pacific railroad during the 1870's. As can be seen, it was converted into a sleeper at night.*

Interior of a Palace Hotel Car used on the Pacific railroad. Sketch by A. R. Waud in HARPER'S WEEKLY, *May 29, 1869.*

ontory across Utah, Eastern passengers glimpsed, many for the first time, the Great Salt Lake Desert. Arid, salty, alkaline, dusty terrain devoid of vegetation swept past the car windows. Alkali and dust billowed upward from the track and permeated the cars. Across Nevada the train rolled over more desert and sagebrush. So much sagebrush grew in the West that a foreigner might well ask if it were America's principal crop.

After crossing the California border, the Express began ascending the Sierra Nevada. The air became cooler and cleaner. Two engines puffed and hissed valiantly to pull the train up the 2.2 per cent grade. The cadence of wheels clicking over rail joints gradually slowed. Deep-blue Donner Lake drifted eastward hundreds of feet below the right of way. Through long Summit tunnel roared and clattered the train. Rounding "Cape Horn," the

cars seemed to hang in space as they swung along the narrow right of way fourteen hundred feet above the American River. An anonymous passenger wrote in 1870, "the cars pass on a high embankment around Cape Horn and nervous passengers begin to look around anxiously peering with evident trepidation into the depths below."

The train then began the long grade downward on the western slopes of the Sierra Nevada toward Sacramento. Of this descent one passenger wrote: "And now the train at accelerated speed moves downward ... The steam is shut off, the brakes put on and as the Eagle sets his wings and floats, we slide swiftly and smoothly down the mountains." Four days and seven hours after leaving Omaha, the Pacific Express rolled into Sacramento and seemed to sigh as released steam hissed from the locomotive.

Interior of an old sleeper-diner car on the Central Pacific, 1869.

Central Pacific Silver Palace Sleeping Car at Jackson and Sharp Delaware Car Works, CIRCA 1870.

Precipitous Cape Horn towering over the American River in the Sierra Nevada. From HARPER'S MAGAZINE, *May 1872.*

To some the journey may have been jolting and tiresome, but to others it was an exhilarating delight. According to the following report published by *Appleton's Railway Guide to the United States and Canada* in 1870, rail travel was pleasant:

> *In no part of the world is travel made so easy and comfortable as on the Pacific Railroad. To travelers from the East it is a constant delight and to ladies and families it is accompanied with absolutely no fatigue or discomfort. One lives at home in the Palace car with as much true enjoyment as in the home drawing room ... The slow rate of speed, which averages but twenty to thirty miles per hour day and night, produces a peculiarly smooth, gentle, and easy motion, most soothing and agreeable.*

Not all passengers considered the Palace cars a delightful experience. Much depended upon the passengers' backgrounds and whether they had previously passed that way by stagecoach. An English Viscountess recorded some caustic observations about the Central Pacific's Silver Palace Sleeping Cars. One complaint was that "there are no special cars for ladies and if your opposite neighbor is a gentleman in the day, in all probability you will have him on your shelf at night [in the upper berth, no doubt] and it will be well with you if he does not snore." Informality and lack of privacy on American trains were a bit disturbing to the Viscountess:

> *Everyone is obliged to retire to rest at a certain hour and rise ditto, for all the beds must*

269

Central Pacific train descending Cape Horn in the Sierra Nevada, CIRCA 1870.

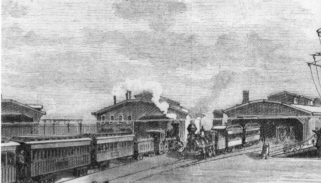

The wharf at Oakland and the terminus of the Central Pacific Railroad, opposite the city of San Francisco.

go up and come down together. Then follows waiting one's turn at the silver lavatory, which consists of two basins, a palatial roller-towel and a piece of soap. There is a silver tap whence you procure clean water—and wash the basin too if a score of your neighbors have used it before you. Particular people select the cleanest portion of the towel or carry their own. In the same luxurious manner you are accommodated with comb, brush, nailbrush and toothbrush. I saw a lady take from her pocket a very handsome set of teeth, clean them carefully with the brush provided by the company, and place the teeth in her mouth. "I don't sleep in them," she remarked. "It uses them out so bad and they are right expensive."

The lavatory is situated at the entrance of the car and cannot be made private either

from without or within, and anything like a good wash is out of the question. You cannot even tuck up your hair or roll up your sleeves but some gentleman or conductor is sure to pounce upon you and remark, "Very refreshing to get a good wash."

Meals on trains west of Promontory were not as elaborate as those served east of Promontory, but food was plentiful. "Fresh vegetables may run short but everything that can be pickled, preserved or carried in cans you can order. Bread and cake are baked twice a day in the train and are always hot," wrote the Viscountess.

Contemporary rail travelers underwent hazards other than the gamblers and vices of Promontory. Another was personal safety. Coaches were

Sacramento's first Central Pacific depot.

Head-on collision between a Western Pacific (Central Pacific subsidiary) passenger train and an S. F. & Alameda passenger train on November 14, 1869.

fabricated of wood and splintered easily into kindling that impaled or crushed passengers in a train crash. Fire-burning heaters added the danger of fire after a derailment or crash. Brakes were still hand operated. If the engineer wished to slow or stop a train, he signaled by whistle and brakemen scrambled to the braking wheels mounted at the end of the coach and twisted and tugged at the wheel. Emergency stops were impossible. George Westinghouse had perfected his air brake by 1869, but very few trains of the early 1870's were equipped with this efficient brake that could lock the wheels of an entire train from the locomotive.

Derailments were frequent but usually were just a jolting annoyance. Since trains moved slowly, derailed cars infrequently left the right of way. They merely bounced over the ties. Few passengers were injured or killed by ordinary derailments, but they caused delays that trainmen

BOTTOM: Central Pacific train passes laborers and snowsheds in the Sierra Nevada.   OPPOSITE TOP: Central Pacific Railroad train schedule in 1868. OPPOSITE BOTTOM: Temporary railroad bridge near Nebraska City, CIRCA 1870.

No. 2. CENTRAL PACIFIC RAILROAD. 1868.
HUMBOLDT DIVISION.

For the Government and Information of Employes only, and is not intended for the information of the Public. The Company reserves the right to vary the same as circumstances may require.

EASTWARD		1 Through Freight	3 Through Freight	5 Passenger	STATIONS.	2 Through Freight	4 Passenger	6 Through Freight	WESTWARD	
Distances.										
3	3	5.15 A M	1.50 P M	6.20 P M	Leave..WADSWORTH..Arrive	7.40	12.20	5.25 A M	3	136
6	9	5.55 "	2.05 "	† 6.29 "	2 MILE STATION	7.30 "	† 12.13 A M	5.15 "	6	133
11	20	6.30 "	2.35 "	6.55 M	DESERT	6.43 M	† 11 46	4.45 "	11	127
8	28	7.30 "	3 30 "	† 7.34 "	HOT SPRINGS	5.55 "	† 11.07 "	3..0 "	8	116
7	35	8.15 "	4.10 "	† 8.05 "	MIRAGE	5.20 "	† 10.36 "	3.10 "	7	108
12	47	8.55 "	4.45 M	† 8.32 "	WHITE PLAINS	4.45 M	† 10 10	2.30 "	12	101
7	54	10.05 "	5.10 "	9.20 M	BROWN'S	3.30 2.45	9.20 M	1.30 "	7	89
9	63	10.50 "	6.50 "	† 9.50 "	GRANITE POINT	2 25	† 8.50 "	12.50 A M	9	82
4	67	11.35 "	7.30 "	10.25 "	LOVELOCK'S	1.50 "	8.16 "	12 05 "	4	73
7	74	12 00 "	7.50 M	† 10.40 "	BRIDGE	1.30 "	8.00 M	11.45 "	7	69
11	85	12.55 P M	8.35 "	11.10 M	OREANA	12.55 M P M	7.28 "	11.15 10.45 M	11	62
11	96	1.55 "	9 30 M	† 11.55 "	RYE PATCH	12.00 "	† 6.45 "	9.30 M	11	51
12	108	2.50 "	10 25 "	12.40 A M	HUMBOLDT	11.05 "	6.00 "	8.25 "	12	40
7	115	3.55 "	11.30 "	1.28 "	MILL CITY	10.05 "	5.13 "	7.15 "	7	28
10	125	4.45 M	12.10 A M	† 1 58 "	RASPBERRY CREEK	9.25 "	4.45 M	6.30 "	10	21
11	136	5.35 M	1.00 "	† 2 36 "	ROSE CREEK	8.35 "	† 4 05 "	5.35 M	11	11
		6.30 "	1 55 "	3.20 "	Arrive..WINNEMUCCA..Leave	7 40 A M	3.20 P M	4.40 P M		Distances.

If Trains are not Met at the Regular Meeting Place, approach Sidings Carefully, until they are Met.   In cases of Uncertainty, always take the Safe Side.

The letter "M" set against a Station signifies a Meet—"Ps," Pass—"Psd," Passed. Meeting and Passing places are Stopping Places. Trains will arrive at Stations on time, as given in the Table, and leave as soon thereafter as business will permit.

Passenger Trains will stop at all Stations against which figures are set, except those marked †, at which they will stop to leave and on signal to take passengers. No. 4 Passenger Train will leave Winnemucca every day in the week except Saturday.

JOHN CORNING, Ass't Gen'l Sup't.   **C. CROCKER, General Sup't.**

Courtesy Nebraska State Historical Society

recklessly attempted to regain. One nervous passenger's thoughts about such an engineer's race to make up lost time were recorded by August Mencken in *The Railroad Passenger*:

The engine driver ran extra risks to make up the time lost and the descent from Summit Station to Sacramento was made with exceptional rapidity. The velocity with which the train rushed down this incline and the suddenness with which it wheeled around the curves produced a sensation which cannot be reproduced in words. The axle boxes smoked with friction and the odor of burning wood pervaded the cars. The wheels were nearly red-hot and in the darkness of the night they resembled discs of flame. Glad though all were to reach Sacramento, not a few were especially thankful to have reached it with whole limbs and unbruised bodies.

Accidents were surprisingly infrequent, but not as infrequent as railroad passenger accidents today. Rail passengers were mangled or burned in wooden coaches all too often.

An accident on the morning of November 14, 1870, was somewhat typical. A train of eight cars was puffing eastward from San Francisco in a dense fog. Suddenly a westbound train loomed ahead in the fog on the same track. Both locomotives reared upward like two fighting stallions. Both were engulfed in a deafening roar, blinding fire and smoke and toppled into a creek alongside the right of way. Several cars were twisted into splinters. One car telescoped the coach in front

Burlington Engine No. 7 at Broken Bow, Nebraska in the mid-1880's.

of it, with thirty passengers, and ground and screeched to within six feet of the end of the telescoped car. Seats and passengers were hurled and twisted forward into that remaining six feet. Only those sitting in the six-foot area were uninjured. Fourteen were killed and many injured; most of the casualties occurred in the telescoped car. No help arrived for an hour.

Contemporary passengers experienced other bizarre and unusual happenings. A passenger leaving Oakland by train underwent what must set a record for bizarreness. "Just after getting started out of Oakland on his way home, a tramp's legs were cut off, the result of an attempt to steal a ride.... Later a sick man yielded up the ghost. After leaving Sacramento a man died of consumption. Still later ... the crack of the playful pistol announced another tragedy. ..." Quoted from the *Central Pacific and Southern Pacific Railroads* by Lucius Beebe.

In August 1869, the Central Pacific posted the following fares:

Sacramento to Omaha	**$111.00**
Sacramento to Chicago	130.00
Sacramento to New York	150.00

These were the rates if paid for in currency; if paid in gold, the fare to New York, for instance, was reduced to $112.50. Silver Palace sleeping accommodations from Sacramento to Promontory were:

Double lower berth	**$ 5.00**
Double upper berth	5.00
Staterooms	12.00

Double berths accommodated two; staterooms, four. Children under twelve went half fare; under five, free.

So this was railroading when the first trains rolled to the Far West. They were faster, safer and more comfortable than stagecoaches and faster than steamboats. Judged by current standards these early day railroads were relatively dangerous, uncomfortable and slow. Yet the railroads opened a whole new world to far westerners, who were, in general, enthusiastic and content with their new mode of transportation.

Bibliography

HISTORIES AND GENERAL WORKS

Abdill, George B. *This Was Railroading.* Seattle: Superior Publishing Co., 1958.

Bancroft, H. H. *History of California*, Vol. VI, 1848-1859. San Francisco: The History Company Publishers, 1888.

Barra, E. I. *Tale of Two Oceans. An account of a voyage from Philadelphia to San Francisco, around Cape Horn, 1849-50.* San Francisco: Eastman & Co., 1893.

Beebe, Lucius W. *The Central Pacific and Southern Pacific Railroads.* Berkeley: Howell-North, 1963.

Beebe, Lucius and Charles Clegg. *Hear the Train Blow.* New York: E. P. Dutton & Co., 1952.

————. *When Beauty Rode the Rails.* New York: Doubleday, 1962.

Best, Gerald M. *Iron Horses to Promontory.* San Marino, Calif.: Golden West Books, 1969.

Billington, Ray Allen. *The Far Western Frontier, 1830-1860.* New York: Harper and Bros., 1956.

Blass, Roy S. *Pony Express — the Great Gamble.* Berkeley: Howell-North, 1959.

Chamberlain, William H. and Harry L. Well. *History of Sutter County, California.* Oakland: Thompson and West, 1879.

————. *History of Yuba County, California.* Oakland: Thompson and West, 1879.

Chapman, Arthur. *The Pony Express.* New York: G. P. Putnam's Sons, 1932.

Conkling, Roscoe P. and Margaret B. *The Butterfield Overland Mail, 1857-1869.* Glendale, Calif.: The Arthur H. Clark Co., 1947.

Cutler, Carl C. *Greyhounds of the Sea; the Story of the American Clipper Ship.* New York: G. P. Putnam's Sons, 1930.

Delay, Peter J. *History of Yuba and Sutter Counties, California.* Los Angeles: Historic Record Company, 1924.

Donovan, Frank. *River Boats of America.* New York: Thomas Y. Crowell Co., 1966.

Drury, Clifford Merrill. *Marcus Whitman, M.D., Pioneer and Martyr.* Glendale, Calif.: The Arthur H. Clark Co., 1963.

————, ed. *First White Women Over the Rockies; Diaries, Letters, and Biographical Sketches of the Six Women.* Glendale, Calif.: The Arthur H. Clark Co., 1963. 2 vols.

Duffus, R. L. *The Santa Fe Trail.* London, New York, Toronto: Longman's, Green & Co., 1930.

Eggenhofer, Nick. *Wagons, Mules and Men.* New York: Hastings House, 1961.

Ellis, W. T. *Memories, My Seventy-Two Years in the Romantic County of Yuba, Calif.* Eugene: The University of Oregon, 1939.

Frederick, James Vincent. *Ben Holladay, the Stage Coach King, A Chapter in the Development of Transcontinental Transportation.* Glendale, Calif.: The Arthur H. Clark Co., 1940.

Galloway, John D. *The First Transcontinental Rail-Road.* New York: Simmon-Boardman, 1950.

Gibbs, Jim. *West Coast Windjammers.* Seattle: Superior Publishing Co., 1968.

Greeley, Horace. *An Overland Journey from New York to San Francisco in the Summer of 1859.* New York: C. M. Saxton, Barker & Co., 1860.

Griswold, Wesley A. *A Work of Giants.* New York: McGraw-Hill, 1962.

Hafen, Leroy R. and Ann W. Hafen. *Handcarts to Zion.* Glendale, Calif.: The Arthur H. Clark Co., 1960.

_____. *The Overland Mail, 1849-1869.* Glendale, Calif.: The Arthur H. Clark Co., 1926.

Hinckley, Helen. *Rails from the West; a Biography of Theodore D. Judah.* San Marino, Calif.: Golden West Books 1969.

Hoffman, H. Wilbur. *History of Navigation on California's Feather River.* An M.A. thesis. Sacramento: Sacramento State College, 1963.

Holbrook, Stewart H. *The Story of American Railroads.* New York: Bonanza Books, 1947.

Howard, Robert W. *The Great Iron Trail.* New York: G. P. Putnam's Sons, 1962.

Howells, Rolen S. *The Mormon Story.* Salt Lake City: Bookcraft, 1957.

Howgood, John A. *America's Western Frontier.* New York: Albert A. Knopf, Inc., 1967.

Hungerford, Edward. *Wells Fargo.* New York: Random House, 1949.

_____. *Wells Fargo Advancing the American Frontier.* New York: Bonanza Books, 1949.

Hunter, Vickie, and Elizabeth Hamma. *Stagecoach Days.* Menlo Park, California: Lane Book Company, 1963.

Jackson, W. Turrentine. *Wagon Roads West.* Berkeley and Los Angeles: University of California Press, 1952.

Johnson, Dorothy M. *The Bloody Bozeman.* New York: McGraw-Hill, 1971.

Kemble, John Haskell. *The Panama Route, 1848-1869.* Berkeley: University of California Press, 1943.

Kraus, George. *High Road to Promontory.* Palo Alto, Calif.: American West Publishing Co., 1969.

Lamson, J. *Round Cape Horn. Voyage of the James W. Paige from Maine to California the Year of 1852.* Bangor: O. F. & W. H. Knowles, 1878.

Lane, Carl D. *American Paddle Steamboats.* New York: Coward-McCann, Inc., 1943.

Lewis, Oscar. *The Big Four.* New York: A. Knopf, 1938.

_____. *Sea Route to the Gold Fields.* New York: Ballantine Books, 1949.

Loomis, Noel M. *Wells Fargo.* New York: Clarkson N. Potter, Inc., distributed by Crown Publishers, Inc., 1968.

Low, Garrett W. *Gold Rush by Sea,* ed. Kenneth Haney. Philadelphia: University of Pennsylvania Press, 1941.

MacMullen, Jerry. *Paddle-Wheel Days in California.* Stanford: Stanford University Press, 1944.

Mansfield, George C. *History of Butte County, California.* Los Angeles: Historic Record Company, 1918.

McAffee, Ward. *California's Railroad Era, 1850-1911.* San Marino, Calif.: Golden West Books, 1973.

McGowan, Joseph A. *Freighting to the Mines, 1849-1859.* An unpublished Ph.D. dissertation. Berkeley: University of California, 1949.

_____. *History of the Sacramento Valley.* New York and West Palm Beach: Lewis Historical Publishing Company, 1961.

McIllhaney, Edward. *Recollections of a '49er.* Kansas City, Mo.: Hailman Printing Co., 1908.

Mencken, August. *The Railroad Passenger Car.* Baltimore: The Johns Hopkins Press, 1957.

Moody, Ralph. *Stagecoach West.* New York: T. Y. Crowell Co., 1967.

_____. *The Old Trails West.* New York: T. Y. Crowell Co., 1963.

Myer, Carl. *Bound for Sacramento, 1849-1850,* trans. from the German by Ruth Frye Axe. Claremont, Calif.: Saunders Studio Press, 1938.

Newell, Gordon and Joe Williamson. *Pacific Coastal Lines.* Seattle: Superior Publishing Co., 1959.

_____. *Pacific Steamboats from Sidewheelers to Motor Ferry.* New York: Bonanza Books, 1958.

Nichols, Roy F. *The Stakes of Power, 1845-1877.* New York: Hill and Wang, 1961.

Ormsby, Waterman L. *The Butterfield Overland Mail,* eds. L. H. Wright and J. M. Bynum. San Marino, Calif.: Henry E. Huntington Library, 1942.

Otis, F. N. *Illustrated History of the Panama Railroad.* New York: Harper & Brothers, 1862.

Quiett, Glenn Chesney. *They Built the West.* New York: D. Appleton-Century Co., 1934.

Ramey, Earl. *The Beginnings of Marysville.* San Francisco: California Historical Society, 1936.

Root, Frank A., and William E. Connelley. *The Overland Stage to California.* Topeka: 1901 reprint by Long's College Book Co., 1950.

Russell, Don. *The Lives and Legends of Buffalo Bill.* Norman: University of Oklahoma Press, 1960.

Rydell, Raymond A. *Cape Horn to the Pacific.* Berkeley: University of California Press, 1952.

Schott, Joseph L. *Rails Across Panama.* New York: The Bobbs-Merrill Company, Inc., 1967.

Settle, Raymond W. and Mary L. Settle. *Saddles and Spurs — the Pony Express Saga.* Lincoln: University of Nebraska Press, 1955.

Sillcox, Lewis Ketcham. *Safety in Early American Railway Operation, 1853-1871.* Princeton: Princeton University Press, 1936.

Smith, Waddell F. *Stage Lines and Express Companies in California.* San Rafael, Calif.: Pony Express History and Art Gallery, 1965.

_____. *The Story of the Pony Express.* San Francisco: The Experian House, 1960.

Steinheimer, Richard. *Backwoods Railroads of the West.* Milwaukee: Kalmbach Publishing Co., 1963.

Stone, Irving. *Men to Match My Mountains.* New York: Doubleday, 1956.

The Editors of Time-Life Books. *Old Soldiers*, with text by David Nevin. New York: Time-Life Books, 1973.

Walker, Henry Pickering. *The Wagonmasters.* Norman: University of Oklahoma Press, 1966.

Wilson, Neill C. and Frank J. Taylor. *Southern Pacific, The Roaring Story of a Fighting Railroad.* New York: McGraw-Hill, 1952.

Wiltsee, Ernest A. *Gold Rush Steamers.* San Francisco: The Grabhorn Press, 1938.

Windeler, Adolphus. *The California Gold Rush Diary of a German Sailor*, ed. W. Turrentine Jackson. Berkeley: Howell-North Books, 1969.

Winther, Oscar Osborn. *Via Western Express and Stagecoach.* Stanford: Stanford University Press, 1945.

DOCUMENTS, DIRECTORIES, ARTICLES, LETTERS, JOURNALS, AND REPORTS

Chever, Edward E. "The First Settlement of Yuba City," *Quarterly of the Society of California Pioneers,* IX No. 4, Dec. 1932.

City Directory of Sacramento for the Year 1854-5. Bancroft Library, University of California, Berkeley.

Crocker, Charles. *Reminiscences.* California Biographical Manuscripts, Bancroft Library, University of California, Berkeley.

Documents and Manuscripts. Ft. Laramie Museum, Ft. Laramie, Wyo.

Documents and Manuscripts. History Room, Wells Fargo Bank, San Francisco.

Documents and Manuscripts. Pony Express History and Art Gallery, San Rafael, Calif.

Documents and Manuscripts. Scotts Bluff National Monument Museum, Scottsbluff, Neb.

Huntington, Collis P. *Reminiscences and Letters.* California Biographical Manuscripts. Bancroft Library, University of California, Berkeley.

Jackson, W. Turrentine. "Wells Fargo: Staging over the Sierras." San Francisco, *California Historical Society Quarterly,* Vol. 79, June 1970.

Joslyn, David L. "A Trip Across the Sierra Nevada Mountains in 1868," *Railway and Locomotive Historical Society Bulletin 29,* Boston, 1932.

Journals and Reports Regarding Handcart Brigades:

    Addresses of Brigham Young and Heber C. Kimball, November 2, 1856.

    Brigham Young's Address, November 16, 1856.

    Captain Grant's Report from Devil's Gate.

    Harney Cluff's Account of the Rescue.

    Journal of the First Handcart Company.

    Journal of the First Rescue Party.

    McArthur's Report on the Second Company.

    Report by F. D. Richards and Daniel Spencer.

Marysville City Directory, 1855. Packard Library, Marysville, California City Library.

Marysville Directory, 1858. Packard Library, Marysville, California City Library.

Pratt, Julius H. "To California by Panama in '49." *Century Magazine,* Vol. 41, No. 6. New York, April 1891.

The Memoirs of Theodore Cordua, ed. and trans. Erwin G. Gudde. Reprinted from the *Quarterly of the California Historical Society,* XII No. 4. December 1933.

Truman, Ben C. "Knights of the Lash," *Overland Monthly,* XXXI, April and May 1898.

Wooster, Clarence M. "Reminiscences of Railroading in California in the 1870's." *California Historical Society Quarterly,* Vol. 18, No. 4, December 1939.

NEWSPAPERS

Bismarck Tribune (Bismarck, North Dakota), June 1876.

Daily Alta California (San Francisco), 1851, 1852, 1858, 1860, 1865.

Daily Bee (Sacramento), 1851, 1853, 1855, 1856, 1861.

Daily Evening Herald (Marysville, California), 1853-1856.

Marysville Daily Appeal (Marysville, California), 1863, 1864, 1869, 1870, 1871, 1872.

Marysville Daily Herald (Marysville, California), 1854, 1857.

Marysville Herald (Marysville, California), 1850, 1851.

Panama Star (Panama City), 1849-1853, 1854.

Panama Star and Herald (Panama City), 1855, 1860, 1861.

Sacramento Union, 1851-1853, 1855, 1856, 1861, 1868, 1869, 1871.

San Diego Herald, 1857, 1858.

San Francisco Bulletin, 1856.

St. Joseph Gazette (St. Joseph, Missouri), 1849-1852.

The Oregonian (Portland, Oregon), 1852, 1853.

Index